Stakeholder Engagement

Aimee L. Franklin

Stakeholder Engagement

Springer

Aimee L. Franklin
University of Oklahoma
Norman, OK, USA

ISBN 978-3-030-47518-5 ISBN 978-3-030-47519-2 (eBook)
https://doi.org/10.1007/978-3-030-47519-2

This Springer imprint is published by the registered company Springer Nature Switzerland AG
The registered company address is: Gewerbestrasse 11, 6330 Cham, Switzerland

Contents

List of Figures

List of Tables

Chapter 1
Introduction to Stakeholder Engagement

Abstract Stakeholders are people who are influenced by or can influence the activities of others. In many cases, stakeholders are representing their self-interests as well as those of other people, groups, organizations, collectives, or even inanimates such as plants, animals, and future generations. Engaging stakeholders, no matter who or what they are, is crucial since they can influence our actions and disrupt or contribute to our success. Through interactions, we can find out their preferences and see where mutually value-producing solutions are possible. The values that can be produced from stakeholder interactions include representativeness, transparency, accessibility, responsiveness, accountability, and sustainability. These values are essential for individuals, especially when they are dealing with organizations, no matter how big or small or in what sector they operate. This chapter introduces a process-based logic model to understand what inputs and processes are possible for enhancing value through stakeholder engagement.

1.1 Introduction

The thesis of the book is this: For an organization to be sustainable, the leaders of the organization must think strategically about stakeholder engagement and institutionalize regimes to assure that stakeholder input is available to inform decisions.

Stakeholders[1] are anyone or anything that is or can be influenced by the actions of another stakeholder. Most discussions about stakeholders are from the organization's perspective and describe the influence of and on its operations by human stakeholders. However, stakeholders can also be inanimate and can take many forms such as future generations, plants, animals, our homes, or even dead people – for example, when dead people control how warm or cold we keep our home. When a

[1] A common complaint about existing literature is a lack of conceptual precision, leading to puny and disorganized theoretical development in the area of stakeholder participation (Ebdon, 2002, p. 84). Therefore, special attention is paid to defining key concepts and explicitly articulating the boundaries of this endeavor. The term, sustainable, is used to represent the capacity to endure. To be sustainable, an organization must be viable, meaning able to maintain itself (a state of autopoiesis) through value or profit creation and by fulfillment of its potentialities.

A. L. Franklin, *Stakeholder Engagement*,
https://doi.org/10.1007/978-3-030-47519-2_1

non-human thing influences our actions or is influenced by our actions, we call them actants.

The importance of engaging stakeholders, no matter who or what they are, is because they can influence our actions and disrupt or contribute to our success, whether success is more money, a more significant market share, or just the overall happiness we have in our life. Engaging our stakeholders and understanding how our actions may influence them or how their actions might influence us can help us to determine when it is beneficial to interact to have more success (or fewer costs).

People (and organizations) often identify stakeholders when considering a change to the status quo because their actions could impact others and cause these others to act in response. By identifying those stakeholders most likely to act, and the nature of the actions they may take, the organization can strategically interact with specific stakeholders. These interactions reveal similar or dissimilar preferences about changes to the status quo. With this information and through purposeful stakeholder engagement, the stakeholder can identify potential benefits that may be gained or costs that may be avoided.

Stakeholder engagement is a strategic process of interacting with stakeholders to gather information about shared interests, preferences, and the potential for joint action.[2] Learning about what other stakeholders get from us, want from us, or can do to us can contribute to decision-making in a way that is mutually value-producing and enhances sustainability.

Individuals purposefully interact with others every day. However, they seldom create a stakeholder engagement regime featuring a systematic process for identifying stakeholders, selecting mechanisms for and facilitating interactions, and then measuring the value produced by the engagement to compare against what was desired or expected.

Some people may do this. However, for most of us, stakeholder interactions occur organically and are not as deliberate, nor as organized, as what this book describes. For this reason, the focus of this book is on stakeholder engagement and how organizations could practice it. Within organizations are persons tasked with acting on behalf of the organization to foster interactions. Administrators might also be tasked with establishing engaged relationships to improve the sustainability of the organization.

In many organizations, (s)elected[3] officials for the organization make decisions without systematically considering the preferences of stakeholders. Ideally, organizational regimes foster routinized decision-making processes that are informed by the preferences of stakeholders inside as well as outside the organization's boundaries. An institutionalized process for considering stakeholders' preferences when

[2] Individuals have preferences, meaning a preferred course of action from among many potential courses of action. Preferences that are communicated or collected and analyzed to influence an organization's operations are inputs into decisions. Preference data is the output from purposefully gathered and aggregated preferences of many people.

[3] The term (s)elected describes officials who have been selected or elected to fill a position that has decision-making authority on behalf of the organization.

making decisions will influence the overall sustainability of the organization, just like participatory processes influence citizens' quality of life in societies with different governance structures (Koontz, 1999; Stripling, 2013). No matter the decision-making process or governance structure, an organization's activities can be enhanced when the leaders purposefully encourage a philosophy, and commit to an institutional regime, of stakeholder engagement. How to go about stakeholder engagement in a way that makes it valuable to the organization as an independent entity is a topic that has been considered for decades.[4] How to structure a stakeholder engagement function that improves value creation and ensures organizational sustainability is the puzzle motivating this book.

1.2 An Overview of Stakeholders

An organization's stakeholders are not a monolithic group. Stakeholders can include clients, partners, competitors, interest groups, and the public, to name just a few. Some definitions of stakeholders are so expansive as to include every person on the planet, future generations, and even plants and animals who may be threatened by an organization's operations. For analytical purposes, this book takes the approach that stakeholders are only able to interact with an organization when human beings represent them. For this reason, the definition refers to anyone who can influence, or is influenced by, the operations of an organization. This is irrespective of whether they are representing themselves or acting as a representative of other stakeholders, animate or inanimate.

When considering the value that can be created by stakeholder engagement practices, what is essential from the organization's perspective is not identifying and interacting with every stakeholder. One of the traditional ways organizations have identified stakeholder preferences is to create processes that gather preferences from representatives of stakeholders who can be highly influenced by or profoundly influence the organization's actions. This approach tasks a small group of elites to serve the interests of stakeholders through their official positions as owners, board members, or employees. I refer to this group as (s)elected officials, denoting the decision-making authority they have for an organization.

Over time, as organizations have become larger and larger, it has concurrently become unrealistic to expect a small group of (s)elected officials to make decisions that represent the interests of all the organizations' stakeholders. Thus, there is a need for organizations to task administrators with purposefully gathering a representative sampling of stakeholder preference data and then communicating this information to guide decision-making. This idea is similar to Lindblom's and

[4] Clearly an organization is not a human being; leaders and members of the organization make decisions and take actions on behalf of and with authority to obligate the organization. For this reason, scholars often reify an organization, attributing the ability for the organization to "act" as shorthand for those actions taken by humans inside the organization.

Woodhouse's notion of partisan analysis (1968). Preference data does not supplant the ability of (s)elected officials to make decisions based on their individual preferences; instead, this data can inform decisions and provide insight into potential dissent if stakeholders' preferences are not served.

Instead of identifying and interacting with every stakeholder, the organization's efforts should be focused on determining the stakeholders most likely to interact with the organization and how their respective preferences are similar to and different from other stakeholders who will and who will not interact.[5]

This process assists administators in facilitating stakeholder interactions. Facilitated interactions can support dialogue for stakeholders and the organization to exchange information, modify preferences, or reveal areas of overlapping preferences. Sociologists describe ideal social interactions as a dynamic sequence of interactions between individuals or groups who modify their actions and reactions based on the actions of their interaction partner(s). When successful, interactions can result in enthusiasm and a positive emotional attachment that influences the willingness to commit to further social interactions.

When individuals interact, they can do so based on four non-mutually exclusive kinds of interest: their interests, the interests of a group, an organization, or a collective. This distinction between the kinds of interests that motivate stakeholders to interact is vital because the interests that lead a stakeholder to interact with an organization can influence the expectations that stakeholder has about the organization's response.

The interests motivating interactions can also influence the amount of effort the organization may need to make to discover the preferences of non-interacting stakeholders, meaning those who choose not to interact or who choose to communicate their preferences in another venue. Considering stakeholders' values, interests, and how these influence the preference data they communicate creates valences between the policy, administrative, and social responsibilities of the organization and its employees (Buckwalter, 2014; Kooiman, 1993; Ruscio, 1996; Sintomer, Herzberg, & Röcke, 2008).

To be clear, in arguing for purposeful, value-driven, stakeholder engagement practices, I am not suggesting that governance regimes reliant on (s)elected officials to make decisions cannot adequately consider the range of stakeholders' interests for an organization. Instead, I am arguing that what is needed is an enhancement to organizational regimes to support multiple pathways for gathering stakeholder preference data that can inform decision-making.

In the first pathway, (s)elected officials themselves represent stakeholders' interests based on their perceptions of what is best for the stakeholders they represent. In the second pathway, stakeholders provide direct input about their preferences to the (s)elected officials in the organization. The third pathway is via a strategic management function, called stakeholder engagement, that features processes to identify

[5] Interactions are one way for stakeholders to communicate preferences. Preferences can also be communicated in other venues and can be about the activities of a particular organization, satisfaction with a transaction, or about multiple organizations that offer similar goods and services.

different stakeholder perspectives deliberately and to facilitate interactions and develop relationship to gather representative preference by design. There is also a fourth pathway, where an organization administrator (or staff unit) indirectly gathers and aggregates stakeholders' preference data that are communicated in other venues such as through social media or newspaper opinion columns or observations of public gatherings. While each of these pathways provides preference data, the last one does not feature any interactions with identifiable stakeholders and, therefore, precludes the possibility of stakeholder engagement.

1.3 Why Worry About Stakeholder Preferences?

Stakeholders, whether acting alone or as part of a collective,[6] have the power to make an organization succeed, just as they have the power to make an organization fail. Consider this scenario: what do you do when you are dissatisfied with what a public, for-profit, nonprofit, or voluntary organization does to you or sells to you or with how it interacts with you? Many of us will complain to an employee of the organization. However, is that always the case, especially when dealing with public organizations or large international organizations for which it is difficult even to identify a real person with whom to communicate? When faced with a lack of information about whom to communicate with inside the organization, would you be more likely to just "grin and bear it," rationalizing that the organization will not listen to just one person?

Think about a follow-up question: "Why is it people will sometimes complain, but at other times take no action?" Many people may decide to take no action because it is not worth their time to find out how and whom to contact in the organization. Another reason may be that they believe that organizational officials will not listen to just one person (especially in situations where that person receives the organization's services).[7] A third reason may be that people anticipate that the organization's response will be unsatisfactory and determine that it is not worth the effort to interact with the organization.

From an organization's perspective, when many stakeholders make the decision not to communicate their dissatisfaction, the sustainability of the organization is threatened. Dissatisfied customers are less likely to have repeat transactions or

---

[6] The term collective refers to two groupings of people. First, a collective is comprised of people living in a geographically bounded space who identify as part of society. People in a collective voluntarily give up some of their rights and liberties in exchange for the enforcement of shared social conventions, which is achieved by vesting power in the state through a governance structure that upholds these conventions. The second grouping of people, who are in a collective, is those engaged in affiliations with others based on affinity interests. In this type of collective, there is no expectation that an individual's liberties or rights will be abridged. Further, affinity groups seldom govern membership, with members free to come and go as they please.

[7] The term "goods and services" is a shorthand way of referring to the goods, products, services, exchanges, resources, and money an organization creates or uses for transactions and interactions.

continued interactions with the organization. They may also vocalize their dissatisfaction to other customers, thus causing a domino effect creating more people who will not have transactions with the organization. If the pattern continues and other stakeholders decide not to communicate their dissatisfaction with the organization, then at some point, the relationship between the organization and stakeholders will no longer exist, and the long-term sustainability of the organization will be threatened. To avoid this outcome, I argue that all organizations, no matter what sector in which they operate, should create and institutionalize a stakeholder engagement regime.

In the next section, I describe the blurring of organizational sectors that has occurred over time. My argument is that sector blurring makes the type of organization offering a good or service mostly irrelevant when considering stakeholder preferences and their potential impacts on an organization's activities. Further, sector blurring makes stakeholder engagement relevant to all organizations as a means for creating more value for the organization. Following a discussion of sector blurring, I review the concept of stakeholders and introduce a logic model of stakeholder engagement. The ideals desired from, and values created by stakeholder engagement presented in the model, are the structure for the remaining book chapters.

1.4 Organizations Across "Blurred" Sectors

The presence of organizations in society and the role they play in individuals' daily lives have steadily increased over time. It is common practice to group organizations into one of the three sectors: public, for-profit, and nonprofit. There is also a fourth type of organization that does not have a specific sector - the informal organization. Differentiation based on the organizational sector evolves due to changes in factors such as the organization's primary sphere of influence, legal status, purpose, and client type (Bozeman & Bretschneider, 1994). However, no matter the sector, all organizations interact and are expected to interact with their stakeholders (Buchholz & Rosenthal, 2004). Therefore, when it comes to stakeholder engagement, organizations can be considered generically. The following paragraphs describe key elements of organizations in the three sectors, public, for-profit, and nonprofit, to show why they can be considered generically and how all can benefit from stakeholder engagement.

Organizations in the public sector are government organizations. These kinds of organizations are differentiated from organizations in other sectors by the authority they have to act on behalf of society and to use public funds to create value. They are charged with ameliorating the social problems of citizens or individuals living within established geographic boundaries. Generally, government organizations[8]

[8] There is a significant amount of scholarship that strives to achieve definitional clarity for terms like governance, government, and regimes. I do not wish to enter this fray since my focus is on the regimes established to guide stakeholder engagement practices irrespective of the type of organiza-

are responsible for serving the needs of individuals living as a collective in society. When individuals benefit from services provided by or through government organizations, they give up some of their rights and allow the government to act on their behalf for the benefit of the collective.

For-profit organizations must secure a legal status allowing them to sell goods or services for a profit in market-based transactions. For a market-based transaction to occur, two conditions need to be satisfied: first, there needs to be an adequate number of buyers and sellers; and second, a fair price must be established. Seldom do these perfect market conditions exist – in part because transactions do not fully account for externalities.[9] When the externalities impact common pool resources (Ostrom et al., 1994), then the government often takes over the provision of goods or services or regulates the organizations providing the goods and services to assure that the full cost of the transaction includes the cost of externalities.

For-profit organizations can be privately held (meaning that there are a limited number of individuals who have a claim on the wealth of the organization), or they can be publicly held (meaning that stock in the organization is bought and sold in the stock market and stockholders are entitled to the wealth of the organization in an amount proportionate to their investment) (Key, 1999). The perspective that for-profit organizations, whether privately held or publicly traded, need only consider owners'/stockholders' interest has been challenged. Scholars, primarily in the business ethics and strategy areas (Follett, 1918; Freeman, 2010; Kaler, 2003; King, Chilton, & Roberts, 2010; Mellahi & Wood, 2003; Vinten, 2001), argue that for-profit organizations have fiduciary and stewardship responsibilities that go beyond the simplistic consideration of owners'/stockholders' preferences.

Nonprofit organizations, for example, charitable, non-governmental (international aid/development), and voluntary (social, religious, interest-based) organizations, have a unique legal status allowing them to operate with no or reduced tax obligations often while engaging in market-based transactions. This status is given since these organizations produce value for an identified collective, such as disadvantaged persons or organizations that have a need not addressed via market transactions nor government programs. Nonprofit organizations can provide a conduit for philanthropic and social entrepreneurial activities (Park & Wilding, 2014; Robbins, 2013). Nonprofit organizations are governed by a Board of Directors and may or may not have employees.

---

tion, so I merely present my working definitions. "Government" refers to a specific type of organization that must be legally created by elected officials acting on the authority of the state as a representative of the collective. When I speak of "governance," I am referring to the overall regime (imbued with actors, institutions, processes, values, expectations, and regularity) that gives any organization the authority to establish policies and practices for making decisions to secure desired outcomes and assure organizational sustainability.

[9] Externalities are defined as positive and negative effects that spill over from a transaction and impact others who are not part of the transaction as well as the unintended consequences from the transaction.

There are two prominent bodies of theories explaining why nonprofit organizations exist. The first explanation holds that nonprofit organizations exist because a profitable market for the good does not exist. Government failure theory (Young, 2011) provides the second explanation, suggesting that the government cannot afford (or is unwilling to allocate resources) to provide the good or service, so nonprofit organizations develop to fill the gap.

The last category of organization, informal, is used to describe ephemeral organizations. They are groups of people who gather together for a short and intense period of interactions often based upon a single issue, such a protest of a government action that restricts individual rights. An informal organization is generally an ad hoc or temporary gathering of people where there are no criteria for membership, membership ebbs and flows as people move in and out of the information organization, and there are no records kept of members. Demonstrations, flash mobs, and social media groups are examples of informal organizations.

This categorization of organizations by sector is a simplification useful for analyzing transactions, interactions, and value production. I do not find this division by sector to be meaningful for stakeholder engagement since the different legal arrangements, financial structures, and operational processes do not necessitate different stakeholder engagement philosophies or strategies. A similar analogy is the policy stages model (Anderson, 2006) which is a heuristic that provides a basis for shared discussion but has little resemblance to the reality of the complex world we live in.[10] The demarcations between an organization's sector, based on the clients it serves and the goods it produces (Chapman & Cleaveland, 1973), have no bearing on how an organization can or should engage its stakeholders. I would suggest that the sectors have blurred to the extent that all organizations may often serve the same clients with similar goods or services, especially in times when government privatizes or contracts for services from the other sectors and seeks collaboration and co-production with clients and other partners. Further, organizations in all sectors can benefit from deliberate stakeholder engagement. My rationale for these conclusions is presented next.

1.4.1 Antecedents of Sector Blurring

There are many examples of sector blurring for organizations. A body of comparative public policy studies suggests that this is a worldwide trend (DiMaggio & Powell, 1983; Friedman & Miles, 2002; Jing & Besharov, 2014; Meriade & Qiang, 2015; Milward, Provan, Fish, Isett, & Huang, 2009; Stout & Love, 2013). Public value creation (Moore, 1995), generally considered the domain of government organizations, is a concern for-profit and nonprofit organizations when they

[10] "We" refers to an unspecified group of like-minded people including you and me. "I" refers to the author making a normative statement reflecting personal worldviews/preferences. "Us" refers to the author and the reader thinking through the implications of an idea presented herein.

contract and collaborate with the government to provide goods or services (LeRoux, 2009; Lipsky & Smith, 1989). On the flip side, many government organizations, such as the US Postal Service, are expected to compete in a market with other organizations and to make a profit. Nonprofit organizations can provide the same goods and services as public and for-profit organizations, often with the sole distinguishing factor being a targeted, and often vulnerable, clientele (Albanesi, Dukes, & Singlevich, 2013; Ambrose, 2014; Hansmann, 1987; Justice & Tarimo, 2012; Saidel, 1991).

Sector blurring often is the result of the collaboration and partnerships that develop when organizations in multiple sectors interact to produce value for each organization. When this occurs, the organizations gain more through the partnership than what they can achieve independently with their resources. An example of this is the privatization of prisons. Sectors can blur when the actions of one organization are necessary to foster the actions of another organization. The partnership between the City of Omaha, the private entrepreneurs, the NCAA and the schools whose baseball teams participate, and the media that cover the event is necessary for the College World Series to occur each year (Franklin, Krane, & Ebdon, 2013).

Sector blurring can also arise under conditions of competition between organizations in the various sectors. For example, elementary education is a policy area commonly served by organizations in all sectors. Public organizations bear the responsibility of providing elementary education to all children residing in their service area. Nonprofit organizations, such as churches, may offer the minimum state-required curriculum but also provide denomination-based religious instruction. For-profit schools offer another alternative to parents and students if the parents are willing to pay a premium for their child's education since these organizations expect to operate at a profit. When delivering educational services, each of these organizations has to comply with relevant laws and administrative policies (Rainey & Bozeman, 2000; Rudder, 2008).

Organizations in every sector must also consider the preferences of their stakeholders to keep them satisfied (Fletcher, Guthrie, Steane, Roos, & Pike, 2003; Hornbein & King, 2012). All schools strive to convince parents that they can best serve the educational needs of their children, not because of the sector that they operate in, but because of the unique mission and competencies they have that influence the type and quality of education children will receive. Finally, to be sustainable, all organizations are expected to create value for the owners. Based on this, I conclude that no matter the sector, organizations are generic when it comes to stakeholder engagement.[11]

---

[11] Bozeman (1987/2004) argued that all organizations are public, publishing a book of the same name. This claim was in response to claims that generic theories of organizations are possible. In 2000, Rainey and Bozeman offered a synthesis of the arguments and the importance of understanding the "publicness" of all organizations.

1.5 Value Creation Through Stakeholder Engagement

As the elementary school education example suggests, the sector in which an organization operates does not matter when considering stakeholder engagement. What matters is how the organization responds to the expectations its stakeholders have in terms of what value the organization will provide to each of them.

Value is a ubiquitous term; everyone knows what it means. However, when thinking about organizations engaging stakeholders, the construct of value suffers precisely because of its ubiquitousness (Overeem, 2015; Rutgers, 2015; Van der Wal, Nabatchi, & de Graaf, 2015). The term has no precision; value means something to everyone, yet the term does not have the same meaning to anyone. A cursory search of online dictionaries yields around 500 different personal, business, societal, or human nature values.[12] The construct of value is even messier since it is also used to refer to levels of values that can be hierarchical and overlapping (Raadschelders & Franklin, 1999).

Historically, the preponderance of literature on stakeholder participation has focused on government organizations and the public values they are expected to create (Jorgensen & Rutgers, 2015). Creating public value by ameliorating societal problems is challenging since there are multiple, and often conflicting, values held by stakeholders. However, the concern with value tensions has seeped into for-profit and nonprofit organizations as well (Quinn & Rohrbaugh, 1983), bolstering the argument in this book that stakeholder engagement matters to all organizations. To effectively respond to conflicting value expectations of stakeholders, organizations first need to identify and then practice the values they want to guide their operations and conduct their stakeholder interactions accordingly.

Values influence the transactions and interactions in which stakeholders and organizations engage.[13] Organizational values generally reflect the culture of the organization or the way the organization desires to (or does) conduct its activities. Some organizational values are clearly articulated and uniformly upheld by all members of the organization, others are informal and may be endorsed by only a few members or smaller groups within the organization (Franklin & Pagan, 2006). Stakeholders learn the values embedded within the organization's culture from the very first interaction they have with the organization and as they are reinforced through repeated interactions. When organizational values are not clearly articulated, organizational members may use discretion to prioritize the values they will serve in their daily activities, often leading to a stakeholder's claim of inequitable treatment.

Organizations strive to create value in their transactions as a means to assure the sustainability of the organization. The values an organization is expected to create

---

[12] There are also individual websites offering cautionary advice suggesting that each individual has their own reduced set of values that "resonate" with them and undergird decisions in their daily life.

[13] Transactions are an exchange of goods that occur between the organization and a client. Interactions are communications between the organization and a stakeholder.

can vary based on the sector being served in a transaction. For example, when organizations operate as if they are in the public sector (meaning they are wholly publicly funded, or a portion of their funding comes from public sources), transactions might be focused on upholding values such as equity, representation, due process, and efficacy (Behn, 2003; Bozeman & Johnson, 2015). For organizations operating as if they are in the for-profit sector (meaning revenues are expected to exceed expenses), there are often efforts to ensure that operations are economical, efficient, and cost-effective. For nonprofit organizations, the dominant values to be served can include representation, diversity, due process, equality, and client empowerment (Florin & Wandersman, 1990).

There are situations when the values which an organization is expected to create are multi-dimensional (Kujala, 2001). When for-profit organizations engage in transactions in imperfect markets or on behalf of other organizations, such as government, they are expected to do more than just make a profit; they might also need to assure equitable transactions. Increasingly, we expect for-profit organizations to be socially or environmentally responsible and to account for the externalities of market-based transactions. Alternatively, if an organization receives public funding, the organization is expected to uphold the public sector values noted above. Another example of how multiple dimensions of values must be served occurs when several organizations work together and pool resources to achieve outcomes desired by each in the same policy area. Examples can be found in the collaboration required for large-scale civic events (Krane, Ebdon, & Franklin, 2020). In this situation, trust, co-production, and accountability are additional values to be created.

The multi-dimensionality of values is often the source of the conflicting stakeholder values. Organizations may attempt to serve multiple values, but the relative priority of each value must be established. Also, the relative priority could be situational for a specific transaction (Bellone & Goerl, 1992) or contested by different stakeholders. When transactions are involuntary (meaning the individual does not seek out the good or service being provided by the organization) and carried out by a government organization or by its proxy, there is a higher expectation for the organization to be responsive to its stakeholders than there is for nonprofit or for-profit organizations which engage in voluntary transactions. Involuntary transactions occur because the collective has determined that the public value being created justifies the suspension of an individual's rights. However, the collective also supports the notion that those who involuntarily experience abridged rights in a transaction they did not initiate should have the ability to register their dissatisfaction and preferences to assure due process and to inform future interactions.

I describe values and their relationship to an organization's actions not to imply that they are sector bound or that the listings are comprehensive. Instead, I want to alert readers to the relationship of values to stakeholder interactions and organizational sustainability. When there are relatively high levels of congruence between the values pursued by the organization and the value expectations of stakeholders, sustainability will be more likely. Knowing the value preferences of stakeholders, as they are applied to specific interactions and transactions, and then communicating to stakeholders the organization's efforts to serve these values, increases the likelihood that stakeholders will support the organization's decisions – even when there is an incongruence in value rankings.

This discussion of organizational values and stakeholders' expectations has two purposes. First, it is intended to suggest that purposeful stakeholder engagement can reduce an organization's costs of operations by aligning preferences and reducing dissatisfaction, thus enhancing its long-term sustainability. Second, I argue that stakeholder engagement should be value-producing for both the organization and the stakeholders. Where there is a mutual value production, then stakeholder interactions are reinforcing, and trust-based relationships between the organization and stakeholders can develop. Should this occur, the relationships between stakeholders and the organization themselves now have value since they create shared meaning. So, even though I start with a thesis statement about the importance of strategic stakeholder engagement for organizational sustainability, I will finish by arguing that, from a normative perspective, mutually value-producing stakeholder engagement is also a desirable outcome.

1.6 The Construct of Stakeholder Engagement

To convince you of the potential for stakeholder engagement to enhance organizational sustainability, it is necessary to articulate what it means clearly. The concept of stakeholder engagement is defined as a process where the organization strategically promotes these values when interacting with stakeholders: representative, transparent, accessible, responsive, and accountable. When these values are achieved, the sustainability of the organization's operations is enhanced, and mutually value-producing relationships with stakeholders are developed. Let us carefully examine each of the elements in this definition since they are the topics of the remaining chapters.

The next chapter examines the value of an organization when stakeholders are representative. Representative is the degree to which the stakeholders who interact with the organization provide input that represents the preferences of a more extensive grouping of stakeholders. Ideally, the organization will compare who is likely to interact with who is unlikely to interact. This will allow for understanding how preference data that is communicated by self-selected stakeholders may miss essential perspectives. I suggest a model of factors that influence stakeholder motivation to participate. When an organizational administrator facilitates interactions, the potential for gathering representative preference data is improved.

An organization is transparent when stakeholders can discover information about the organization's policies and administrative practices as well as the processes and mechanisms available for providing input into decisions. The transparency that comes when stakeholders know how to communicate their preferences is vital to the organization in order to gauge the magnitude and sincerity of these preferences, as well as the stakeholders' willingness to pay for the organization to accommodate these preferences. In Chap. 3, I describe how transparency is a prerequisite for accessibility, meaning that stakeholders can select from a variety of participation activities outside of the organization.[14] They may also invite people within the organization to communicate their preferences.

Accessibility refers to the understanding and perceptions stakeholders have about how they can communicate their preferences to the organization. To be accessible, the organization first needs to know who their stakeholders are and then to learn about the stakeholders' preferences that may influence the success of the organization's transactions and interactions. An individual stakeholder's interests often exist in varying combinations representing a mosaic of individual, group, organizational, and collective-based concerns. In Chap. 4, I identify the kinds of things that can motivate stakeholders to interact with the organization. A perception of accessibility can influence stakeholders' motivations positively to interact with the organization.

An organization is responsive when administrative processes are purposefully designed to facilitate stakeholder interactions with the organization. Facilitated participation can encourage a group of stakeholders representing a wide variety of interests into interactions as well as to avoid perceptions of undue influence by stakeholders highly motivated to participate. Also, facilitated interactions can be structured to provide representative preference data for decision-making as well as provide value by increaseing stakeholders' efficacy for future interactions. Chapter 5 describes facilitated interactions and how an organization can assess the relative costs and benefits of this strategic management function designed to engage stakeholders.

One of the outcomes of stakeholder engagement should be an accountable organization. When this value is served, stakeholders' participation experiences yield the expected results, namely, that these values - representative, transparent, accessible, and responsive - are increased via a stakeholder engagement regime. The regime should provide data that informs decisions and communicates how stakeholder preferences were considered. Additionally, a commitment to stakeholder engagement is institutionalized within the organization.

As discussed in the final chapter, to be sustainable, stakeholder engagement should also be mutually value-producing. For this to occur, the administrator will orchestrate a confluence of processes that serve the economic and social performance goals for the organization.

1.6.1 Building the Case for Stakeholder Engagement

Borrowing from the black box metaphor of Easton (1965) in public policy scholarship, Table 1.1 introduces a logic model reflecting the interrelationships between the concepts that constitute the stakeholder engagement construct.

[14] Participation can occur outside of the organization in a variety of venues. However, when individuals communicate preference information specific to an organization, then they have self-identified as a stakeholder. However, the organization may have a more expansive definition of stakeholders, taking into consideration those who do not interact with the organization but who can or are influenced by organizational operations and decisions.

Table 1.1 The black box of stakeholder engagement

	Activities occurring within the black box of the organization		
Inputs →→→	Processes →→→	Outputs/ Outcomes →→→	Impacts →→→↓↓
Stakeholders Participation Activities Motivations (push)	Motivations (pull) Facilitated Interactions	Stakeholder Engagement	Representativeness ↓ Transparency ↓ Accessibility ↓ Responsiveness ↓ Accountability ↓ Sustainability ↓
Recursive Adjustments	← ← ← Feedback (Organization)	← ← ← Feedback (Institution)	← ← ← Feedback (Collective)

Looking at the first column, we see the inputs that exist in the operating environment of the organization – namely, stakeholders and participation activities. In the first and second columns, participation motivations are represented as both processes and inputs. Inputs feed into the transformation processes that occur within the organization via purposeful facilitated interactions. Facilitated interactions are a means for the organization to gather input from a representative group of stakeholders while also being responsive to stakeholders who voluntarily seek to provide input. This makes facilitated interactions with stakeholders a process variable that transforms the inputs into stakeholder engagement.

When the organization's purposeful interactions with stakeholders provide usable information to guide decision-making, then a stakeholder engagement regime can be institutionalized to provide the value of accountable as an output derived from organization processes. When the organization improves accountability via stakeholder engagement activities and the interactions are mutually value-producing, this can also enhance the outcome of sustainability.

Each of the chapters in the book begins with the development of a taxonomy for the substantive topic and then develops a typology that can be a useful analytical tool for the administrator tasked with stakeholder engagement. The taxonomy provides a meta-level description of the substantive topic based on empirical observations and includes a classification scheme. The typology extracts generalizable themes from the taxonomy and puts them in the context of the ideal condition for an organization to be sustainable. Organizational administrators can use the typology to reflect on processes and practices, to consider how stakeholders' ideas about the substantive topic can have utility in specific operating contexts and to reflect on how different alternative actions differentially serve the organizational values and preferences. Challenges related to the administrative processes described in the chapter are presented as is potential trajectory for overcoming the challenges and moving toward more robust stakeholder engagement.

A trenchant question guiding this project is: How can the community of scholars and practicing professionals improve upon and institutionalize stakeholder engagement practices to improve organizational outcomes and enhance value creation?

To begin answering this question, I undertake my analysis with the intended result of suggesting new ways to perform this management function as well as identifying directions for continuously developing theory and informing practice, recursively (Franklin & Ebdon, 2005). Fundamental to this endeavor is the assumption that all current forms of participation in organizations are legitimate and appropriate. However, I also think we can improve the interactions between an organization and its stakeholders. In this sense, my purpose is to supplement, and not supplant, the ways that organizations engage stakeholders to promote the sustainability of the organization.

References

Albanesi, H., Dukes, R. L., & Singlevich, M. (2013). With strings attached: Philanthropic funding and greater inclusiveness. *The Social Science Journal, 50*, 235–243.

Ambrose, J. (2014, September 9). New hope for solving social issues. *Norman Transcript*, 5.

Anderson, J. E. (2006). *Public policymaking: An introduction* (6th ed.). Boston: Houghton Mifflin Company.

Behn, R. D. (2003). Why measure performance? Different purposes require different measures. *Public Administration Review, 63*(5), 586–606.

Bellone, S. M., & Goerl, G. F. (1992). Reconciling public entrepreneurship and democracy. *Public Administration Review, 52*(1), 130–134.

Bozeman, B., & Johnson, J. (2015). The political economy of public values: A case for the public sphere and progressive opportunity. *The American Review of Public Administration, 45*(1), 61–85. https://doi.org/10.1177/0275074014532826

Bozeman, B., & Bretschneider, S. (1994). The "publicness puzzle" in organization theory: A test of alternative explanations of differences between public and private organizations. *Journal of Public Administration Research and Theory, 4*(2), 197–223.

Bozeman, B. (1987). All organizations are public: Bridging public and private organizational theories. San Diego, CA: Fondo de Cultura Económica.

Bozeman, B. (2004). All organizations are public: Comparing public and private organizations. Washington, DC: Beard Books.

Buchholz, R. A., & Rosenthal, S. B. (2004). Stakeholder theory and public policy: How governments matter. *Journal of Business Ethics, 51*, 143–153.

Buckwalter, N. D. (2014). The potential for public empowerment through government-organized participation. *Public Administration Review, 74*, 573.

Chapman, R. L., & Cleaveland, F. N. (1973). The changing character of the public service and the administrator of the 1980's. *Public Administration Review, 33*(4), 358–366.

DiMaggio, P. J., & Powell, W. W. (1983). The iron cage revisited: Institutional isomorphism and collective rationality in organizational fields. *American Sociological Review, 48*(April), 147–160.

Easton, D. (1965). *A framework for political analysis*. Englewood Cliffs, NJ: Prentice-Hall.

Ebdon, C. (2002). Beyond the public hearing: Citizen participation in the local government budget process. *Journal of Public Budgeting, Accounting and Financial Management, 14*, 273–294.

Fletcher, A., Guthrie, J., Steane, P., Roos, G., & Pike, S. (2003). Mapping stakeholder perceptions for a third sector organization. *Journal of Intellectual Capital, 4*(4), 505–527. https://doi.org/10.1108/14691930310504536

Florin, P., & Wandersman, A. (1990). An introduction to citizen participation, voluntary organizations, and community development: Insights for empowerment through research. *American Journal of Community Psychology, 18*(1), 41–54.

Follett, M. P. (1918). *The new state: Group organization, the solution to popular government*. London: Longman Publishers.

Franklin, A. L., & Ebdon, C. (2005). Practical experience: Building bridges between science and practice. *Administrative Theory & Praxis, 27*(4), 628–639.

Franklin, A. L., Krane, D., & Ebdon, C. (2013). Multilevel governance processes–citizens & local budgeting: Comparing Brazil, China, & the United States. *International Review of Public Administration, 18*(1), 1–24.

Franklin, A. L., & Pagan, J. F. (2006). Organization culture as an explanation for employee discipline practices. *Review of Public Personnel Administration, 26*(1), 52–73. https://doi.org/10.1177/0734371X05277335

Freeman, R. E. (2010). *Strategic management: A stakeholder approach* (2nd ed.). Cambridge, UK: Cambridge University Press.

Friedman, A. L., & Miles, S. (2002). Developing stakeholder theory. *Journal of Management Studies, 39*(1), 1–21.

Hansmann, H. (1987). Economic theories of the nonprofit sector. In W. W. Powell & R. Steinberg (Eds.), *The nonprofit sector* (pp. 27–42). New Haven, CT: Yale University Press. http://www.law.yale.edu/documents/pdf/Faculty/Hansmanneconomictheories.pdf.

Hornbein, R., & King, C. S. (2012). Should we be teaching public participation? Student responses and MPA program practices. *Journal of Public Affairs Education, 18*(4), 717–737.

Jing, Y., & Besharov, D. J. (2014). Collaboration among government, market, and society: Forging partnerships and encouraging competition. *Journal of Policy Analysis and Management, 33*(3), 835–842.

Jorgensen, T. B., & Rutgers, M. R. (2015). Public values: Core or confusion? Introduction to the centrality and puzzlement of public values research. *The American Review of Public Administration, 45*(1), 3–12. https://doi.org/10.1177/0275074014545781

Justice, J., & Tarimo, F. J. (2012). NGOs holding governments accountable: Civil-society budget work. *Journal of Public Budgeting, Accounting and Financial Management, 12*(3), 204.

Kaler, J. (2003). Differentiating stakeholder theories. *Journal of Business Ethics, 46*, 71–83.

Key, S. (1999). Toward a new theory of the firm: A critique of stakeholder "theory". *Management Decision, 37*(4), 317–328. https://doi.org/10.1108/00251749910269366

King, S. M., Chilton, B. S., & Roberts, G. E. (2010). Reflections on defining the public interest. *Administration and Society, 41*(8), 954–978.

Kooiman, J. (1993). *Social-political governance: Introduction*. London: Sage.

Koontz, T. M. (1999). Administrators and citizens: Measuring agency officials' efforts to foster and use public input in forest policy. *Journal of Public Administration Research and Theory, 9*(2), 251–280.

Krane, D., Ebdon, C., & Franklin, A. L. (2020). Social entrepreneurship and the challenge of collaborative governance of civic events: Brazil, Korea, and the United States. In M. N. Iftikhar, J. B. Justice, & D. B. Audretsch (Eds.), *Urban studies and entrepreneurship* (pp. 119–142). Cham, Switzerland: Springer International Publishing. https://doi.org/10.1007/978-3-030-15164-5_7

Kujala, J. (2001). Analysing moral issues in stakeholder relations. *Business Ethics: A European Review, 10*(3), 233–247. https://doi.org/10.1111/1467-8608.00237

LeRoux, K. (2009). Paternalistic or participatory governance? Examining opportunities for client participation in non-profit social service organizations. *Public Productivity and Management Review, 69*, 504–517.

Lindblom, C. E., & Woodhouse, E. J. (1968). *The policy making process*. Englewood Cliffs, NJ: Prentice-Hall.

Lipsky, M., & Smith, S. R. (1989). Nonprofit organizations, government and the welfare state. *Political Science Quarterly, 104*(4), 625–648.

Mellahi, K., & Wood, G. (2003). The role and potential of stakeholders in "hollow participation": Conventional stakeholder theory and institutionalist alternatives. *Business and Society Review, 108*(2), 183–202.

Meriade, L., & Qiang, L. Y. (2015). Public values on the public/private boundary: The case of civil servant recruitment examinations in China. *International Review of Administrative Sciences, 81*(2), 282–302. https://doi.org/10.1177/0020852314546581

Milward, H. B., Provan, K. G., Fish, A., Isett, K. R., & Huang, K. (2009). Governance and collaboration: An evolutionary study of two mental health networks. *Journal of Public Administration Research and Theory, 20*, i125–i141.

Overeem, P. (2015). The concept of regime values: Are revitalization and regime change possible? *The American Review of Public Administration, 45*(1), 46–60. https://doi.org/10.1177/0275074013510771

Park, C., & Wilding, M. (2014). An exploratory study on the potential of social enterprise to act as thei institutional glue of network governance. *The Social Science Journal, 51*, 120–129.

Quinn, R. E., & Rohrbaugh, J. (1983). A spatial model of effectiveness criteria: Towards a competing values approach to organizations. *Management Science, 29*(3), 363–377.

Raadschelders, J. C. N., & Franklin, A. L. (1999). Serving the public interest: The reality of serving multiple publics. *Global Virtue Ethics Review, 1*(3), 1–14.

Rainey, H. G., & Bozeman, B. (2000). Comparing public and private organizations: Empirical research and the power of the a priori. *Journal of Public Administration Research and Theory, 10*(2), 447–469.

Robbins, B. (2013, November 20). Finding solutions to climate change. *Norman Transcript*, 4.

Rudder, C. E. W. (2008). Private governance as public policy: A paradigmatic shift. *The Journal of Politics, 70*(4), 899–913.

Ruscio, K. P. (1996). Trust, democracy, and public management: A theoretical argument. *Journal of Public Administration Research and Theory, 6*(3), 461–477.

Rutgers, M. R. (2015). As good as it gets? On the meaning of public value in the study of policy and management. *The American Review of Public Administration, 45*(1), 29–45. https://doi.org/10.1177/0275074014525833

Saidel, J. R. (1991). Resource interdependence: The relationships between state agencies and nonprofit organizations. *Public Administration Review, 5*(6), 543–553.

Sintomer, Y., Herzberg, C., & Röcke, A. (2008). Participatory budgeting in Europe: Potentials and challenges. *International Journal of Urban and Regional Research, 32*(1), 164–178.

Stout, M., & Love, J. M. (2013). Relational process ontology: A grounding for global governance. *Administration & Society, 47*(4), 447–481. https://doi.org/10.1177/0095399713490692

Stripling, B. (2013). Should democracy be direct? *Public Administration Review, 73*(1), 48–49. https://doi.org/10.1111/puar.12011

Van der Wal, Z., Nabatchi, T., & de Graaf, G. (2015). From galaxies to universe: A cross-disciplinary review and analysis of public values publications from 1969 to 2012. *The American Review of Public Administration, 45*(1), 13–28. https://doi.org/10.1177/0275074013488822

Vinten, G. (2001). Shareholder versus stakeholder—Is there a governance dilemma? *Corporate Governance, 9*(1), 36–47.

Young, D. R. (2011). Chapter 12: Government failure theory. In J. S. Ott & L. A. Dicke (Eds.), *The nature of the nonprofit sector*. Boulder, CO: Westview Press.

Moore, M. H. (1995). Creating public value: Strategic management in government. Cambridge, MA: Harvard University Press.

Ostrom, E., Gardner, R., Walker, J., Walker, J. M., & Walker, J. (1994). Rules, Games, and Common-pool Resources. University of Michigan Press.

Chapter 2
Identifying Stakeholders

Abstract From a normative perspective, all stakeholders have a right to voice their preferences. Not doing so can diminish loyalty and may even lead to an exit from transactions with the organization (Hirschman, Exit, voice, and loyalty. Cambridge, MA: Harvard University Press, 1970). This chapter tackles the question of why organizations may purposefully identify missing stakeholder perspectives and take action to invite input from those whose perspectives are missing. Two methods for the identification and analysis of stakeholders are presented. The first starts by identifying stakeholders the organization regularly interacts with then moves on to identify stakeholders who could be influenced by or influence the success of organizational activities but do not interact. The second uses three categories of stakeholders based on their position relative to the organization, external, mixed, or internal, to identify stakeholders who could represent the interests of multiple stakeholders and who could provide proxy preference information to make stakeholder engagement more cost-efficient.

2.1 Introduction

Who are the individuals or members of groups and organizations who can or do have an impact on, or influence over, your actions? Are these the same people who are influenced by your actions or upon whom your actions have an effect? The answers to these questions often depend on the issue or potential action you are considering. For each action, there is a wide range of people with whom you could interact to enhance the value created by your actions.

I define stakeholder as anyone who or anything (represented by a human) that can influence, or is influenced by, the activities or behaviors of another stakeholder. From an organization's perspective, stakeholders are an input into engagement since these individuals already exist outside the organization, even though an organization may not currently be interacting or engaging with specific stakeholders.

Stakeholders can be people as well as inanimates. When we describe stakeholders as people, we may be talking not only about those who are alive now, but we could also be considering the interests of future generations. Discussions about the need for sustainable human activity are very much focused on the need to preserve the environment for our childrens', childrens', children. When we describe

A. L. Franklin, *Stakeholder Engagement*,
https://doi.org/10.1007/978-3-030-47519-2_2

stakeholders as inanimates, we are acknowledging the impact that nonhuman things may have in our everyday life and consider how they influence our activities. Some examples of nonhuman stakeholders include animals, plants, the environment and common-pool resources, geography, or geographical features of a location, physical structures, social structures, and even the past. Any of these inanimates can impact on our activities.

I refer to these inanimate stakeholders as actants. An *actant* is a nonhuman actor who influences the activities of humans. Here is an example of the influence of an actant on my activities. While hiking in the desert, my hiking group members learned that a rattlesnake was enjoying the shade under a cactus on the path ahead. The presence of the rattlesnake caused the entire group of hikers to change their path to avoid direct interaction. Considering the flip side of this interaction, the rattlesnake had a stake in our behavior. If the group decided to stay on the path, then the rattlesnake could have chosen to stay put under the cactus, move away, or strike at one of the hikers. I wasn't willing to take the chance that the rattlesnake would not take the third option, so I was influenced by the shared interest in survival I had with the rattlesnake and modified my actions appropriately!

Of course, stakeholder interactions can only occur between living people. But these people can be acting for themselves, as delegated representatives of other stakeholders, or as members of groups, organizations, or a collective, such as society. Inanimate stakeholders, by their very nature, rely on human stakeholders to identify and represent their interests. Individuals acting in their own interests or acting in the interest of other stakeholders do so to influence, impact, or react to the impacts stakeholders have on their activities.

The taxonomy in this chapter presents a theoretical arrangement of six continua of stakeholders. The continua are arranged in a way that allows for the systematic identification of a universe of stakeholders. Identifying a wide range of stakeholders informs your selection of which stakeholder(s) with whom you might interact. From this description, a typology is developed that arranges common types of stakeholders within the operating context and demonstrates how a stakeholder may interact differently based on the frequency and nature of the contextual interaction.

Robust identification via the taxonomy and placement of stakeholders within the typology can enable an organization to anticipate who is likely to be influential or impactful. Knowing more about who the stakeholders are for an organization, an administrator for the organization can consider proactively inviting interaction on a particular issue. Stakeholder engagement processes increase the likelihood that the interests of all stakeholders impacted by or impacting the organization's activities can be identified and considered. Purposefully identifying stakeholders and comparing with whom you currently interact to whom you could strategically interact can make the organization more accessible. Identifying a universe of stakeholders can also shed light on strategies to increase the input organizations voluntarily receive from stakeholders for representing a diverse array of interests and preferences.

2.2 The Universe of Stakeholders

The term stakeholder is ubiquitous, yet there is no consensus about what the word means. Academic literature began to systematically address the role and influence of stakeholders on public- and private-sector organizations in the twentieth century. In 1984, Freeman contributed to the business management literature arguing for the need to differentiate between business owners (and/or stockholders) and stakeholders. In 1996, Najam furthered our awareness of definitional differences in the stakeholders for public, corporate, and nonprofit organizations.

A meta-analysis by Miles (2017, p. 29) of 593 definitions of stakeholders identified 16 definitional categories that could be organized within four hyponyms – a stakeholder as an influencer, claimant, collaborator, and/or recipient. These labels are a few of many depicted on a typical stakeholder map. Standard representations of stakeholders place an organization at the center of a diagram with a universe of stakeholders surrounding the organization (Franklin, 2001a). Then other stakeholders are randomly arranged like a solar system with the ones that the organization deals with the most depicted closer to the organizational sun of the solar system.

Within the rings of Fig. 2.1, we can identify stakeholders representing those who are influencers, claimants, collaborators, and/or recipients suggesting the different relationships an organization has with a wide range of stakeholders. Drawing from various strands of literature, in this chapter, I create a more robust taxonomy that arranges stakeholders along six commonly described continua to better capture characteristics of the relationships and suggest why some stakeholders are viewed as influencers or collaborators while others are labeled claimants or recipients.

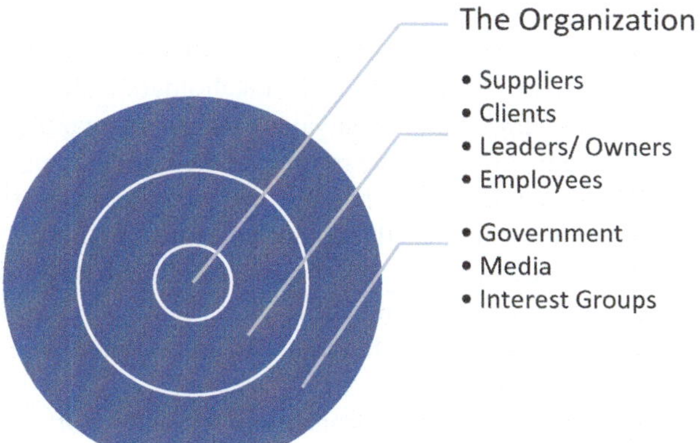

Fig. 2.1 A bulls-eye approach to stakeholder identification

2.2.1 Continuum #1: Relationship to the Organization

In this Chapter, we use six continua to arrange stakeholders based on their position relative to the organization. Stakeholders are often classified based on the nature of the interactions they have with another stakeholder. On Continuum #1, stakeholders can be placed anywhere between involuntary to voluntary interactions. Anyone who buys from a local business is a voluntary stakeholder. However, someone who lives near a business production facility where noise or high traffic flows are issues is an involuntary stakeholder. Taxpayers are another example of involuntary stakeholders, since everyone who works, lives, or shops in a governmental jurisdiction must pay income, property, sales, and/or use taxes.

Most stakeholder interactions are voluntary, meaning one stakeholder chooses to interact with another. Customers making a food purchase are an example of a voluntary stakeholder. Consider the different ways you could purchase food. You could go to a restaurant, a grocery store, the farmer's market, have the food delivered to you and so on. Your choice depends on the timing and type of food you wish to eat. To create value, food vendors consider how to make interactions satisfying to you in the hope that a transaction will result. The process of food vendors identifying stakeholders with whom they interact can provide valuable information about unserved needs and potential product innovations that could increase the likelihood of a transaction with you.

2.2.2 Continuum #2: Interests of the Stakeholder

In the academic literature, there has been discussion about who legitimately has an interest in a stakeholder's actions and how this translates into interactions. Stakeholders with direct interests typically engage in routine transactions. Stakeholders can also have indirect (or derivative) interests. For example, in the legal system, courts require a party to a legal matter to demonstrate standing individually, or as a member of a class of impacted persons, before they can be involved in legal action. Interactions with stakeholders with indirect interests can prove valuable for avoiding diminished value creation by making changes in activities planned by an organization that the indirect stakeholders oppose.

The consideration of indirect interests is particularly important for government organizations since "… the body of persons to whom it is accountable (and, thus, to whom it needs to report on its finances) is much larger and more diverse than that of a business or not-for-profit entity …" (Mead, 2013, p. 95). Indirect stakeholders for government are the people within the jurisdiction who receive goods or services or pay taxes or fees.

Issues related to an environmental ecosystem often include interactions between stakeholders acting as agents for other stakeholders who have no voice. In their representation of actants, the participating stakeholder has indirect interests.

Consider the example of wind energy turbines and the reduction in avian populations that occur near where they are installed. A wildlife protection group that seeks to protect local bird species is an indirect stakeholder for the electric company purchasing the alternative energy. This same group is also an indirect stakeholder for the nonprofit university that owns the wind farm, as well as for the government organization regulating tax credits associated with installing the wind turbines.

A stakeholder may have both direct and indirect interests in the actions of another stakeholder. The wind turbine example demonstrates these overlapping interests. The owner of the land where the turbine is installed has a direct interest in the decisions of the electric company, the university, and the tax agency. If that same landowner is also a member of a wildlife protection group, she simultaneously can interact with these same three organizations as a stakeholder with indirect interests.

As this example suggests, interests often overlap, especially for stakeholders who have dual roles inside and outside the organization, such as a nonprofit board member. For some issues, a direct interest will be specific to a transaction or organizational activity. For other issues, especially when policy issues are being considered, interactions may be based on indirect interests. For this reason, identifying stakeholders who have direct as well as indirect interests can contribute to enhanced value creation.

2.2.3 Continuum #3: Location of the Stakeholder

The third type of classification suggests a delineation between those who are internal to the organization (demonstrated by the closest proximity to the center) and those who are external (shown by the distance away from the center). Typical internal stakeholders for an organization include employees – either as a general label or by named groups of employees such as managers, supervisors, frontline employees, occupational specialists, and line and staff units. External stakeholders often include regulatory agencies, competing organizations, interest groups, unions, professional organizations, vendors, partners, clients, customers, suppliers, and citizens. If we were to identify stakeholders for an individual person, internal stakeholders could be partners, family members, or even pets. External stakeholders could be friends, employers, food vendors, future family members, etc.

Categorizing stakeholders, as internal or external, is overly simplistic. In a time when partnerships, collaboration, and co-production are being emphasized (Agranoff & McGuire, 2003), the internal or external dichotomy does not capture the stakeholders who are simultaneously internal and external for a specific stakeholder. This mix of roles can result in multiple and perhaps conflicting interests.

Recognizing this, Continuum #3 includes a third type of stakeholder – the mixed stakeholder. If you were invited to serve as a member of a nonprofit community art board because you are also an artist, you are a mixed stakeholder for the nonprofit. You are an internal stakeholder as a board member but also an external stakeholder, just like all other artists who support community arts. Identification of mixed stakeholders can be a means for discovering areas of overlap in the interests of internal versus external stakeholders. Identifying all three types of stakeholders, external, mixed, and internal, can be important for understanding who the organization's actions impact and who can influence the organization's actions.

The first three continua allow the organization to inventory the stakeholders with whom they do (or should) regularly interact. Creating a stakeholder inventory is a multistage process that begins by identifying a stakeholder and then determining where the stakeholder should be placed relative to the ongoing activities of the organization and not when a decision about policy or organization activities is under consideration.

Once the stakeholder is identified, the placement in Table 2.1 can be made by answering three questions (in a process similar to a decision tree):

1. Does the stakeholder have a voluntary or involuntary relationship with the organization?
2. Does the stakeholder have or experience direct or indirect influence from the ongoing activities of the organization?
3. What is the relationship of the stakeholder to the organization, and is the stakeholder an external, mixed, or internal stakeholder?

The answers to these questions may be quite easy for most stakeholders, but thought-provoking for other stakeholders who may fall into more than one category for a particular issue or activity. Choosing the correct type is not a concern. You could choose to place any stakeholder in multiple categories if you think they are interacting with the organization as an individual as well as an agent for another stakeholder.

Table 2.1 Identifying stakeholders by characteristics

#1 Relationship to the Organization											
Involuntary						**Voluntary**					
#2 Interests of the Stakeholder											
Indirect			**Direct**			**Direct**			**Indirect**		
#3 Location of the Stakeholder											
E	M	I	E	M	I	E	M	I	E	M	I

In Table 2.2, I present an example drawn from my experience as a board member for the local Meals on Wheels organization. I identified eight stakeholders with whom the organization regularly interacts and labeled them A–H. For each stakeholder, I noted in brackets the decision I made on each of the questions for Continuum #1, #2, and #3. Then, I plotted the stakeholders in Table 2.2.

- A = Staff (voluntary, direct, internal)
- B = Board members (voluntary, indirect, mixed)
- C = Drivers (voluntary, direct, mixed)
- D = Clients (voluntary, direct, external)
- E = Meal preparer (voluntary, direct, external)
- F = Donors/funders (voluntary, indirect, external)
- G = Community service volunteers (voluntary, indirect, internal)
- H = Meal providers for vulnerable populations (involuntary, indirect, external)

Reviewing the table, I wondered why stakeholder H (other meal providers for vulnerable populations) was the only stakeholder on the involuntary side of the table. This would prompt me to try to identify other stakeholders with whom the organization does not interact regularly. If there were others, then I would view this as an opportunity to invite interactions to get additional input for the organization, especially if there were involuntary relationships with stakeholders who were directly influenced by our activity.

Table 2.2 above is a useful way to identify stakeholders who can or should regularly interact with the organization based on the first three continua. Research has demonstrated that some stakeholders engage in repeated and/or nearly continuous interactions with an organization. One reason for this is quite simple: the stakeholders already have the contact information for providing their preferences. Frequent interactions or transactions can lead to an awareness of more opportunities to interact as well as more interactions, creating a cadre of stakeholders labeled the usual suspects (Franklin, 2001a). It is relatively easier for an organization to develop an invitation list for interacting with the usual suspects than with unfamiliar stakeholders for whom contact information is not yet known. Also, prior interactions with the usual suspects build relationships over time and make future interactions likelier (Orr, 2014).

Table 2.2 Typical stakeholders for Meals on Wheels

#1 Relationship to the organization											
Involuntary						Voluntary					
#2 Interests of the stakeholder											
Indirect			Direct			Direct			Indirect		
#3 Location of the stakeholder											
E	M	I	E	M	I	E	M	I	E	M	I
H						D	C	A	F	G	G
						D					

Unfortunately, the usual suspects may not represent the interests of all stakeholders who can or will be impacted by another stakeholder's actions. The challenge is to determine the impacts to and responses by non-represented stakeholders if there are no interactions. Next, I describe three additional continua helpful for considering who is likely to interact with the organization and why they may choose to interact when the organization is considering changes to its current activities.

2.2.4 Continuum #4: Interests Being Represented

In Chap. 1, I argued that it is advantageous for organizations to encourage stakeholder engagement through interactions. These interactions can occur between organizational members and individuals acting on their own or with people representing groups and organizations or even having more abstract representation of institutions and ecological systems as proxies for a collective or society. At any of these levels, a stakeholder can interact with other stakeholders based purely on their own direct and individual interests. Generally, this takes the form of a transaction.

Often, a stakeholder's self-interests are blended with the interests of others who share similar interests. In this case, the stakeholder can represent shared interests through an agency relationship. Research has identified many kinds of agency relationships for groups of stakeholders who have shared or similar indirect interests. These include the role of profession-based organizations (Kahane, Loptson, Herriman, & Hardy, n.d., p. 8; Ogata, 2017), identity groups (Valentinov, Roth, & Will, 2019), and voluntary membership organizations (Krawczyk & Sweet-Cushman, 2017) who represent a community of interest to improve value creation for those they serve.

Stakeholders who interact as an agent for specific groups of stakeholders tend to represent their own interests as individuals as well those of the organized group they represent. Several authors (Baiocchi & Ganuza, 2014; Craw, 2017; Miller & Evers, 2002; Salahudin & Zumitzavan, 2017; Sulkowski, Edwards, & Freeman, 2018) have recognized the importance of stakeholders who act as intermediaries, such as civil society advocacy organizations (Michels, 2017) for the less privileged and vulnerable persons in society (Morone, 1990; Stenberg, 1972, p. 192).

This situation also applies to stakeholders who interact on the behalf of inanimates and for the public in general. Prohl's (1997, p. 77) reporting of 102 cases of local government participation in an international network of 10 countries suggests that citizens become involved when decisions are made to improve government services and create a better community for all residents. The Institute for Local Government (n.d.) notes the importance of knowing the interests stakeholders have for the collective since it articulates the kind of community, infrastructure, and programs that residents want. It is also a way for stakeholders to recognize and assert their duties as citizens and as vital members of society (King et al., 1998; Schlupp & Franklin, 2014).

2.2.5 Continuum #5: Focus of Organizational Action

Proposed changes in activities may cause a stakeholder to seek out interactions with the organization. The organization may be considering one of two kinds of proposed actions: a policy or an activity change to enhance activities and improve value creation. Policy issues arise when the current course of action for an organization, group, or social system is not creating sufficient value. This can lead to consideration of new activities to enhance value creation. Policy issue-based interactions often lead to decisions by (s)elected officials authorizing the enactment of new laws, rules, policies, practices, and/or the deliberate realignment of tangible and intangible resources for a more sustainable future. These policy decisions are abstract statements of intent and, sometimes, will reference specific outcomes desired. Decisions on policy issues seldom provide details about how to get those outcomes.

Administrative issues, on the other hand, relate to the processes and practices necessary for implementing policy decisions and engaging in transactions or interactions. Stakeholders providing input on the organization's activities are typically limited to those stakeholders who are already engaging in, or who have newly become eligible to participate in, transactions and thus have a direct interest in how organizational activities will be conducted. The value being produced for each stakeholder in the transaction is easy to estimate for activities. Based on this, decisions about current or proposed activities can focus on the value-enhancing potential that can be produced for different kinds of stakeholders involved in a transaction.

2.2.6 Continuum #6: Impact of Organizational Action

Any change in the activities of the organization is expected to have positive effects and to create more value for the organization. However, the organization must also consider the potential adverse impacts on the organization, especially if a proposed change will alter the behavior of stakeholders who now engage in transactions with the organization.

Changes in the activities of the organization may improve transactions with stakeholders leading to more positive outcomes. However, changes may lead to transactions that could have negative or mixed impacts on stakeholders who are directly interacting with the organization. The introduction of externalities could also lead to unintended consequences and spillover effects that impact stakeholders who are not a direct party to the transaction. Therefore, the effects of a proposed change in organizational activities on a stakeholder can range from negative to mixed to positive, as shown in Continuum #6.

In Table 2.3, the taxonomy is expanded to include all six continua. In the far left column is Continuum #4, depicting if the stakeholder is acting in their own interest or as an agent for another organization, a group, or a collective. The next column to the right is for Continuum #5. Stakeholders are divided based on the focus of the

Table 2.3 Identifying activity-specific stakeholders

		#1 Relationship to the organization												
		Involuntary						Voluntary						
		#2 Interests of the stakeholders												
		Indirect			Direct			Direct			Indirect			
		#3 Location of the stakeholder												
		E	M	I	E	M	I	E	M	I	E	M	I	
Collective	Policy													Negative
Group														
Org.														
Individual														Negative
	Admin													Mixed
														Positive
Organization	Policy													Positive
Group														
Collective														
#4 Interest Repr'd	#5 Org's action													#6 Impact of Org's action

organization's proposed action; i.e., is it a policy change or a change in activities? Continuum #6 is in the last column on the right. In this column, the impacts, negative, mixed, or positive, from the proposed change are displayed based on whether it is a change to policy or administration and whether the stakeholder is representing his/herself or others.

2.3 Using the Taxonomy

By systematically identifying stakeholders and plotting them on the six continua, it is possible to identify who have ongoing interests and will continue transactions or interactions for the foreseeable future. The first three continua were useful for determining the usual suspects with whom the organization regularly interacts. The second three continua help estimate stakeholder reactions when the organization is considering a change to policy or to their activities.

Systematically identifying stakeholders with whom the organization does not regularly interact could help determine where invitations to interact may be needed. These invitations are particularly important for stakeholders who will be directly impacted by a decision, but with whom no interactions are currently taking place. The invitation to interact also matters to stakeholders who may not be aware that changes to policies or activities are being considered and that they can provide input into the decision-making process.

Let's return to the Meals on Wheels example and use the expanded taxonomy to consider a new activity being proposed. Imagine that Meals on Wheels is considering adding new delivery areas for eligible persons in the growth areas of the city. The challenge is that one of the growth areas is between 5 and 10 miles away from the current meal preparation location. Further, it is hard to attract drivers and to develop routes to deliver the food on time to clients in this area.

The new delivery plan is to develop partnerships with churches and other non-profits in the growth area who would host a centralized location for a Meals on Wheels food provider to deliver the meals. Then the clients could come to that location and share a congregate meal, or volunteer drivers living in that geographic area could deliver the meals, which would reduce the time and expense of traveling an extra 10–20 round-trip miles to pick up the meals.

To analyze the impact of this proposed change, we first consider stakeholders who have already been identified:

- A = Staff (voluntary, direct, internal + indiv, admin, mixed + org, policy, mixed)
- B = Board members (voluntary, indirect, mixed + org, policy, mixed)
- C = Drivers (voluntary, direct, mixed + collective, policy, positive)
- D = Clients (voluntary, direct, external + indiv, admin, positive)
- E = Meal preparer (voluntary, direct, external + org, policy, mixed)
- F = Donors/funders (voluntary, indirect, external + group, policy, positive)
- G = Community volunteers (voluntary, indirect, internal + org, policy positive)
- H = Meal providers (involuntary, indirect, external + collective, policy, positive)

Next, we add three new stakeholders who could be influenced by or might influence the success of the proposed change and plot them in Table 2.4:

- I = Second meal preparer (voluntary, direct, external, group, policy, positive)
- J = Churches (voluntary, indirect, external, group, policy, mixed)

Table 2.4 Activity-specific stakeholders for Meals on Wheels

		#1 Relationship to the organization												
		Involuntary						Voluntary						
		#2 Interests of the stakeholders												
		Indirect			Direct			Direct			Indirect			
		#3 Location of the stakeholder												
		E	M	I	E	M	I	E	M	I	E	M	I	
Collective	Policy													Negative
Group														
Org.														
Individual														Negative
	Admin									A				Mixed
								D						Positive
Organization	Policy							E		A		B	G	Positive
Group								I	C		J			
Collective		H						K	G		F			
#4 Interest Repr'd	#5 Org's action													#6 Impact of Org's action

- K = Food and shelter (voluntary, direct, external, collective, positive)

With the expanded stakeholder typology, the only stakeholder of concern is the MOW staff since the proposed service expansion, as an additional administrative duty, will require them to identify and manage more clients, more drivers, and more food preparers. Plus, the staff will have to interact with the MOW board during the policy decision process to assure that there are sufficient resources or that additional resources can be secured to cover the additional administrative costs.

Having reviewed these six different dimensions for identifying and classifying stakeholders, it may be easier to understand why organizations find robust identification of other stakeholders overwhelming. Buzz Lightyear's famous tag line "To infinity and beyond!" seems appropriate since, in today's increasingly interdependent global society, everyone and everything in the universe potentially can be considered a stakeholder.

The taxonomy provides a means for visualization to anticipate who is most likely to interact and then to place these stakeholders in the graphic. Doing this provides visual cues about where there may be unidentified stakeholders who can provide essential perspectives on the effects, positive and negative, of proposed activities.

2.4 A Typology for Analyzing Groupings of Stakeholders

The taxonomy of stakeholders is valuable for systematically identifying stakeholders who would be placed in categories that currently have no interaction nor representation but who may be influenced by or could seek to influence organizational activities. In this section, I introduce a typology for categorizing stakeholders that can be helpful for organizations to analyze who can be expected to, or who needs to, interact with the organization to fully understand the impacts of current or proposed activities. The type of stakeholder, external, mixed, or internal, is carried forward from Continuum #2 of the taxonomy and displayed on the horizontal axis. Since these types of stakeholders were discussed in the taxonomy, the discussion about the typology is limited to the focus and frequency of interactions that a stakeholder has with the organization, starting at no frequency and ending at a frequency that is nearly continuous. This arrangement allows for the identification and analysis of groups of stakeholders who may have shared interests based on the focus of the activity. Identifying stakeholders with shared interests can reduce the burden to the organization related to collecting data that are representative of many stakeholders' interests.

2.4.1 The Nature of Stakeholder Interactions

The vertical axis of Table 2.5 portrays the focus of interactions ranging from non-participating to continuously interactive. Analyzing interactions is important because expectations about the frequency with which stakeholders will interact are not the same across stakeholders or decisions/activities. Some stakeholders interact with the organization nearly continuously while others are passive, interacting when their self-interests are threatened. Alternatively, some act as principals and delegate their interactions to another stakeholder who acts as their agent. The agent is generally someone who is already interacting and perceived to be more influential. Lastly, some stakeholders may not interact, but for whom an invitation may be sufficient to encourage interactions.

2.4.2 *External Stakeholder Analysis*

The second column of the typology displays a listing of typical external stakeholders. In this column, we can see that external stakeholders could be an individual acting for their own self-interests; an individual who is a member of a group, organization, or collective; or an official representative of a group, organization, or collective. And, when stakeholders provide input into an organization's decisions or activities, they may be doing so based on a combination of interests.

Another observation is that the identities of some external stakeholders, such as the public, citizens, and inanimates, are unknown. The stakeholder's identity becomes known when she/he, or a delegated representative (an agent), contacts the organization about current or future activities or decisions. A specific stakeholder's identity can also be determined when the organization reaches out to people who are eligible to receive the organizations' goods or services as well as those who may experience externalities from organizational activities. One example for stakeholders who experience externalities is residents in a coastal area near an oil spill. The organization responsible for cleaning up the oil spill will likely be mentioned in media reports. With this information, people who suffered harm from the spill may contact the organization directly. Or, the organization may get a list of property owners in the area and reach out to them to explain the cleanup activities.

2.4.2.1 Nonparticipating Stakeholders

Starting in the first row of the external column, the category nonspecific describes stakeholders who may not interact but who have an (usually involuntary and) indirect interest in an organization's activities as a member of a collective. Often they choose not to or are unable to interact as stakeholders of an organization (Franklin, 2001a).

There can be several explanations for nonparticipating stakeholders. Some may feel that their interests are already represented or that the organization already knows their preferences (Ebdon, 2002). Others may be unaware of decision-making that impacts them or do not know that their input would be considered (Yankelovich, 1991). Or, it may just be a logistical problem, like an inconvenient meeting place or time (Franklin, 2001b). A more concerning explanation for not participating may be that individuals fear co-optation or pseudo-empowerment (Arnstein, 1969), describing a situation where stakeholders are pressured to accept the status quo or the views of the majority of stakeholders (Environmental Protection Agency, 2001).

Nonparticipating stakeholders can have a direct but unknown interest in organizational activities. When they discover this interest, they can choose to interact with the organization at any time. When they do decide to interact, then the individual's stakeholder type would shift to a different location in both the taxonomy and the typology. Likewise, there may be times when the organization wants to reach out to individuals who are representative of nonparticipating stakeholders and invite interactions. In this situation, it would be reasonable for the organizations' public relations or customer or stakeholder relations function to develop communication materials to reach a broad, but a nonspecific, audience.

2.4.2.2 Case-Specific Stakeholders

In the second row, the organization interacts with a specific stakeholder based on she/he being a case, which involves a transaction with a particular client, customer, consumer, collaborator, or their representative. The interaction can be initiated by external stakeholders who are directly impacted or by their agents; by mixed stakeholders such as ombudspersons or administrative law judges who mediate or adjudicate a dispute; or by internal stakeholders such as line employees in the organization who have responsibility for delivering goods or services. Generally, the interaction is related to concerns about current transactions or organizational activities. In this situation, the organization may decide to allow a variation from the status quo for this one person (case), or the organization may determine that this change should become a regular practice for handling all other similar cases.

2.4.2.3 Policy or Organizational Activity Decisions and Regularized Interactions

Beginning with the third row of the typology, we see a shift in the interactions from interacting on specific decisions to providing input on activities not related to a particular case. Interactions to communicate preferences may occur when multiple stakeholders are impacted as a group (or class) by the organization's activities. Should the organization change its activities (as shown in the third row of the typology), the change would then apply equally to all comparable cases.

Stakeholders providing input into policy decisions are identified in the fourth row of the typology. This type of interaction is different from that related to organizational activities since the stakeholders may provide insights about changes in the organization's operating environment that may necessitate policy changes. It is also likely that more stakeholders will communicate their preferences and that conflicting preferences will be revealed when policy decisions are considered since the impacts may extend beyond the current cases being served.

Scheduled interactions with (s)elected stakeholders (row 5) can be related to policy changes or routine activities. These interactions differ from those in rows three and four in terms of the external stakeholders who are involved. These individuals are typically invited by the organization to provide input for a specified time as part of an established group of people who interact at regular intervals. Also, the input that is received is much more focused on making incremental changes to organizational activities than to considering new policies.

2.4.2.4 Continuous Interactions

The last row features external stakeholders who have regularized interactions, both on a scheduled and on an infrequent basis, and the input occurs informally on a nearly continuous basis as the organization. The stakeholders work together do so to produce value for each, respectively. Interactions that occur with an almost continuous frequency can include external stakeholders, like vendors, suppliers, and collaborators with whom the organization regularly transacts as part of the supply chain for the organization. Typically, these stakeholders are the first to be invited to interact with the organization to provide feedback and input on emerging issues about activities or policy decisions. Higher frequency interactions help to align interests since there is a continuing relationship and the prospect for future transactions is high.

2.4.3 Mixed Stakeholder Analysis

In the mixed stakeholder column of Table 2.5, I list persons who have professional credentials, skills, or training directly related to their interactions with the organization. The mixed stakeholders' affiliation with the organization generally occurs by an invitation that is based upon some combination of an individual's knowledge, skills, and abilities. For example, since the Sarbanes-Oxley legislation was enacted in 2002 (P.L. 107-204), nonprofit organizations have had to be much more deliberate in identifying potential members for the board of directors since they must assure that there are stakeholders who have the background necessary to fulfill specific financial stewardship requirements.

The first observation for the mixed column is that all the individual stakeholders interact with the organization based on their profession or because they have an oversight or regulatory role for the organization. From the perspective of the organization, interactions with mixed stakeholders can be more influential in policy decisions than input from external stakeholders. Mixed stakeholders can have expectations for deciding or the ability to compel organizational action. The scholarly literature alludes to three kinds of mixed stakeholders without assigning the label of mixed stakeholder: intermediaries, interpenetrating positions, and

Table 2.5 Stakeholder typology

Stakeholder type			
Interactions	External	Mixed	Internal
1. Nonspecific, may not interact	Public Citizens Constituents Inanimates	Elected officials	Public relations
2. Case-specific	Clients, customers, consumers	Ombudspersons, administrative law judges	Caseworker Customer service
3. Administrative decisions	Advocates Competitors	Compliance Regulatory organizations	Street-level bureaucrat
4. Policy decisions	Industry groups Watchdogs, media Interest groups	Professional associations	Subject matter experts
5. Regularly scheduled with (s)elected stakeholders	Advisory groups – members of boards, councils, commissions	Owners Board of directors, principals in agency relationships	Programs and staff units
6. Continuous	Vendors, suppliers, collaborators	Unions Partners Contractors	Executive leaders Decision-makers

interlocking relationships. We consider the characteristics of each of these groupings next.

2.4.3.1 Intermediaries

Mixed stakeholders represent the interests of internal and external stakeholders. This can be helpful for reconciling disputes about the organization's activities. An intermediary can represent the interests of an individual stakeholder or the interests of a group (or class) of stakeholders. An example is a lawyer contacting the organization about his client's transaction with the organization. However, even when represented by an intermediary, stakeholders do not give up their rights to directly interact with the organization. This first type of intermediary does not have the authority to compel organization action.

The second type of intermediary is independent of both the internal and external stakeholders. These stakeholders have formal authority to resolve a case-based dispute between an individual stakeholder and the organization. An example is an administrative law judge. Some mixed stakeholders, like the administrative law judge, make their determination based on an examination of the policies or the practices of the organization. Other intermediaries, such as officials in compliance and regulatory agencies, monitor the activities of an organization and can compel corrective action or enforce sanctions when violations are discovered. In both situations, the mixed stakeholder is acting to preserve group or collective interests (which includes nonparticipating as well as case-specific external stakeholders).

Another activity for third-party intermediaries is to use their substantive knowledge and professional expertise and experience to monitor organizational activities, persuasively present evidence for policy or organizational activity changes, and enhance accountability to individuals, groups, and the collective (Mead, 2013, p. 111).

Involving an intermediary, whether the intermediary does or does not have the authority to compel organization action, can be an additional source of input about the operating environment. Their perspective can inform decision-making and enhance the value created by the organization's activities. On the other hand, the involvement of an intermediary can result in a loss of control and higher transaction costs to the organization since an additional stakeholder is now involved in and may have authority over the organization's decisions and activities. However, all intermediaries provide insight into what is desired by other stakeholders and how these preferences relate to the organization's activities, so they are labeled mixed stakeholders.

2.4.3.2 Interpenetrating Positions

As we move toward the bottom of the mixed column, we find stakeholders who have a vested interest in the sustainability of the organization. Thus, the interactions between these stakeholders and the organization are more collaborative than are those of third-party intermediaries. Interpenetrating positions occur when a formal or informal arrangement exists for a person to simultaneously serve multiple organizations in an official capacity (Follett, 1918, p. 54). Formal arrangements occur when someone is asked to fill a position on the organization's board of directors.

When inter-penetrating relationships occur within a policy community or a collaborative network of production partners, formal arrangements are less likely. Typical examples are employees involved with professional associations, unions, partnership collaborations, and contractors. At the National Weather Center building on my campus, it is quite common for weather researchers to have two official positions – one with one of the NOAA agencies housed in the building and the other as a staff or faculty member of the University of Oklahoma. There are also sequential interpenetrating positions that exist when a person leaves an organization in one sector to work with an organization in another sector based on an established pattern of interactions between the organizations but continues to serve as a board member of the first organization.

When mixed stakeholders with interpenetrating positions provide feedback on the decisions being made or activities of the organization, they can act based on individual interests as well as group or collective interests. When this happens, these stakeholders may experience tension when attempting to align their interests with those of the organization simultaneously.

2.4.3.3 Interlocking Relationships

Interlocking relationships reflect formal organizational arrangements where a member of a board of directors serves on the boards of other organizations (known as multiple directorships). The interests of these stakeholders can be direct if the director is an executive of one of the organizations or indirect if two directors both sit on the board of a third organization. Within Table 2.5, owners, members of the board of directors, and principals in agency relationships such as those of elected officials and government programs would participate in interlocking relationships.

Interlocking relationships can raise questions about the independence of a stakeholder's preferred decision outcome. There can also be social justice concerns because of the de facto creation of an elite community of interest. This is a particular concern when corporate elites are appointed to the boards of government and nonprofit organizations based on influence rather than to assure representation of the stakeholders directly served by the organization.

Mixed stakeholders may have positions of authority that can compel an organization to take some action or to cease some activity. Or, they may have positions of influence whereby the mixed stakeholder's input tends to be more heavily weighted than those of other stakeholders. Mixed stakeholders can also have standing as a member of an organized group invested with the right to negotiate the terms of transactions the organization has with internal or external stakeholders. Identifying mixed stakeholders and learning their preferences can be a valuable way to avoid challenges to organizational decisions or activities brought by external stakeholders in venues that are outside the organization's boundaries.

2.4.4 Internal Stakeholder Analysis

The internal stakeholder column identifies the units in an organization that typically have interactions with mixed and external stakeholders at each of the different frequency levels. As suggested above, the employees tasked with the public relations function can assist with the identification of nonparticipating stakeholders. They can devise methods of communication to promote transparency and, when desired, to invite interactions.

Gathering input about current cases from the employees who directly engage in client transactions can improve internal operations at the administrative and policy levels. Direct goods or service delivery employees and subject matter experts in functional and staff units of the organization are best positioned to identify patterns in the organization's activities that are suggestive of systematic impacts (externalities) on a group or class of stakeholders.

Executives and leaders are listed in the last row because they often play an important role in decision-making on behalf of the organization. These internal stakeholders are boundary spanners who can provide insights on preferences based on interactions with internal, mixed, and external stakeholders.

When reviewing the list of internal stakeholders, however, it is important to remember that all employees, as individuals, are voluntary stakeholders who have individual as well as organizational interests. The literature on public (Perry & Wise, 1990) and nonprofit organizations (LeRoux & Bernadska, 2014) suggests that employees also have varying levels of service motivation and altruism that influences them to consider collective interests as well as their own and the organization's interests.

The listing of internal stakeholders in the typology suggests segmentation between organizational units based on the different frequencies of interactions. At the top of the column are administrative decisions that relate to the provision of goods or services to a specific case. Internal stakeholders often attempt to make each transaction uniform to gain economies of scale by treating like cases alike, thereby reducing transaction costs.

As the kind of interaction moves from administrative decisions about a specific case to more abstract discussions about policy decisions, we can expect that the input of program employees in line units will be reduced in favor of input from employees in centralized staff units as well as those at the apex of the organization. Input from process owners is still essential, but often the reallocation of resources is necessary. Resource reallocation generally requires the approval of higher levels of organizational officials. As input is gathered from more employees of the organization, one challenge is that interactions with each additional internal stakeholder increase the time necessary to make the decision. Besides, the employee will not be entirely self-interested. Many employees are advocates for those they serve or for group or collective social interests such as human rights or environmental sustainability. In this situation, the employee's input may also represent the interests of an outside group or organization or collective.

2.4.5 Stakeholder Groupings That Overlap Columns

Table 2.6 places examples of different kinds of stakeholders within the cells in the typology for illustrative purposes, without any attempt to ensure that the categories are mutually exclusive or exhaustive. You could likely identify other stakeholders to include or may place stakeholders in a different cell. The purpose of the typology is not to argue that stakeholders can correctly be placed in the table. The purpose is to suggest a way to organize information and discern patterns for analysis. In the next figure, I have superimposed boxes on the stakeholders in the cells of the typology to identify overlapping stakeholder groups for analytical purposes.

Several different labels for overlapping stakeholder groups have been presented in the literature. Heclo (1978) first introduced the label of the iron triangle to describe a cozy relationship between congressional staffers, industry groups, and agency administrators. Cozy relationships are an excellent way for stakeholders to get the policy or administrative outcomes they desire (Schattschneider, 1960). Other labels for cozy relationships include issue networks (Berry, 1990), policy elites

Table 2.6 Stakeholder groupings

Stakeholder type			
Interactions	External	Mixed	Internal
1. Nonspecific, may not interact	Public Citizens Constituents Inanimates	Elected officials	Public relations
2. Case-specific	Clients, customers, consumers	Ombudspersons, administrative law judges	Caseworker Customer service
3. Administrative decisions	Advocates Competitors	Compliance/regulatory organizations	Street-level bureaucrat
4. Policy decisions	Industry groups Watchdogs, media Interest groups	Professional associations	Subject matter experts
5. Regularly scheduled with (s)elected stakeholders	Advisory groups – members of boards, councils, commissions	Owners Board of directors, principals in agency relationships	Programs and staff units
6. Interactive	Vendors, suppliers, collaborators	Unions Partners Contractors	Executive leaders Decision-makers

(Pierce, Lovrich, & Matsuoka, 1989), policy communities (Dowding, 1995), and the usual suspects (Franklin, 2001b). These labels similarly describe situations where external and mixed stakeholders directly interact to influence policy and administrative decisions.

In Table 2.6 the overlapping stakeholder group that extends from the External column in rows 3 and 4 to the Mixed column in rows 2 and 3 contains stakeholders who have been given authority to represent other external stakeholders, so they are labeled Delegated. Stakeholders in this overlapping group often provide input about transactions related to a specific case or activities impacting all of the organization's stakeholder. They might also be engaged in policy deliberations on behalf of involuntary and voluntary stakeholders. Indirect, group, organizational, or collective interests will generally guide the delegate's actions. External stakeholders acting as a delegate seldom have the authority to make decisions that bind the organization. Mixed stakeholders, however, may have formal authority to act on behalf of external stakeholders who wish to challenge a decision of the organization.

The box that includes the entire Internal column, as well as portions of rows 4, 5, and 6 of the Mixed and External columns, is used to denote stakeholders who receive compensation as part of their interactions with the organization. Compensated stakeholders are voluntary stakeholders. Most are directly impacted by the organization, as well as being individually and organizationally interested.

Within the grouping of compensated stakeholders, the external stakeholder's role is typically informal and advisory. The mixed stakeholder's role is usually formal and vested with binding authority (granted by the organization or delegated from the internal/external stakeholders they represent). There is variation among the internal stakeholders in terms of the degree to which their input is advisory or binding.

2.4.5.1 Mediating Institutions

Third-party intermediaries do not have official status to work with stakeholders to assist in providing input to the organization are presented in the External column. When the third-party intermediary, such as a civil society organization, has a formalized relationship with the organization to assist in gather stakeholder input, or when they have some level of influence over the employees of the organization, such as a government or professional organization accrediting entity, then they become mediating institutions.

In the Mixed column, I list mediating institutions with some overlap between individuals who also participate in interpenetrating relationships. An example of a mediating institution (Berger & Neuhaus, 1996) is a professional association that acts on behalf of specific individuals who have an involuntary, indirect, and passive relationship to an organization. Mediating institutions in the Mixed column enjoy a privileged relationship with the organization causing their input to be valued more highly. Or, the mediating institution may be able to compel action.

Organizations tend to collaborate more frequently with those in overlapping stakeholder groups since they are easier to contact, have a stated interest in the organization, and have more detailed knowledge about organizational policies and activities, making their input more immediately useful. A disadvantage is that it is difficult to judge the concordance of motives and preferences between stakeholders in the overlapping groups with other external and mixed stakeholders who do not benefit from a cozy relationship with the organization (Lando, 1999). Without the organization deliberately inviting input from a representative group of stakeholders, the interests of stakeholders in these overlapping groups may unduly influence organizational decisions and activities.

Using the typology has value for the organization by retrospectively analyzing the stakeholders who predictably interact with the organization. If there are cells in the typology that are blank, then representatives of the missing stakeholders, based on the Focus column, can be identified and invited to interact. Doing this also reveals stakeholders who could provide useful preference data concerning future policy decisions and changes to organizational activities. The typology is an analytical tool that can be used independently of the taxonomy as a quick guide for identifying stakeholders for a specific decision by focusing on the relevant row and then gathering input from a combination of external, mixed, and internal stakeholders.

2.5 Summary

In this chapter, I present two methods for the identification and analysis of the universe of stakeholders. The first starts with identifying stakeholders the organization regularly interacts with then moves on to identify stakeholders who could be influenced by or influence the success of proposed changes in organization activities but do not interact. To assist in the identification of stakeholders, I developed a taxonomy utilizing categories of stakeholders arranged on six different continuums.

In the typology section, I narrowed the analysis to consider stakeholders based on the focus and frequency of interaction with an organization. Starting with three simple categories of stakeholders derived from their position relative to the organization, external, mixed, or internal, overlapping groups of stakeholders within the table were identified, and ways in which these groupings could enlighten stakeholder analysis were described.

Using these analytical tools, the number of potential stakeholders may first seem as vast as the universe. However, not every stakeholder will want to interact on every issue. Further, stakeholders will experience different levels of impact from an organization's activities or could differentially influence organizational decision-making. Finding efficient ways to identify stakeholders and consider gaps and overlaps allows for greater precision in determining with whom the organization might interact on any issue or upcoming decision. Over the long-term, when the organization considers how to meaningfully increase the representativeness of input into activities, the prospect of sustainability is enhanced.

Determining the gap between who does provide input and who may need to provide input is vital for organizations to thrive. From a normative perspective, all stakeholders have a right to voice their preferences. Not doing so can diminish loyalty and may even lead to an exit from transactions with the organization (Hirschman, 1970). Identifying stakeholder perspectives not currently offered nor gathered is one way for the organization to target an administrator's activities to gather the information that is missing but will be informative. The question of how to do this systematically is one that has not received a sufficient amount of attention by scholars nor practitioners. In Chap. 3, we consider how to categorize the kinds of participation activities available and then to strategically design a data collection routine to make sure that stakeholder input is representative and available to inform organizational decisions.

References

Agranoff, R., & McGuire, M. (2003). *Collaborative public management: New strategies for local government*. Washington, D.C.: Georgetown University Press.

Arnstein, S. R. (1969). A ladder of citizen participation. *American Institution of Planners Journal, 35*(7), 216–224.

Baiocchi, G., & Ganuza, E. (2014). Participatory budgeting as if emancipation mattered. *Politics and Society, 42*(1), 29–50. https://doi.org/10.1177/0032329213512978

Berger, P. L., & Neuhaus, R. J. (1996). *To empower people: From state to civil society* (2nd ed.). Washington, D.C.: American Enterprise Institute.

Berry, J. M. (1990). Citizen groups and the changing nature of interest group politics in America. *Annals of the American Academy of Political and Social Science, 538*, 30–41.

Craw, M. (2017). Institutional analysis of neighborhood collective action. *Public Administration Review, 77*(5), 707–717. https://doi.org/10.1111/puar.12707

Dowding, K. (1995). Model or metaphor? A critical review of the policy network approach. *Political Studies, 43*(1), 136–158.

Ebdon, C. (2002). Beyond the public hearing: Citizen participation in the local government budget process. *Journal of Public Budgeting, Accounting & Financial Management., 14*, 273. https://doi.org/10.1108/JPBAFM-14-02-2002-B006

Environmental Protection Agency. (2001). *Stakeholder involvement & public participation at the U.S. EPA*. Washington, D.C.: U. S. Government Printing Office.

Follett, M. P. (1918). *The new state: Group organization, the solution to popular government*. New York: Longman Publishers.

Franklin, A. L. (2001a). Involving stakeholders in organizational processes. *International Journal of Public Administration, 24*(4), 385–403.

Franklin, A. L. (2001b). Serving the public interest: Federal experience with participation in strategic planning. *American Review of Public Administration, 31*(2), 126–138.

Heclo, H. (1978). Issue networks and the executive establishment. In A. King (Ed.), *The new American political system*. Washington, D.C.: American Enterprise Institute.

Hirschman, A. O. (1970). *Exit, voice, and loyalty*. Cambridge, MA: Harvard University Press.

Institute for Local Government. (n.d.). Public involvement in budgeting: Options for local officials. *Western City, November* (2008). cailg.org/PublicInvolvementBudgeting.

Kahane, D., Loptson, K., Herriman, J., & Hardy, M. (n.d.). Stakeholder and citizen roles in public deliberation. *Journal of Public Deliberation, 9*, 37.

King, C. S., Stivers, C., & Collaborators. (1998). *Government is us: Public administration in an anti-government era*. London: Sage Publications.

Krawczyk, K. A., & Sweet-Cushman, J. (2017). Understanding political participation in West Africa: The relationship between good governance and local citizen engagement. *International Review of Administrative Sciences, 83*(1_suppl), 136–155. https://doi.org/10.1177/0020852315619024

Lando, T. (1999). Public participation in local government: Points of view. *National Civic Review, 88*(2), 109.

LeRoux, K., & Bernadska, A. (2014). Impact of the arts on individual contributions to U.S. civil society. *Journal of Civil Society, 10*(2), 144–164.

Mead, D. M. (2013). Accounting and financial reporting. In J. R. Bartle, W. B. Hildreth, & J. Marlowe (Eds.), *Management policies in local government finance* (6th ed., pp. 93–116). Washington, D.C.: ICMA Press.

Michels, A. (2017). Participation in citizens's summits and public engagement. *International Review of Administrative Sciences, 85*, 211. https://doi.org/10.1177/0020852317691117

Miles, S. (2017). Stakeholder theory classification, definitions and essential contestability. In D. M. Wasieleski & J. Weber (Eds.), *Stakeholder management* (Vol. 1, pp. 21–48). Bingley, UK: Emerald Publishing Limited.

Miller, G. J., & Evers, L. (2002). Budgeting structures and citizen participation. *Journal of Public Budgeting, Accounting & Financial Management, 14*(2), 233–272. https://doi.org/10.1108/JPBAFM-14-02-2002-B005

Morone, J. A. (1990). *The democratic wish: Population participation and the limits of American government*. New York: Basic Books.

Najam, A. (1996). NGO accountability: A conceptual framework. *Development Policy Review, 14*(4), 339–353.

Ogata, K. (2017). Stakeholder responses to government austerity: What happens when strong stakeholders fail to react? *International Review of Administrative Sciences, 83*(1), 129–148. https://doi.org/10.1177/0020852315576711

Orr, S. K. (2014). *Environmental policymaking and stakeholder collaboration*. Boca Raton, FL: CRC Press.

Perry, J. L., & Wise, L. R. (1990). The motivational bases of public service. *Public Administration Review, 50*, 367–373.

Pierce, J. C., Lovrich, N. P., & Matsuoka, M. (1989). Support for citizen participation: A comparison of American and Japanese citizens' activities and elites. *The Western Political Quarterly, 43*, 39–59.

Prohl, M. (1997). *International strategies and techniques for future local government. Practical aspects towards innovation and reform*. Gütersloh, Germany: Bertelsmann Foundation Publishers.

Salahudin, S., & Zumitzavan, V. (2017). A relationship between local government and civic groups on budget planning in Malang City. In *Proceedings of the International Conference on Ethics in Governance (ICONEG 2016)*. Makassar, Indonesia. https://doi.org/10.2991/iconeg-16.2017.54

Schattschneider, E. E. (1960). *The semisovereign people*. New York: Holt, Rinehart and Winston.

Schlupp, J., & Franklin, A. L. (2014). Civic engagement motivations: Understanding why some do and some don't. *Oklahoma Politics, 24*, 21–44.

Stenberg, C. W. (1972). Citizens and the administrative state. *Public Administration Review, 32*, 190–198.

Sulkowski, A. J., Edwards, M., & Freeman, R. E. (2018). Shake your stakeholder: Firms leading engagement to co-create sustainable value. *Organization & Environment, 31*(3), 223–241. https://doi.org/10.1177/1086026617722129

Valentinov, V., Roth, S., & Will, M. G. (2019). Stakeholder theory: A Luhmannian perspective. *Administration & Society, 51*(5), 826–849. https://doi.org/10.1177/0095399718789076

Yankelovich, D. (1991). *Coming to public judgment. Making democracy work in a complex world*. Syracuse, NY: Syracuse University Press.

Chapter 3
Selecting Participation Activities

Abstract Stakeholder engagement requires the sharing of information about preferences between stakeholders and the organization. This can be accomplished through many kinds of participation activities. Some are passive and not specifically shared with the organization. Others are active and can range from one-way to two-way interactions that serve a variety of purposes. Organizations can design data collection strategies that fit the purposes for which they need information. They can also consider the venue in which stakeholder inputs can be gathered. Stakeholder participation can be influenced by the availability of data, time required, nature of the interaction, and intended use of the inputs. Because of this, the relative costs of gathering stakeholder preferences using different activities vary. Deliberately designing participation activities can enhance the transparency of the organization's activities and increase the representativeness of the data to inform decisions.

3.1 Introduction

All organizations communicate information about the goods and services they offer as a way to generate the transactions necessary for the organization to be sustainable. Many organizations also communicate financial data and performance reports, or information about recent policy or administrative decisions, by making these documents publicly available or sending information out to a list of stakeholders. Fewer organizations commit to communicating the processes for stakeholders to transmit their preferences to the organization. Often this occurs because the organization does not have a regularized process for gathering stakeholder data or seeking input or has not adopted a uniform stakeholder engagement policy and different organizational units have different processes.

Releasing publicly accessible documents or communicating directly with specific stakeholders is a means for fostering transparency. Communicating instructions about ways to participate or extending an invitation for participation suggests that the organization values accessibility as well as transparency. Accessibility assures that stakeholders are aware of opportunities for offering input should they choose to do so. If stakeholders want to provide input or are viewed as a source of preference data for decisions, then organizations should strive to be both accessible and transparent.

A. L. Franklin, *Stakeholder Engagement*,
https://doi.org/10.1007/978-3-030-47519-2_3

The topic for Chap. 3 is participation activities, which is a second input into the stakeholder engagement logic model. Organizations gather information through a range of participation activities in which stakeholders provide input that communicates their preferences. Inputs are information suggesting what a stakeholder wants the organization to do, while preferences are the course of action the stakeholder prefers the organization to take in its activities. Input information, as well as stakeholder-specific preferences, can be communicated in many different venues. These communications can be abstract, such as a policy preference, or can be specific to organization activities or even about the organization's processes.

Stakeholder engagement is an activity that I recommend to be a formal and institutionalized organization process. This is not to say that an individual could not create and benefit from adopting a stakeholder engagement regime. However, if they did so, it would likely be because they regularly take part in stakeholder engagement activities that contribute to success in their profession or in their business. In this case, the stakeholder engagement regime is purposefully undertaken with the intention of enhancing professional outcomes to assure sustainability and not to influence a single transaction or interaction.

Consider the example of people who are (or want to be) social influencers. These people would benefit from undertaking the stakeholder engagement activities described in this book. However, people who are not interested in being social influencers probably would not put forth the effort to get the largest visibility for their social media posts. Instead they would be posting for fun and interacting with people whose ideas they like and perhaps arguing with, or blocking interactions with, people whose ideas they do not like. In this book, I take the organization's perspective. This means that stakeholder engagement is accomplished through interactions with stakeholders who the organization influences or who influence the organization's activities.

Stakeholders can engage in transactions related to the exchange of a good or service. Stakeholders can also interact with the organization to provide input about the organization's activities or to convey their preferences for decisions being made. Transactions and interactions can be done by stakeholders anonymously, but we will be considering the impact on the organization of a stakeholder's actions whether or not the stakeholder is identifiable.

In this chapter, I describe and analyze different kinds of participation activities that can gather input from stakeholders to inform decision-making. The chapter starts with a discussion of common reasons why organizations and stakeholders interact. Then, I describe the venues available for participation activities. Next, I analyze the kinds of activities available to stakeholders to interact with organizations and for the organization to promote accessibility and transparency. The analysis then turns to an examination of the activities available to foster interactions and the challenges related to making organizations accessible based on active participation mechanisms organizations commonly offer. The trajectory suggests ways to institutionalize participation activities to gather preference data strategically.

3.2 Reasons to Gather Stakeholder Preference Data

Organizations in all sectors regularly offer a variety of participation activities to gather information from stakeholders. There are many reasons why organizations choose to make the organization accessible via these mechanisms. Many government organizations routinely offer participation opportunities due to legal requirements. A ubiquitous example is the public hearing required before the budget is adopted by city officials (Berner & Smith, 2004). At the federal level, there are laws such as the Administrative Procedures Act of 1946 spelling out requirements for participatory processes. There are also uniform standards for participation opportunities, such as publishing proposed rules in the *Federal Register* and notifying the public of the comment process and timelines for commenting. Publicly traded organizations hold annual board meetings to which all stockholders receive invitations to attend. Organizations in the not-for-profit sector often host annual meetings to recognize their accomplishments, to honor their volunteers and donors and to announce new strategies and policies for the upcoming time period.

Participation opportunities may also be encouraged based on the language of official documents like a mission statement. For the US Forest Service, the mission statement contains a requirement to "...listen to people and respond to their diverse needs in making decisions" (U.S. Forest Service, n.d.). The Johnson & Johnson mission statement is that "our credo stems from a belief that consumers, employees and the community are all equally important" (https://mission-statement.com/johnson-johnson/).

Official organization positions such as these communicate an expectation of responsiveness to stakeholder preferences. They also suggest an organizational culture that values the relationships that can be established when expectations for interactions or institutionalized. Gathering input from stakeholders is often done voluntarily by organizations since it can be informative in gauging the viability of current activities as well as learning what stakeholders desire from a specific decision that the organization is considering. In either case, learning stakeholder preferences can help in the design of future policies and in the activities of the organization to reduce the disruption that comes from dissatisfied stakeholders.

3.3 Kinds of Participation

There are two main kinds of participation activities – passive and active. As the term passive suggests, stakeholders can indicate their preferences, even though they are not directing the input to a specific stakeholder or organization. There may not even be any interaction between stakeholders or with the organization. In this case, the preference information is learned by the organization through purposeful activities to collect existing data.

Posting to Internet websites and social media platforms is a passive participation activity that has become more prominent for stakeholders to communicate preferences. Modern technology allows anyone to get involved in organizational decision-making. Providing input can be accomplished by liking items posted online, sending a message to an organizational official, giving money to a mediating institution, or objecting and launching counter-objections via crowdsourcing mechanisms (Kamensky, 2015; Lovejoy, Waters, & Saxton, forthcoming; Santaniello & Amoretti, 2013). As Rethemeyer (2007) observed, one response to people who make objectionable comments is to just "unfriend" them. When you do this, you no longer are exposed to ideas with which you disagree or find objectionable.

When stakeholders decide to "unfriend" the organization and communicate their preferences in other venues, the organization loses the opportunity to preserve stakeholder interactions and maintain expected future transactions. The incidence and prevalence of passive participation is a trajectory to monitor since it can diminish the desired future communication of preferences.

On the other hand, stakeholders can actively initiate participation activities and interact with other stakeholders or with the organization, synchronously, or asynchronously. Based on this, the term participation activities refers to situations where a stakeholder initiates the process of revealing preferences but may or may not directly communicate these preferences through interactions with the organization.

Stakeholder-initiated participation activities are contrasted with organization-initiated participation mechanisms, which are deliberately selected and structured activities offered by the organization to gather stakeholder preference data to inform decisions. In this respect, mechanisms are a subset of participation activities.

There are many different mechanisms for gathering preference data. Some require no direct interaction between the organization and the stakeholder; others feature one-way or two-way interactions. Interactions are a dynamic sequence of social exchanges between individuals, groups, or organizations that reveal stakeholder's preferences. Interactions can be accidental, repeated, regular, or regulated and can include a feedback component.

There are two types of stakeholder interactions: conducting transactions and interacting to provide preference data. Transactions are the activities that take place as part of the exchange of goods and services between the organization and the stakeholder. They do not imply stakeholder participation in the organization's decision-making process via the provision of preference data (Datta, 2003). Transactions are also unlikely to modify a stakeholder's preferences. However, they can, such as when a stakeholder selects a substitute good because they are unhappy with the cost or quality of the goods or services offered. Interactions feature direct communication between the organization and the stakeholder about a particular concern related to the organization's activities or to provide input into a decision.

An organization does not always have to interact with stakeholders to gather preference data. For example, the organization can systematically gather pre-existing preference data that has been passively or actively communicated by stakeholders. However, stakeholder participation generally occurs through direct interactions with the organization, although it can take many different forms.

Organizations often use a combination of activities and mechanisms to gather information. Some of these are institutionalized, such as transaction feedback mechanisms, like a customer satisfaction survey, while others gather input on an ad hoc basis (Van Meter, 1975, p. 806). An example of an ad hoc approach may be a waste management firm considering enhancements to a recycling program. The organization may hold a series of meetings anyone can attend and can send out a survey to explore what options are attractive and what level of charges will be acceptable to users. The meetings can gather broad-based stakeholder input from a range of potential stakeholders, and the survey of existing customers collects concentrated data from current stakeholders (Folz, 1991). This example invites stakeholder input on a specific decision and utilizes ad hoc data collection techniques. Institutionalized participation opportunities provide information for recurring decisions, such as meetings for the annual budget adoption.

Organizational officials initiate some interactions, and some are self-initiated by stakeholders. When interactions are *proactive*, the organization generally seeks input into decisions that will change the status quo. Another type of proactive interaction is when the organization, as part of their regular business practices, seeks feedback about its current activities and how they could be improved. In either case, (s)elected officials or administrators will purposefully seek out stakeholder input.

When interactions are *reactive*, the organization is responding to stakeholder-initiated communication, often due to dissatisfaction with a proposed policy or a current activity of the organization. In this situation, the organization can use the interaction to inform and then craft a response to the concerns provided by the stakeholder. The organization can communicate the response to other stakeholders who are in a similar situation as well.

Whether obtained passively or actively through transactions or interactions, when preference data are collected and inform decisions, the transparency of the organization is enhanced. The various forms of participation described in this chapter exist, in part, because of the multitudinous venues available to stakeholders for communicating preferences.

3.4 Venues

A venue is a space, either tangible or intangible, that people use to communicate and where something happens based on these communications. Baumgartner and Jones defined venues as "…institutional locations where authoritative decisions (about a policy) are made" (1993, p. 32). My definition of venues does not require an authoritative decision. Instead, stakeholder participation venues are where people communicate their satisfaction with the status quo or their preferences for the future on any topic of their choosing. The communication de facto encourages others to respond, even if the response is to not make any change in the status quo.

The rules and procedures governing venues vary widely, ranging from venues with highly formal rules to those governed by informal rules. Rules for participating in venues can become barriers to participation. When barriers exist, the information that is communicated in a particular venue may not represent the range of stakeholders' preferences on an issue. These rules, procedures, and norms can create structures of bias that give some interests more access to the venue than others (Hall & Taylor, 1996).

Some venues require direct interactions with the organization. In contrast, other venues are useful for applying pressure on an organization through indirect interactions. These interactions are indirect since the communication is not directly provided to the organization. However, someone who learns about the preferences of others from that venue may share information with the organization. For our purposes, I have identified two types of venues: public and decision-making.

Public venues exist outside of the organization's control and are defined similarly to the entertainment industry's use of a venue. They are a space where people can proactively or reactively communicate ideas and preferences that are not specific to any one organization using self-selected participation activities. Public venues consist of, but are not limited to, passive as well as active participation activities, and public venues can accommodate any number of stakeholders if physical space allows. The identity of participants in public venues may not be discernible, especially when the stakeholder takes steps to remain anonymous.

Decision-making venues are more in line with the legal use of the term venue where evidence is presented, persuasive arguments are made, and a decision is rendered. Many decision-making venues foster a marketplace of ideas, but with the last man standing, winner takes all mentality. Bryson (2011) describes three types of decision-making venues: arenas, forums, and courts. Arenas are unstructured venues hosting discussions in which anyone can engage. This type of venue facilitates information transparency and educational activities. However, participants may choose to comment rather than interact with others. Forums involve a select group of stakeholders who are allowed to engage in a facilitated dialogue to make a decision. Forums facilitate two-way interactions. Stakeholders must have standing on the issue to participate in venues called courts. Deliberation within this venue occurs between a select few participants, and the rules that govern the deliberation and decision-making process are pre-established. Courts generally feature adversarial interactions.

Stakeholders can choose from an array of participation activities for providing input and communicating preferences. Just as the preferred type of participation activity limits the method of interacting, the type of venue will limit the type of participation activity since different venues facilitate different types of participation. Both stakeholders and organizations make strategic choices about venue selection considering factors such as (1) the intended purpose of the participation activity, (2) the number of stakeholders who have standing or who can be mobilized to interact in a specific venue, and (3) the decision-making process and rules of the particular venue. In Table 3.1, I describe venues external to an organization and suggest the different purposes for which the venue can be useful.

For the most part, venues exist continuously and are not situation, stakeholder, nor organization specific. Venues become specific, however, when (1) a stakeholder

Table 3.1 Participation venues and purposes

Participation venues	Purposes
Arena – participants can decide to be anonymous No limits to number of participants	
Public commentary	Promote preferences
Media	Identify the problem, set agenda, force change
Social movements	Protest or build momentum for change
Financial contributions	Influence decisions
Consumer market pressure	Influence transactions
Forum – stakeholders must be invited to interact The number of participants is established by the organization hosting the forum	
Partnering with organizations	Influence decisions
Financial collaborations	Mobilize and aggregate preferences
Industry or profession groups	Influence organization-specific transactions
Mediating institutions	
Court – stakeholders must have standing to participate Interaction is limited to a single issue or case	
Policymaking institutions	Consider a change in policy
Administrative law proceedings	Force changes
Laws, regulations, and court rulings	Determine the validity of different claims
	Application or setting of precedent

is motivated to engage in some type of participation activity based on a desire to influence an organization's decision and (2) the stakeholder is making a decision about how and where she should participate. The motivations driving stakeholder participation and venue selection are discussed further in Chap. 4.

3.5 An Overview of Participation Activities

In this section, I first describe common participation activities by dividing them into two categories: passive and active. I use the term passive to describe two kinds of situations. In the first situation, the stakeholder is able to collect information about the organization's activities or about decisions that are being considered and to communicate their preferences in an indirect way without having to interact directly with the organization. In the second situation, the organization is able to gather data that already exists and use this data as proxy indicator for stakeholder satisfaction and preferences. Additionally, the organization can use technology-assisted methods that publicly invite participation for anyone who is interested. These preference data are submitted to the organization without any direct interaction between an organizational representative and the stakeholder.

Active participation is a label for participation activities that require stakeholders to take individually identifiable action to provide input about their preferences specific to an organization's current or proposed activities. Active participation can be initiated by either the stakeholder or the organization. Passive participation, since it can be indirectly or directly related to an organization, can be initiated by a stakeholder, the organization, or even a third party, such as a response to a blogger about what an organization is doing.

3.5.1 Passive Participation Activities

The amount of passive participation activities has been steadily increasing over time. Advances in technology have introduced participation activities that communicate information, actively or passively, to other stakeholders, or the organization. Examples include blogs, discussion boards, tweets (Herian, 2014), and online petitions such as whitehouse.gov. Technology has fostered the sharing of information between organizations for a one-stop-shop concept, or publicly accessible portal, that is beneficial for organizational clients and stakeholders (Ho & Ni, 2004). Examples include the Bank of America promoting Merrill Lynch's services and discounts for their customers on the Bank of America homepage as well as notifying customers of deals offered by their cashback reward partners.

Some passive participation activities, such as commenting on the organization's website or submitting responses to requests for comment posted in *the Federal Register*, are fairly convenient for stakeholders to use and have the added advantage of being able to gather input at very low cost (U. S. General Accounting Office, 2003). However, these mechanisms generally require the organization to have adequate information systems as well as the expertise necessary to design an interactive website. They also require more time for stakeholders to review background materials and provide comments. Sending out a draft document to stakeholders an organization has worked with before has a better likelihood of getting stakeholders to respond.

Passive participation activities have increased the indirect study of consumer behavior via publicly observable data. In this situation, the stakeholder is unaware that they are providing preference data to an organization. For example, Franklin, Mott, and Williams (2013) describe how social media posts can inform military personnel who are in transit to a hostile destination, and Dunbar and her colleagues (2013) describe transportation surveillance screening connected to social media posts.

Advances in Internet technology, combined with developments in computer-based analytics programming, have created another non-traditional passive participation activity called big data analytics. An example is marketing research that provides input about current and potential consumers via the analysis of Internet and website browsing patterns, which are mashed together with social media or geospatial tracking data to tailor what appears on the web browser and encourage transactions. Organizations can determine where a person's mouse lingers and how they "sequentially" visit the website pages and subpages as well and mash it with data from past purchases and then suggest items the customer may want to purchase.

Organizations in all sectors find big data analytics helpful. One example in my town is an annual observational census to determine current, but unfilled, needs within a geographical service area to provide information to homeless organizations and alliances. There are other examples of information that can be used as non-traditional preference data, such as identifying and profiling the purchasers of a bond issue (Hildreth & Zorn, 2005) or tracking organization evaluation data generated by consumers' intermediaries (such as *Consumer Reports* ratings or Morningstar stock reports). The list seems to grow every day!

With this kind of information, organizations can custom-tailor potential clients' browsing experiences so that they see content that is of particular interest to them. Doing this makes it more likely that additional transactions with the sponsoring organization or its partners may be possible. These pre-existing data sources do not require any interaction with the stakeholder. However, the use of big data analytics can impact stakeholders in unintended ways. When this occurs, the stakeholders' response is unpredictable. Consider the case of a parent who is upset because his underage daughter is receiving advertising and discounts from a major retailer for diapers, which leads to the parent discovering that the daughter was pregnant. From the organization's perspective, pre-existing data represents an opportunity to enhance transactions and perhaps lower transaction costs, but it can also present a risk of adverse stakeholder reactions.

Studies have identified several other activities described as participation that have no expectation of a time commitment for participation by stakeholders. In these activities, information concerning the organization and its activities is made available to the general public. Activities in this category include public information offices; public education activities; public relations strategies (Folz, 1991, p. 225); and public outreach including annual reports, newsletters, brochures, management/performance report cards and satisfaction surveys, media campaigns, and participation in fairs or trade shows (Denton & Woodward, 1990; Koontz, 1999, p. 267; Wheeler, 1994).

Organizations can make a wide range of information available via technology such as meeting videos, meeting summaries, and by offering downloads of organizational documents or reports, citizen's guides, or budget summaries (Marlowe, 2005; Yusuf, Jordan, Neill, & Hackbart, 2013), or offering the budget in public places such as libraries or on organizational websites (Berner & Smith, 2004). Organizations can also get assistance from third parties in making information available. For example, when there is a media report about an organization, it is common for the media outlet to include a link to the organization's websites (Goldsmith & Eggers, 2005).

Stakeholder outreach can also occur as a passive participation activity. This can occur through the use of public access television to provide information on organizational activities, as well as public officials' participation in community organizations and attendance at meetings held by other organizations.

All of these passive participation activities enhance the organization's transparency. When properly communicated, they can also make stakeholders aware of how to interact with the organization, thus increasing accessibility. The advantage of passive participation activities is that large numbers of stakeholders can communicate, or the organization can indirectly learn, their preferences at a very low cost.

3.5.2 Active Participation Activities

The next level of participation activities is active. They can range from a one-shot time commitment by stakeholders to nearly continuous interactions. Included in this category are mechanisms like participating in a stakeholder workshop, educational events like a "Meet the Candidate" forum sponsored by the League of Women Voters (Kathlene & Martin, 1991, p. 58), a field trip, or a Pride program. Other participation activities are possible, including providing comments on proposed rules or regulations (Gordon, 1996; Koontz, 1999, p. 254); attending a public hearing or a meeting on a specific issue (Lukensmeyer & Brigham, 2002); completing a customer comment card or sending an email providing feedback to an organization about its service; registering a compliant; participating in a protest activity (Timney, 1996); writing a letter to the editor about organizational activities; voting; calling a stakeholder hotline number (Stenberg, 1972, p. 193); serving on a jury; interacting formally or informally with organizational officials (Ebdon, 2003); attending activities or receiving services at a neighborhood mini-city hall (Stenberg, 1972, p. 193); participating in a focus group or simulation (Irland, 1975, p. 31); and completing a survey (Glaser & Hildreth, 1996).

For many mechanisms, such as surveys, it is possible to invite large numbers of respondents (Ebdon, 2002b; O'Toole, Marshall, & Grewe, 1996). Citizen surveys can provide responses that are more representative (Johnson, 1998; Miller & Miller, 1991; Simonsen & Robbins, 2000; Webb & Hatry, 1973); however, they may also have the unintended consequence of creating issues that mobilize formerly acquiescent stakeholders (Daneke & Klobus-Edwards, 1979, p. 421).

Attendance at public meetings is often low, and many times it is a small group of citizens who show up regularly with the same or self-interested complaints, leading to a reduction in credibility with organizational officials (Ebdon, 2002a). If decisions are made solely on the basis of this input, there can be charges of undue influence by a select few with their own personal agendas. Mechanisms such as advisory boards and committees encourage more collective-interested involvement, and the participants can be selected purposefully to gather data reflecting the preferences of different groups of stakeholders (Thomas, 1995). Holding summits and conferences is another mechanism that can ensure a larger and, hopefully, more representative sample of participants. However, these mechanisms have weaknesses to consider as well since with more participants they can be very expensive to conduct.

The third level of stakeholder time commitment features activities that require more than one meeting; however, the meetings are clustered together in a short time. This category includes activities like participating in a citizen's academy (Lun, 2004), working with a government official or ombudsperson's office on casework activities, commenting as part of a regulatory (Berry, Portney, & Thomson, 1993, p. 40) or citizen review panel (Fiorino, 1990, p. 235) or lay jury, becoming involved in neg reg (negotiated regulation) (Berry et al., 1993, p. 38), engaging in service-learning while attending school, serving as an expert from the for-profit or nonprofit sectors, and being a member of an ad hoc workgroup (Irland, 1975, p. 266) or study circle for a specific issue (Buck, 1984, p. 471; Koontz, 1999, p. 256; Leighninger, 2002; McCoy & Scully, 2002).

The fourth level in the taxonomy suggests a time commitment that involves multiple participation activities over an extended time. Examples of repeated participation include membership in citizens interest groups like rotary or economic development councils (Jones, 1938, p. 176) or special interest groups, legal challenges to organizational actions, representation on neighborhood, district or agency advisory boards (Reidel, 1972), or planning councils or councils of government (Stenberg, 1972, p. 193). Often these interactions are supported by extranets that allow access to the organization's e-systems for transactions and interaction with partners/customers (Clark, Brudney, & Jang, 2013; Franklin et al., 2013; Streib & Navarro, 2006).

The last level of time commitment requires nearly continuous interaction with an organization in a pre-established and ongoing official role. Examples of ongoing activities include government research organizations such as the National Municipal League (Jones, 1938, p. 176); official duties as a citizen member of a government board, council, or commission; volunteer activities; co-production; and collaboration with a government organization (Mattson, 1986; Whitaker, 1980).

Some recurring participation mechanisms, such as the gathering of client feedback or distributing of customer comment cards, provide more of an open forum with looser control of the type of feedback generated. In this situation, input may be more self-interested based on the individual participant's experience with that organization.

Some mechanisms, whether passive or active, require participants to have prior knowledge or to be provided with background information before they can provide input (Thomas, 1995). Informal meetings with organizational officials seldom require extensive knowledge of a wide range of topics. Serving on a lay jury or as part of a citizens' review panel, on the other hand, requires wide ranging prior knowledge to provide informed input. Citizen advisory committees are one mechanism where education efforts can be necessary but also worthwhile because the participants are purposefully selected to represent different stakeholders. Committee members may need education efforts to get up to speed with the knowledge of other stakeholders. Selecting mechanisms that can also educate participants (O'Toole et al., 1996), especially about issues and choices related to decisions (Roberts, 1997), is one way to overcome this challenge.

3.6 A Taxonomy of Participation Activities

To organize the wide variation in participation activities and mechanisms from which the organization can gather data, I construct a taxonomy based on the type of interaction fostered and the amount of time required. With this arrangement, we can analyze the nature of the relationships created through different kinds of participation activities. We can also suggest potential directions for the development and more effective use of a combination of mechanisms.

No matter whether interactions are organization or stakeholder initiated, participation activities vary in the amount of time required. Some require no or very little time commitment; others require nearly continuous involvement. Table 3.2 displays participation activities arranged on the vertical axis from no time commitment to nearly continuous interactions. Across the horizontal axis are different activity purposes, details about who is involved, and the direction of information flows.

Starting on the left-hand side of the table, the first two columns present stakeholder and organization activities that passively make preference data available, including the provision of information or preference data and advising stakeholders about organization activities and upcoming decisions. The next two columns feature a one-way information exchange. The first is a request from a stakeholder to the organization. In the second, the organization asks stakeholders for input. In neither of these exchanges is there any dialogue, nor any follow-up communication describing how the input was used. In the last two columns, there is a two-way dialogue and interaction with feedback between the stakeholders and the organization.

3.6.1 The Nature of Stakeholders' Interactions

By studying Table 3.2, we can discern differences in the nature of stakeholders' interactions (as shown in the second row of the table). Either a stakeholder or the organization can be the initiator, and the purpose of the interaction may differ based on who is the initiator. One-way participation activities transmit information between stakeholders without any assurance that action will be taken in response. Two-way participation activities make it more likely that preference data will inform decisions and spur action (Schaller, 1964, p. 176).

One-way participation is advisory not binding. Further, there is no guarantee of feedback about how the input influenced the decision. Two-way participation makes organizations more responsive since it creates an atmosphere that reduces the defensiveness of organizational employees by providing constructive criticism combined with a purpose-driven exchange of ideas. Some of these activities result in preferences that are binding such as legal actions. Or the preference information can be advisory, such as the results from a lay jury (Bingham, Nabatchi, & O'Leary, 2005). Even though the two-way input is advisory most of the time, one can argue that there is a more tangible commitment by the organization to attempt to incorporate stakeholder input than there is for one-way interactions since resources have been expended by the organization to get the data.

Another difference exists between one-way and two-way participation activities – the two-way activities tend to require increased time commitments from the stakeholders. More frequent interactions make it more likely that an ongoing relationship between the stakeholder and the organization will occur. As interactions increase, there is also an increased likelihood that the organization will provide more real-time feedback about how preference data informs decisions (Dusong, 1997).

Table 3.2 Participation activities by time commitment

	Type of activity					
Time commitment ↓	Info/data (S to S, S to Org)	Advise (org to S)	Request (S to org)	Ask (org to S)	Discuss (2-way)	Resolve (2-way)
Continuous	Social media	Social media	Research organizations		Volunteers, co-production, collaboration	Boards and commissions
Multiple over time	Newsletters, analytical reports	Newsletters, financial reporting	Citizens interest groups, special interest groups		Advisory boards, planning councils, councils of government	Legal challenges
Clustered	Volunteers Special issue meetings/protests	Citizens' academy		Special issue meetings	Service-learning, private and nonprofit expert advisors, ad hoc and workgroups	Ombudsperson, casework, lay jury, regulatory review, review panel, negotiated rules
One-shot	Calls to action *Donations* Displays sharing	Pride programs, *education events*, field trips, workshops, transactions	Voting petitions *Public hearings*, client complaints, protests, letters to the editor	Request for comments, customer or client feedback, census	Invited meetings, *informal interactions*, mini-city halls, focus group, simulation, survey	Jury duty, stakeholder *hotlines*
None	Crowdsourcing Scraping Mashing	PR activities, public documents, public access TV, outside meetings				

In addition, spending more time on the dialogue that occurs during two-way interactions can encourage trust-based relationships (Dusong, 1997; Ebdon & Franklin, 2006). When you trust someone, you are more likely to be honest in your communications and be willing to discover shared preferences. On the other hand, when you do not trust someone, you may be rigid in your preferences. Establishing trust can be crucial for successful stakeholder engagement. Since it takes time to develop, two-way interactions and a more substantial stakeholder time commitment are vital antecedents to engagement.

Organizations and stakeholders have a vast array of participation activities from which they can select. The participant's selection of an activity can be influenced by two factors – the time commitment and the purpose of the interaction. The amount of time required to participate is wide-ranging, with some activities requiring no time at all since the activity is being undertaken for a different purpose or only a one-shot meeting to others that necessitate an ongoing time commitment. Participation activities can support different purposes, from informing to requesting, asking, discussing, and resolving. All these participation activities share the same desired outputs: making information available, increasing transparency about preferences, and fostering accessibility. In the next section, I consider how these different participation activities foster stakeholder interactions and engagement.

3.7 Interactions Fostered by Participation Activities

Several theorists have suggested arrangements for the different kinds of participation activities. Whitaker (1980, p. 242) describes three kinds: requesting assistance, providing assistance, and interacting to change expectations and actions, also referred to as mutual adjustment. Nagel (1987) arranges participation into four categories: doing, advising, deciding, and supporting. Utilizing the taxonomy's dimensions of time commitment and type of interaction, I identify three kinds of participation interactions. First, some activities are neutral since they convey information or provide education but do not require further action on the part of the stakeholder or the organization. Others are adversarial since these activities force the organization to choose between the preferences of different stakeholders. The third kind of interaction encourages cooperation for improving organizational activities. Table 3.3 highlights the cells of the taxonomy that represent each of these three kinds of participation interactions.

Neutral interactions are primarily located in the Info/data and Advise column. These activities are often informational and can foster a cooperative or adversarial attitude toward the organization. Since most lack interaction, there is little direct stakeholder input to the organization. However, these activities are often the precursor to participation interactions that occur in the remaining columns of the typology. The time commitment for neutral interactions ranges from no time commitment to events clustered within a short time.

Table 3.3 Interaction types by time, interaction, and input

Type of interaction	Time	Interaction	Input
Neutral: informational	None	None	None
Neutral: educational	One-shot to clustered	One-way	Often a precursor to input activities
Adversarial	One-shot to continuous	One-way or two-way	Advisory or binding
Cooperative	One-shot to continuous	Two-way	Advisory

There are six cells in the typology in Table 3.2 representing adversarial participation activities. Many organizations, especially those that offer government programs with involuntary clients or have a regulatory function, have adversarial relationships with their stakeholders. Another type of adversarial relationship can occur when the preferences provided by one stakeholder are in direct opposition to the preferences of another stakeholder. Within the adversarial category, the interactions feature a controverted decision and no discussion to discover mutually shared preferences. Three of these adversarial cells require only a one-shot time commitment on the part of the stakeholders and can take the form of a one-way or a two-way exchange. The other three adversarial cells are in the right-hand column, where multiple activities to resolve a dispute over preferences are involved. Within the adversarial category, there is a mix of expectations regarding the utilization of stakeholder input. In some cases, the input is advisory. In others, it is binding. Binding stakeholder input usually occurs when an intermediary, such as an ombudsperson, is involved.

Cooperative interactions occur in two-way interaction settings and appear in the Discuss column. By their very nature, cooperative activities suggest a search for alternatives preferred by most participants with the goal being that everyone is (somewhat) satisfied with the decision. The four cells representing cooperative interactions feature the most variation in the amount of time required on the part of the stakeholders ranging from one-shot to continuous. Additionally, activities in the cooperative category tend to produce advisory preference input.

Table 3.3 organizes information about the types of participation activities based on the time commitment for stakeholders, the nature of the interaction, and the input received. Looking at this table, we can conclude that for each type of stakeholder relationship, there are many different participation activities with varying time commitments from which a stakeholder can choose to offer or exchange information or to interact. The type of participation activity, on the other hand, determines the preferred method of interacting. Informational activities will not feature two-way interactions but can lead to future interactions. Cooperative participation activities must, by their very nature, include two-way interaction. Finally, binding input is the outlier rather than the norm for most participation activities. Table 3.3 shows the relationships between time, the direction of the interaction, and the type of input.

When analyzing the typology as a whole, there are two additional points to make before moving into a discussion of potential participation trajectories. First, the request column features activities by stakeholders with primarily collective interests influencing them to interact with the organization over multiple meetings. There are a variety of reasons why stakeholders may initiate requests, including (1) seeking data that can determine if clients' needs are met, (2) requesting a change in organizational activities dues to negative spillover effects, or (3) suggesting mutually beneficial changes in policy organizational activities. These different reasons for requesting organizational action represent informational, adversarial, and cooperative participation activities, respectively. Therefore this cell should be classified as having a mix of the three types of participation activities.

Second, there are two exceptions in the labeling of the relationships represented by particular cells. Negotiated rulemaking, called neg reg, found in the clustered time x resolve cell, is not considered to be an adversarial interaction. Neg reg is a participation mechanism that brings all impacted parties together to determine regulatory standards cooperatively. The standards are then binding on all parties to the agreement. This participation activity is used primarily in the area of consumer protection regulation. This type of interaction was introduced as an alternative to adversarial approaches that frequently resulted in costly and lengthy legal challenges in the regulatory arena. Another exception in the typology is found in the four cells in the bottom row. Since the stakeholder is not willing to make any time commitment, input cannot be provided. For this reason, no activity, neutral, cooperative, or adversarial in nature, is possible in this part of the typology.

Analyzing stakeholders using this typology uncovers three kinds of relationships that can occur when stakeholders interact with the organization. Administrators can use knowledge about adversarial, neutral, and cooperation stakeholder relationships to manage participant expectations when stakeholders communicate their preferences. Also, administrators can attempt to align the time commitment, interaction fostered, and input generated with the purpose of stakeholder interaction.

3.8 Challenges Associated with Participation Activities

One thing that decision-makers value is stakeholder input that ranks a wide range of solutions and then indicates the magnitude of preferences of the stakeholders. Some mechanisms meet this need, but the challenge is that all mechanisms have strengths as well as weaknesses. Surveys are quick, but the questions should be structured to learn the intensity of participants' preferences (Thomas, 1995). Focus groups, while more time consuming, provide opportunities to explore preferences and to interpret reactions to proposals. Budget simulations are useful for educating and making participants determine what trade-offs they would make to balance the budget. These kinds of participation activities can suggest the strength of opinion about specific issues but only for those who participate. Further, many mechanisms do not reveal sincere preferences, often assumed to be the willingness to pay for services (Glaser & Denhardt, 1999).

Lastly, like surveys, some mechanisms can be repeated over time to reveal trends (Miller & Miller, 1991; Webb & Hatry, 1973). Repeated data collection can provide critical information about stakeholders' willingness to pay the costs of changes to organizational goods or services or about changes in the relative level of support that exists for different policy and program alternatives. Unfortunately, since few mechanisms are institutionalized, it is hard to gather this trend data. The need for institutionalization is a possible trajectory for participation activities.

As calls for accountability to stakeholders' preferences increase, administrators will need to consider how to balance the costs and risks associated with being transparent and accessible. Doing this systematically may require that the organization commit, especially with resources, to a program that uses a variety of active and passive participation activities. Determining which or how many participation activities to offer can be a function of how much stakeholder input is desired. One must also consider whether sufficient preference data is already known or passively available (Thomas, 1993). Some decisions are made without stakeholder input. However, the organization can increase transparency by communicating the decision publicly. In other cases, decision-makers may desire input drawn from a representative group of stakeholders. What determines the appropriate level of stakeholder interactions is situation specific.

Gathering information and making it publicly available or transmitting it to a select group of stakeholders will require organizations to divert resources from direct service delivery – thus increasing transaction costs. Transparency in decision-making can also make proprietary information more vulnerable to accidental release to a competing organization. Selecting an appropriate combination of participation activities makes it more likely that organizations will be able to identify and consider stakeholders' preferences when making decisions, while balancing sustainability concerns is an important component of a stakeholder engagement commitment.

3.9 Summary

Participation activities are one of the two inputs into stakeholder engagement processes. There are many different participation activities. Some are passive and others are active, meaning the stakeholder and the organization are interacting. The interactions may take place in different venues, each with its own rules about who can participate and how information will be used and decisions made. In this chapter, I present a taxonomy describing the range of participation activities. This taxonomy considers the time commitment required and the type and purpose of the interaction.

From this taxonomy, I develop a typology based on the nature of the interactions encouraged by different activities. Participation activities that provide information foster neutral interactions. Adversarial interactions result in a situation in which some stakeholders' preferences are adopted over others. Cooperative interactions feature an attempt to find solutions that satisfy most stakeholders' preferences. Using this typology, I conclude that the majority of currently used participation mechanisms foster adversarial relationships, but from a theoretical perspective, the typology identifies cells where no participation activities are currently offered. Becoming aware of this gap may offer the potential for more cooperative interactions.

Both the taxonomy and typology reveal the potential for using a combination of participation activities to gather data about stakeholders' preferences. Some of these will be low-cost since data can be collected passively and continuously from existing sources. Others will have higher costs since they may require frequent and two-way interaction. However, offering a wider variety of participation activities and tailoring data collection to the organization's needs will increase the representativeness of stakeholder input as well as the transparency of an organization.

In Chap. 2, I described many kinds of stakeholders and analyzed how to get information that is representative of the stakeholder who is impacted by or can impact the organization's activities. This chapter offered insights into participation activities and how to strategically utilize them to gather input to inform decisions. One question that remains unanswered is how to connect the two inputs for stakeholder engagement to succeed. Like the farmer's vision in the movie the Field of Dreams: If you build it, will they come? In Chap. 4, we explore the motivations that can encourage stakeholders to come to the organization and to participate to provide input that informs decisions.

References

Baumgartner, F., & Jones, B. D. (1993). *Agendas and instability in American politics*. Chicago: University of Chicago Press.

Berner, M. M., & Smith, S. (2004). The state of the states: A review of state requirements for citizen participation in the local government budget process. *State and Local Government Review, 36*(2), 140–150.

Berry, J. M., Portney, K. E., & Thomson, K. (1993). *The rebirth of urban democracy*. Washington, D.C.: Brookings Institution Press.

Bingham, L. B., Nabatchi, T., & O'Leary, R. (2005). The new governance: Practices and processes for stakeholder and citizen participation in the work of government. *Public Administration Review, 65*(5), 547–558.

Bryson, J. M. (2011). *Strategic planning for public and nonprofit organizations: A guide to strengthening and sustaining organizational achievement* (4th ed.). San Francisco: Jossey-Bass.

Buck, J. V. (1984). The impact of citizen participation programs and policy decisions on participants' opinions. *Western Political Quarterly, 37*(3), 468–482.

Clark, B. Y., Brudney, J. L., & Jang, S.-G. (2013). Coproduction of government services and the new information technology: Investigating the distributional biases. *Public Administration Review, 73*(5), 687–701.

Daneke, G. A., & Klobus-Edwards, P. (1979). Survey research for public administrators. *Public Administration Review, 39*, 421–426.

Datta, C. (2003). Participation of the people. In A. Cornwall & G. Pratt (Eds.), *Pathways to participation: reflections on PRA* (pp. 54–59). London: ITDG Publishing.

Denton, R. W., & Woodward, G. C. (1990). *Political communication in America*. New York: Praeger.

Dunbar, N. E., Wilson, S. N., Adame, B. J., Elizondo, J., Jensen, M. L., Miller, C. H., et al. (2013). MACBETH: Development of a training game for the mitigation of cognitive bias. *International Journal of Game-Based Learning, 3*(4), 7–26.

Dusong, M. (1997). City of Neuchatel: From the reform of the local management structures to the concept of partnership. In M. Prohl (Ed.), *International strategies and techniques for future local government: Practical aspects towards innovation and reform*. Gütersloh, Germany: Bertelsmann Foundation Publishers.

Ebdon, C. (2002a). Interactive surveys as tools to combine citizen education and preference revelation [working paper].

Ebdon, C. (2002b). Beyond the public hearing: Citizen participation in the local government budget process. *Journal of Public Budgeting, Accounting & Financial Management, 14*, 273. https://doi.org/10.1108/JPBAFM-14-02-2002-B006

Ebdon, C. (2003). Citizen participation in the budget process: Exit, voice and loyalty. In *Encyclopedia of public administration and public policy*. New York: Marcel Dekker.

Ebdon, C., & Franklin, A. L. (2006). Citizen participation in budget theory. *Public Administration Review, 66*(3), 437–447.

Fiorino, D. J. (1990). Citizen participation and environmental risk: A survey of institutional mechanisms. *Science, Technology and Human Values, 15*(2), 226–243.

Folz, D. H. (1991). Recycling program design, management, and participation: A national survey of municipal experience. *Public Administration Review, 51*(3), 222–231.

Franklin, A. L., Mott, T., & Williams, T. H. L. (2013). Coproduction in the U.S. Department of Defense: Examining how the evolution of geographic information systems (GIS) expands non-traditional partner engagement. *Policy & Internet, 5*(4), 387–401. https://doi.org/10.1002/1944-2866.POI345

Glaser, M., & Denhardt, R. B. (1999). When citizen expectations conflict with budgetary reality: Discontinuity between the public's demand for services and its willingness to pay taxes. *Journal of Public Budgeting, Accounting and Financial Management, 11*(2), 276–310.

Glaser, M. A., & Hildreth, W. B. (1996). A profile of discontinuity between citizen demand and willingness to pay taxes. *Public Budgeting & Finance, 15*(4), 96–113.

Goldsmith, S., & Eggers, W. D. (2005). *Governing by network: The new shape of the public sector*. Washington, D.C.: Brookings Institution Press.

Gordon, M. C. (1996). Different paradigms, similar flaws: Constructing a new approach to federalism on Congress and the courts. *Yale Law and Policy Review and Yale Journal on Regulation, Symposium Constructing a New Federalism*.

Hall, P. A., & Taylor, R. C. R. (1996). Political science and the three new institutionalisms. *Political Studies, 44*(5), 936–957. https://doi.org/10.1111/j.1467-9248.1996.tb00343.x

Herian, M. N. (2014). Trust in government and support for municipal services. *State and Local Government Review, 42*, 82–90.

Hildreth, W. B., & Zorn, C. (2005). The evolution of the state and local government municipal debt market over the past quarter century. *Public Budgeting & Finance, 25*(4s), 127–153.

Ho, A. T.-K., & Ni, A. Y. (2004). Explaining the adoption of e-government features: A case study of Iowa county treasurers' offices. *The American Review of Public Administration, 34*(2), 164–180.

Irland, L. C. (1975). Citizen participation: A tool for conflict management on the public lands. *Public Administration Review, 35*, 263–269.

Johnson, E. (1998). Recommended budget practices: Incorporating stakeholders into the process. *Government Finance Review, 14*(4), 15–18.

Jones, H. P. (1938). Citizen groups, tool of democracy. *Annals of the American Academy of Political and Social Science, 199*, 176–182.

Kamensky, J. (2015). What if government operated more like Disney? *Government Executive*.

Kathlene, L., & Martin, J. A. (1991). Enhancing citizen participation: Panel designs, perspectives, and policy formation. *Journal of Policy Analysis and Management, 10*, 46–63.

Koontz, T. M. (1999). Administrators and citizens: Measuring agency officials' efforts to foster and use public input in forest policy. *Journal of Public Administration Research and Theory, 9*(2), 251–280.

Leighninger, M. (2002). Enlisting citizens: Building political legitimacy. *National Civic Review, 91*(2), 137–148.

Lovejoy, K., Waters, R., & Saxton, G. D. (forthcoming). Engaging stakeholders through Twitter: How nonprofit organizations are getting more out of 140 characters or less. *Public Relations Review, 38*, 313.

Lukensmeyer, C. J., & Brigham, S. (2002). Taking democracy to scale: Creating a town hall meeting for the twenty-first century. *National Civic Review, 91*(4), 351–356.

Lun, N. (2004). Local government finance and budgeting 101: Encouraging meaningful citizen participation through education. *Government Finance Review, 20*(2), 33–38.

Marlowe, J. (2005). The budget as a communication tool. *International City/County Association IQ Report, 37*(4), 1–19.

Mattson, G. A. (1986). The promise of citizen coproduction: Some persistent issues. *Public Productivity Review, 40*, 51–56.

McCoy, M. L., & Scully, P. L. (2002). Deliberative dialogue to expand civic engagement: What kind of talk does democracy need? *National Civic Review, 91*(2), 117–135.

Miller, T. I., & Miller, M. A. (1991). *Citizen surveys: How to do them, how to use them, what they mean*. Washington, D.C.: International City/County Management Association.

Nagel, J. H. (1987). *Participation*. Englewood Cliffs, NJ: Prentice-Hall.

O'Toole, D. E., Marshall, J., & Grewe, T. (1996). Current local government budgeting practices. *Government Finance Review, 12*(6), 25–29.

Reidel, J. A. (1972). Citizen participation myths and realities. *Public Administration Review, 32*, 211–220.

Rethemeyer. (2007). The empire strikes back: Is the internet corporatizing rather than democratizing policy processes? *Public Administration Review, 67*(2), 199–215.

Roberts, N. (1997). Public deliberation: An alternative approach to crafting policy and setting direction. *Public Administration Review, 57*(2), 124–130.

Santaniello, M., & Amoretti, F. (2013). Electronic regimes: Democracy and geopolitical strategies in digital networks. *Policy & Internet, 5*(4), 1944–2866.

Schaller, L. E. (1964). Is the citizen advisory committee a threat to representative government? *Public Administration Review, 24*, 175–179.

Simonsen, W., & Robbins, M. D. (2000). *Citizen participation in resource allocation*. Boulder, CO: Westview Press.

Stenberg, C. W. (1972). Citizens and the administrative state. *Public Administration Review, 32*, 190–198.

Streib, G., & Navarro, I. (2006). Citizen demand for interactive e-government: The case of Georgia consumer services. *The American Review of Public Administration, 36*, 288–300.

Thomas, J. C. (1993). Public involvement and governmental effectiveness: A decision-making model for public managers. *Administration and Society, 24*(4), 444–470.

Thomas, J. C. (1995). *Public participation in public decisions*. San Francisco: Jossey-Bass.

Timney, M. M. (1996). *Overcoming NIMBY: Using citizen participation effectively*.

U. S. General Accounting Office. (2003). *Electronic rulemaking: Efforts to facilitate public participation can be improved*. Washington, D.C.: U. S. Government Printing Office.

U.S. Forest Service. (n.d.). *What we do: Mission statement*. Retrieved June 10, 2015, from http://www.fs.fed.us/fsjobs/forestservice/mission.html.

Van Meter, E. C. (1975). Citizen participation in the policy management process. *Public Administration Review, 35*, 804–812.

Webb, K., & Hatry, H. P. (1973). *Obtaining citizen feedback. The application of citizen surveys to local governments*. Washington, D.C.: The Urban Institute.

Wheeler, K. M. (1994). *Effective communication*. Washington, D.C.: International City/County Management Association.

Whitaker, G. P. (1980). Coproduction: Citizen participation in service delivery. *Public Administration Review, 40*, 240–246.

Yusuf, J. E., Jordan, M. M., Neill, K. A., & Hackbart, M. (2013). For the people: Popular financial reporting practices of local governments. *Public Budgeting & Finance, 33*(1), 95–113.

Chapter 4
Understanding Stakeholder Motivations

Abstract This chapter identifies two vectors of factors that may push or pull a stakeholder into interacting with an organization. The push factors are specific to an individual and establish whether there is sufficient motivation to participate. The pull factors are organizationally designed and can include incentives that motivate participation from select stakeholders to increase representativeness and accessibility. In addition to offering incentives for participation for specific stakeholders, the organization may purposefully select the venue for interactions to make the process more inclusive. System dynamics theory offers some prospects for making theories of stakeholder motivation more robust. I use the board game Monopoly to model stakeholder motivation since it features interaction effects and a recursive decision-making process. Plus, it takes into consideration dynamic changes in the environment as well as changes in the push and pull factors. Understanding factors that motivate participation is an essential first step to assuring that the preferences communicated to the organization represent the stakeholders who can influence or are influenced by the organization's activities.

4.1 Introduction

In this chapter, I argue that stakeholders must be motivated before they will make an effort to provide preference input to an organization. I define stakeholder motivation as a stakeholder's desire to communicate interests or preferences to individuals, groups, organizations, or a collective in which the individual has an interest.

I examine the topic of stakeholder motivation by integrating multi-disciplinary empirical conclusions to suggest a model for better understanding a stakeholder's participation decision. This framework allows me to identify vectors of push and pull factors that can influence an individual's decision to participate. These vectors make it possible for the administrator tasked with gathering stakeholder input to identify who is most likely to participate. Then the administrator can design strategies to pull stakeholders into participation in order to gather data that represents missing stakeholder preferences.

A. L. Franklin, *Stakeholder Engagement*,
https://doi.org/10.1007/978-3-030-47519-2_4

4.2 Understanding Stakeholders' Motivations to Interact

As defined by Nagel (1987, p. 1), participation is an action through which ordinary members of a political system influence or attempt to influence outcomes. Many factors may influence stakeholders' decisions about whether they will interact with an organization to provide input and communicate their preferences.

There are many reasons why the organization should understand what influences stakeholder motivation and how this contributes to the participation decision. By anticipating who is likely to participate and comparing this information with the universe of stakeholders who are likely to be influenced or attempt to influence an organizations' actions (from Chap. 2), the organization can determine how representative the self-selected stakeholders will be. When representativeness is lacking, efforts can be made to gather input from stakeholders unlikely to participate. Gathering input from stakeholders who do not typically interact with the organization can be especially helpful when stakeholders may experience a negative externality from the organization's activities. Reducing the types of stakeholders who do not provide input may also reduce the likelihood that dissatisfied stakeholders will seek a venue outside the organization's control to voice their preferences.

When the preferences of stakeholders who are not motivated to interact with the organization cause the organization to miss valuable perspectives, then the administrator can invite those not likely to interact to do so. A strategy of purposefully inviting stakeholders into interactions can make the organization more accessible.

4.3 Push Factors Motivating Participation

In the early 1990s, the Arizona Lottery employed the marketing slogan, "You can't win if you don't play." This slogan seems appropriate for opening the discussion on what motivates people to provide input to organizations. If stakeholders do not provide input and communicate their preferences, then the probability of influencing an organization's activities is practically the same as the probability of winning the lottery without purchasing any lottery tickets.

Not everyone in the universe of stakeholders who could potentially influence, or be influenced by, the organization's actions will interact with the organization. Organizational officials often describe interactions with the usual suspects as the norm (Franklin, 2001). What makes some stakeholders think they can win by interacting with the organization, while others choose not to play? To answer this question, we consider the topic of motivation.

Motivation is a construct with many dimensions. Much of the empirical research on motivations in decision-making comes from psychology with a focus on the individual. Simply defined, motivation is the thoughts that guide and cause behavior. In studies of motivation, scholars consider many cognitive and behavioral variables. For example, some authors emphasize the intrinsic factors that a person thinks he can control and that will lead to enjoyable activities (Ryan & Deci, 2000). When a person's actions may lead to the achievement of a self-interested outcome, then a person may be motivated to some behavior (Lawrence, 1981).

Extrinsic factors also influence an individual's choice of what action to take. In this case, an individual can be swayed by the preferences or actions of others, especially if these others are offering incentives that are in addition to an enhanced probability of achieving the desired outcome (Ryan & Deci, 2000). As the behavioral theorist, Pavlov (1927), demonstrated, the prospect of external incentives can reinforce behavior and lead to predictable repeated interactions (Arnold 1990). Identifying intrinsic and extrinsic motivators for stakeholders can help to identify who is likely to participate and to discover situations where incentives may encourage participation.

In addition to psychology, I borrow ideas about motivation from public policy literature. Policy literature suggests that motivation can depend on an analysis of tangible and intangible costs and benefits over the lifetime of the decision (Ekelund Jr., 1968). Decisions with the highest net present value, meaning the alternative where the net benefits are largest, are often chosen as the preferred course of action.

I combine ideas from psychology and public policy with the tourism promotion literature. When considering a vacation, tourism researchers (Prayag & Ryan, 2012) argue that there are push and pull factors that influence an individual's motivation[1].

Push factors are intrinsic, meaning they are specific to an individual's consideration of their situation. When push factors are motivating, the individual is now ready to do something (like go on vacation). Pull factors are extrinsic and influence the choice of what specific action will be taken (like choosing a vacation destination). Pull factors have their roots in sociocultural theories (Vygotsky, 1978), meaning the perceived preferences of others will influence an individual's motivation to take a specific action.

To unbundle the factors that could motivate an individual's participation, I suggest a taxonomy of stakeholder motivation. I offer a word of caution for reviewing this taxonomy. The listing of individual variables in the vectors of push factors is suggestive based on normative arguments or empirical validation. However, the extant literature on variables included in the taxonomy seldom tests the variables as they relate specifically to stakeholders' motivation to participate, instead using the variables as descriptive of who does and does not participate. Therefore, this listing is neither empirically authoritative nor comprehensive since the specific concept of stakeholder motivation is underdeveloped.

The scholarly literature suggests six factors that may motivate or push a stakeholder into participation based on their interests: (1) stakeholder profile, (2) demographics, (3) efficacy, (4) group membership, (5) transaction/issue salience, and (6)

[1]Yang & Callahan, 2007, have also used the push and pull concept. However, they adopt the organization's perspective with push factors influencing an individual to work with the organization and pull factors represented by mechanisms the organization uses to get stakeholder input and customer transactions.

resources. To this list, I add a seventh push factor that integrates these variables: the stakeholder's benefit-cost analysis of the overall effect of the push factors.

Some of these factors can be moderating variables since the characteristics of the individual cannot be changed. Other factors may be mediating factors, meaning they intervene to influence motivation. For example, it is well established that race and ethnicity are correlated with participation and that involvement with special interest groups is also correlated with participation. A person's race or ethnicity is a moderating factor. There is no way to change race or ethnicity in order to influence participation. However, being active in a political party can be a mediating factor that enhances the likelihood of participation as well as incentivizing participation. Understanding how the characteristics of the stakeholder and how different moderating and mediating push factors may influence participation decisions may help to predict an individual's motivation to participate.

4.3.1 Push Factor #1: Stakeholder Profile

In Chap. 2, the taxonomy identified six continua that could be useful for robustly identifying the organization's stakeholders and the interests they may have related to normal activities or specific decisions. The continua in the taxonomy offer clues about what might push a stakeholder into participating. For example, consider a customer who has already had transactions with the organization. Imagine that the customer finds out the organization may raise its price or add a transaction fee in the future. Using the information in Table 4.1, is it possible to estimate the likelihood that the customer will provide input into this decision?

To estimate the likelihood of interaction, we would determine whether the stakeholder's profile places them on the likely or unlikely side of Table 4.1. A customer is a voluntary stakeholder (Axis #1) who is likely to be motivated since she has already chosen to have transactions with the organization. If a particular decision would influence the future transactions of the customer, then she has a direct (Axis #2) as well as individual interest (Axis #4), which would also increase motivation to participate. As an external stakeholder (Axis #3), customers would not be as strongly motivated as mixed stakeholders and those who have two mixed roles with the organization, making their participation unlikely. Administrative decisions (Axis #5)

Table 4.1 Motivation based on the stakeholder's profile

Unlikely	*Chapter 2: Taxonomy continua*	*Likely*
Involuntary	#1: Relationship to organization	Voluntary
Indirect	#2: Interests of the stakeholder	Direct
External/internal	#3: Location of the stakeholder	Mixed, overlapping
Collective, group	#4: Interests being represented	Individual, organization
Policy	#5: Focus of organizational action	Administrative
Positive	#6: Impact of organizational action	Negative, mixed

that would influence future transactions have immediate impacts on those who engage in transactions with an organization, making this customer more likely to participate than for a policy decision.

Moreover, if the client is likely to experience negative or mixed externalities (Axis #6), then she would also be more likely to participate in an attempt to mitigate the externalities. Overall, the client's profile makes her likely to participate based on five out of the six axes for this push factor. A similar analysis could be possible for other stakeholders to identify who is likely to be pushed to participate.

4.3.2 Push Factor #2: Demographics

One conclusion scholars have consistently reached is that older individuals are more likely to participate. Younger members of the community participate, but not in "(... [t]raditional passive participation mechanisms such as voting, attending civic meetings, or running for city council [since they] do not capture the cultural forms of participation that are more likely to involve [them].)" (Kathlene & Martin, 1991, p. 322). More advantaged persons (as measured by things such as education and wealth) are disproportionately over-represented in stakeholder participation as well (Buck, 1984, p. 472; Verba & Nie, 1972). Those with low socioeconomic status are less likely to participate, although age and education are more significant than income (Almond & Verba, 1965; Milbraith, 1965; Gittell, 1980, p. 21). Verba, Schlozman, and Brady (1995) suggest that race and ethnicity are correlated. Other scholars (Dalton, 1996; Pierce, Lovrich, & Matsuoka, 1989; Pye, 1958; Reed, 2002; Schatteman, 2012; Van Ryzin, 2013) reach similar conclusions. They note that ideology may be an important predictor, concluding that conservatives are more likely to participate based on self and organizational interests and liberals tend to base their participation decision on collective interests. By considering these correlations, the administrator can identify the groups of stakeholders likely to provide input voluntarily.

4.3.3 Push Factor #3: Stakeholder Efficacy

I define the term efficacy as being successful in producing an intended result. The concept of efficacy is essential in the medical arena as a standard for testing the success rate of prescriptions or medical interventions (Ciociola et al., 2014). Efficacy comes from a variety of factors, such as gaining knowledge about a topic that makes a person feel confident engaging with others, having a positive self-image that gives one a sense that he is worthy of being in a discussion as a peer, and being comfortable with social interactions.

Efficacy is self-reinforcing; when a person participates and thinks that his participation was successful, then his efficacy increases. There is support for the notion that stakeholder engagement increases efficacy (Reidel, 1972). An active engagement process can be transformative (Thurmaier & Ceka, 2019, p. 4) since it features dialogue that helps to learn sincere preferences and willingness to pay. For example, people who live in states that let citizens vote directly on legislation tend to have higher levels of political efficacy and higher voter turnout (Donovan & Bowler, 2004). Differences in efficacy levels are found even after controlling for a whole set of other individual push factors such as education.

In the political arena, efficacy suggests someone who possesses a self-image necessary to believe they can understand and engage in politics and to feel that their participation makes a difference (Kirlin, 2005). Political efficacy correlates positively with participation (Campbell, Converse, Miller, & Stokes, 1960). Higher levels of efficacy often lead many people to believe they can affect what the government does (Hirlinger, 1992). There is also a relationship between efficacy and participatory budgeting empowerment (Gilman, 2016; Lerner, 2014). The *Empowerment Sourcebook* (Narayan-Parker, 2002, p. 4) defines empowerment as the "… the expansion of assets and capabilities of poor people to participate in, negotiate with, influence, control, and hold accountable institutions that affect their lives." Empowerment is a push factor for the disadvantaged who are unlikely to participate, ceteris paribus (Franklin, Krane, & Ebdon, 2013).

4.3.4 Push Factor #4: Group Membership

Motivation to participate is expected to be more persuasive if an individual is active in political parties, campaigns, and elections or has membership in interest groups or civic, social, or affiliation groups. In the political arena, the level of political interest and strength of one's identification with a party or political activity can outweigh wealth or education as factors motivating participation (Adams, 2007; Moyser & Parry, 1989; Rowley & Moldoveanu, 2003). Stakeholders who represent groups also tend to mobilize as a member of the group, causing the organization to work with networks of stakeholders rather than in dyadic relationships (Cole, He, McCullough, Semykina, & Sommer, 2011; Rowley, 1997).

However, the power of group membership as a factor pushing individuals into participating may be less potent than in the past (Skocpol, 2000). The conclusion that people prefer *Bowling Alone* was made famous by Putnam (2000), referring to the fact that individuals are less and less likely to be involved in social organizations such as bowling leagues. Alternatively, people may purposefully opt-out of participation because of the contentiousness of public action (Skocpol & Fiorina, 2004) and the sentiment that it is an insiders' game where one person cannot effectively pursue their preferences (Coleman, 2014; Schlupp & Franklin, 2014). However, the argument for the bridging and bonding that occurs when people identify with a group still has traction in extant literature (Uslaner, 2005).

4.3.5 Push Factor #5: Transaction/Interaction Salience

There are also situation-specific conditions that must be present before an individual is motivated to act (labeled individual initiative by Shingles, 1981, p. 78). Situational motivations are divided into two categories: instrumental or expressive (Lawrence, 1981, p. 334). Instrumental motivations have as their goal achieving the outcome of interest or reducing the dissatisfaction a stakeholder has with an organization (Olsen, 2015), such as influencing the organization to make a decision aligned with a stakeholder's preference. Expressive motivations, on the other hand, are inherently rewarding and cause stakeholders to value participation.

Thomas (1982, p. 504) concludes that citizen-initiated contact with government organizations tends to have instrumental motivations based on perceived needs. When stakeholders contact the organization, instrumental motivation is higher than expressive motivation since there is the expectation of self-interested benefits. While self-interests can be powerful motivators, expressive motivations can be powerful as well. One example is my friend who successfully ran for a 5-year term on the school board at a time when her children were no longer in the public school system. Individuals can be pushed into participation by group-based as well as organizational and collective interests. When a particular situation combines instrumental and expressive interests, the salience of interaction will be higher, increasing the likelihood of participation.

Thus, a motivated individual may decide to communicate their preferences passively and in non-organizational venues. Alternatively, the same person may decide to interact directly with the organization, increasing the likelihood that their preferences can inform an organization's decision-making. In this case, motivation may be considered individually and in combination with the choice of participation activities when an individual is making a participation decision.

4.3.6 Push Factor #6: Resources

The motivation to participate is contingent on the resources available to stakeholders (Greenwald, 1977, p. 266). Research has shown that specific stakeholders are excluded from participation (Aberbach & Rockman, 1978, p. 505), simply because they lack the resources to become involved. Disadvantaged or marginalized groups are the least likely to participate (Gittell, 1980; Hausknect, 1962) because they find it challenging to gain access to the participation process due to a lack of resources. The provision of transportation and childcare to attend organization-sponsored participation events is critically essential in participatory budgeting processes in Brazil (Souza, 2001). If participation requires attendance at a time that is inconvenient or requires attendance at multiple events, then many persons in the working classes are excluded from participation de facto (Schlupp & Franklin, 2014). The lack of participation by some, and reduced participation by others, has led to ongoing discussions among scholars about how to get not just more, but also broader, and more representative involvement (Pateman, 1970).

The technological revolution has had a mixed effect on how resources influence participation (Tao, 2013). Mechanisms that allow for participation in an asynchronous time frame enhance opportunities to participate; however, digital mechanisms must be accessible to all kinds of stakeholders. Accessibility is an essential consideration for groups of stakeholders who do not have the hardware or software necessary to participate. The digital divide has become less of a concern as increasing percentages of the world's population have smartphones with access to social networking sites. In this venue, preferences motivate participation based on push factors such as dissatisfaction and regret. Participation is less motivated by pull factors like the attractiveness of alternatives or mooring factors like switching costs (Chang, Liu, & Chen, 2014). Even though technology can be a resource for participation, there are concerns related to government monitoring and censorship of Internet-based transmissions. These can mute the expression of preferences in the name of national security, such as the Chinese government's ability to, and proclivity for, removing postings from Sina Weibo.

4.3.7 Push Factor #7: Benefit-Cost Analysis

When thinking about participation, a stakeholder examines the benefits and costs of participation. The stakeholder may be more likely to provide input if doing so is anticipated to provide more benefits than costs. In Table 4.2, I suggest the benefits and costs that may be considered for each push factor.

Table 4.2 Influence of push factors on a stakeholder's motivation to participate

Push factors	Gain in potential benefits	Reduce potential costs
Stakeholder profile	Increases goods or services directly received individually or as agent	Avoid externalities and spillovers from changes
Demographics	Increases voice for individual and those they (passively or actively) represent and likelihood better decision outcomes	Preserve favorable terms of current transactions
Efficacy	Improves confidence to interact with other stakeholders and organizations and can be a pathway to active engagement	Neutral effect
Group membership	Acting with others raises the visibility of the issues and can become a tipping point	Avoid contentious actions
Transaction issue salience	Increased benefits or reduced costs if successful and can feel like making a difference	Neutral effect
Resources	Neutral effect	Lack of access if interactions are not facilitated and opportunity costs

If the stakeholder directly benefits from interacting, this suggests self-interested behavior. However, the participation decision is not motivated solely by benefits or costs to the individual. Stakeholders may also communicate their preferences based on group, organization, or collective interests. Participation based on these motivations suggests that the benefits of participating can be compounded with little increase in the costs. However, an additional cost, an opportunity cost, can also be identified. Opportunity costs arise when individuals forfeit the ability to engage in other activities in which they could choose to spend their time (Kweit & Kweit, 1980).

Kahneman and Tversky (1979, p. 279) offer additional guidance predicting that risk aversion will cause the individual to choose more certain alternatives. Additionally, they maintain that the utility curve related to the probability of loss is steeper than that of gains. Fear of loss may lead the stakeholder to overweight the status quo and the probability of short-term costs but undervalue delayed or long-term benefits. Empirical research lends support to this prediction with findings that many people perceive a high cost to participate, no matter what level of resources they currently experience (Kweit & Kweit, 1980; Schlupp & Franklin, 2014).

Applying these conclusions about benefit-cost analysis to an individual's decision on whether or not to participate, a stakeholder may evaluate the six factors sequentially. In doing so, he could conclude that each push factor may produce benefits such as a successful outcome, an outcome with fewer negative externalities, or increased self-efficacy. The push factors may also have costs related to the process of communicating preferences, participating, or not achieving the desired outcome.

Using a typical benefit-cost analysis process, once the benefits or costs of each push factor are recognized, then the individual attempts to determine the overall net value produced from participation.

Kahneman and Tversky (1979) theorized that the decision logic process for an individual is different from a benefit-cost analysis an organization would conduct for something like a purchasing decision. The individual assigns values to potential gains and losses and then determines the probabilities or each. For the organization, the decision criterion is the net present value.

There are other ways that individuals differ when analyzing costs and benefits such as (1) people seldom assign monetary values to each cost and benefit related to a decision. However, they will assign a relative valuing to different costs and benefits. Also, individuals tend to value different outcomes irrationally (Ariely, 2009). Also, people are not good at discounting for the influence of time. Thus, it should not be surprising to learn that an individual's preferences are not consistent in similar situations or at different points in time (Thaler & Sunstein, 2008). The organization's consideration of the costs and benefits of facilitating stakeholder interactions that may reduce perceived costs of participation and pull stakeholders into participating is our next topic.

4.4 Pull Factors Motivating Participation

The tourism literature alerts us to the fact that push factors are seldom sufficient to spur concrete action. The pull factors also influence the decision to act by establishing the preferred form of action. When the combined push and pull factors are strong enough, then action will occur. Reviewing extant literature, I have identified seven pull factors that can influence a stakeholder's motivation to participate: (1) stakeholder invitation, (2) other active stakeholders, (3) participant development, (4) issue salience, (5) active venues, (6) incentives, and (7) benefit-cost analysis.

Some pull factors can be understood as mediating factors on the motivation decision since the stakeholder takes into consideration actions by others that attempt to pull her into participation through an invitation, opportunities for knowledge development, or incentives. When these pull factors work, the stakeholder considers how it may further her own goals or increase the probability of a successful outcome. Pull factors can also be extrinsic motivators since they offer the prospect of enhanced efficacy that comes from interacting with others active on issues that have high salience, primarily when the interaction occurs in venues perceived to have a higher probability of a successful outcome in terms of preference satisfaction.

Here is an example of how pull factors influence decisions about my leisure time: I like hiking at moderate altitudes in places with water features and perfect weather (as defined by Goldilocks). I will nearly always be *pushed* into hiking on the Mogollon Rim in Arizona during the spring and fall. I am less likely to be *pulled* into hiking in high altitudes and steep inclines (mountain hiking) in or near Arizona unless I have resources and preparation for that type of hiking, appropriate equipment, a guide, and the ability to hike at the right time of year to avoid extreme weather (which is what Goldilocks does not prefer).

4.4.1 Pull Factor #1: Stakeholder Invitation

Rudder (2008) claims that stakeholders need to know about the opportunity to participate. Communicating opportunities is one area where many organizations fall short. Communication is the most powerful way to notify stakeholders about organizational activities and the options available for providing input. Fostering knowledge and participation happens when the organization or other active stakeholders reach out to individuals and invite them to participation opportunities (Communities Scotland, 2014; Rice, 2001). The positive power of an invitation from the organization was evident in Midwestern cities with people who started participating in resource allocation processes after someone in government invited them to participate (Ebdon & Franklin, 2004). The power of invitations was reconfirmed a decade later in a project that queried citizen advisory board members about who invited them to participate. Almost uniformly, they responded that an elected official or an administrator invited them. When this happened, stakeholders accepted (Franklin & Rickard, 2016; Schlupp & Franklin, 2014). Organizations realize that people with whom they currently have transactions can be a vital source of information and can lead to future interactions. As a result, they regularly invite these stakeholders to provide input. Over and over again, I have learned through research that the most prominent critics often evolve into powerful program advocates once they participate.

4.4.2 Pull Factor #2: Other Active Stakeholders

One of the push factors identified above was group membership. From the cradle, we take cues from our family and peers who model behaviors and attitudes about participation. Group membership can also be a pull factor when people in a group we like to invite us to participate or other stakeholders have already decided to participate. As technology evolves, individuals in groups and organizations are better able to encourage others to get involved (Stecklein, 2014). Examples that can mobilize participation include social media postings, professional association calls to action, and informational websites like www.badvoter.org (a website allowing anyone to check the voting history of candidates who are on the ballot).

Specific characteristics of an interest or advocacy group can influence a person to become involved, primarily when the group communicates information on a policy issue or a future decision (Moe, 1980). The group characteristics more likely to pull someone into participation include a broad constituency that is politically active, a constituency willing to make financial contributions to political candidates, an established long-term trust relationship with public officials, a staff dedicated to full-time activism, a group of professionals with subject matter and technical expertise who can use their knowledge to influence organizational processes, favorable publicity, and an acknowledged stake, or legal standing, in the activities of a public program (Beatty, Doerksen, & Pierce, 1978, p. 339; Schmid, 1971, p. 2). Identifying with the group's characteristics could influence a stakeholder to join the group's efforts since the standing of the group may better serve its members' interests over other stakeholders, not in the group (Uslaner, 2005).

The potential for other stakeholders to pull someone into participation is also more pronounced when individuals are close to people, especially family and friends, directly impacted positively or negatively by an organization's activities. I have the first-hand experience of this pull factor. Shortly after enrolling my father in the Meals on Wheels program and seeing the improvement in his health (and also benefitting from a phone call from the organization when he did not open the door to get his meal one day), I became a client representative on the Board of Directors.

4.4.3 Pull Factor #3: Participant Development

As described above, groups and organizations perceived to have better resources can lead to someone joining and participating in the group. Groups and organizations purposefully offer resources to members designed to increase an individual's issue knowledge and participation efficacy or to overcome resource limitations. Examples of these participation development activities are education and training programs provided as part of organizationally sponsored participation mechanisms (Gilman, 2016). Scholars (Dervitsiotis, 2003; Fung, 2003; Jones, 2015; Theiss-Morse & Hibbing, 2005; Westheimer & Kahne, 2004) recommend that organizations provide resources and learning experiences in a nurturing participatory environment to pull people into participating as well as to make the self-interested stakeholder more collective-minded.

As described in Chap. 2, there are mixed stakeholders, in particular mediating institutions and intermediaries, who provide knowledge, that can pull people into participation. For example, since 2013, Arizona State University has hosted a website, iCivics.org, with games to enhance citizens' knowledge about society and how to become active. Many groups and organizations provide educational materials, communicate information (such as policy analysis results), and create discussion boards for sharing ideas with other members. Yang and Callahan (2007, p. 256) found that participant development activities such as these overcome obstacles to participation. Having sufficient knowledge to participate also correlates with increased trust in the organization, which facilitates the stakeholder's development (Levin & Cross, 2004).

4.4.4 *Pull Factor #4: Issue Salience*

Another pull for stakeholders' participation is media, organization, or interest group coverage of an upcoming participation opportunity or decision. King (2010, p. 963) argues that public interest is aroused when policy-tipping points emerge and are communicated. Also, individuals are more likely to become involved when there is an exciting decision agenda or an issue perceived as being politically divisive (Wang, 2001). As Johnson and Ward note: "[S]ocial dynamics are constantly changing… and the intensity of participation is situational…" based on the amount of turbulence in the environment (1972, p. 24).

Additionally, the salience of an issue or decision can be raised when there are concerns about the accountability of an organization (Khagram, Fung, & DeRenzio, 2013). Information about organization performance comes increasingly from third parties (like the media) as well as from unofficial sources rather than from the organization directly. Individuals regularly post evaluations of transactions and interactions on the Internet (Porumbescu, 2013). First-person reviews can be problematic for organizations, especially when information is erroneous or purposively misleading (Hothschild & Einstein, 2015).

4.4.5 *Pull Factor #5: Active Venue(s)*

In Chap. 3, I introduced the concept of venues for participation and described how they could be useful conduits for stakeholders to register their preferences for organizational activities. Over time, and assisted by technology, the venues available for participation have been multiplying. So too has the power of a particular venue to pull a stakeholder into participation (Fung, 2003). This is especially true when the venue is already actively gathering and reporting stakeholder preferences on a particular decision or issue of salience to the stakeholder.

The venues that stakeholders consider for communicating their preferences are generally tied to the venue's decision-making process (arena, forum, or court) as well as to the probability that an individual stakeholder's preferred policy solution is possible. For example, in the public policy arena, the solution that a court offers can differ dramatically from that of a legislative body or government organization. When thinking about how venue selection influences stakeholder motivation, another consideration is the time frame in which the decision (and resulting policy change) can occur. Twitter posts, as a public dialogue arena, can trend in an exceedingly short time and can capture the attention of other stakeholders. Court decisions, on the other hand, are released on their own unpredictable timeline.

Advocacy groups have been found to prefer some venues over others. The choice often depends on members' beliefs about the most effective means for change or the suitability and sustainability of certain kinds of policy solutions. Of the stakeholders who have actively been involved with government, it has been found that there are different preferences for which branch of government they will contact (Berry, 1977; Cooper, Nownes, & Roberts, 2005; Yackee, 2006). Often the preference is based on previous successful experience (Kohlmeier, 1969), but it can also be based on shared professional ties (Vogel, 1980). In either situation, these established relationships offer the prospect of uniformity and consistency in interaction processes and outcomes. They also can provide access that is easier than trying to work with multiple organizational officials (Smith, 1985).

Most stakeholders know about everyday participation activities, especially those that encourage passive participation. Likewise, most know that they can directly contact organizational officials via different mechanisms for stakeholders to interact with and to provide input to the organization. When examining different potential participation activities, the stakeholder may analyze which activities are in venues deemed likely to lead to successful outcomes. If there is a high percent of venues likely to lead to successful outcomes, then the probability of being pulled into participation rises. Therefore, the choices of venue and participation activity will be based on the stakeholders' preferred outcome and perceived probability of success.

4.4.6 Pull Factor #6: Participation Incentives

An incentive is a stimulant or inducement that encourages or motivates someone. To be effective, incentives related to stakeholder participation need to provide value to the stakeholder. There are three types of incentives found to be useful for getting someone to do something: (1) material, when a tangible reward is offered; (2) solidary, when affiliating with someone is rewarding (these incentives can also be selective such as the elite status that can be achieved by affiliating with a high-profile/

powerful organization); and (3) purposive, when the reward is related to goal achievement (Clark & Wilson, 1961).

The literature supports the importance of incentives as pull factors. Stakeholder participation studies suggest that citizens are positively influenced by the presence of incentives (Folz, 1991). For example, citizens want to participate more in government (Creighton, 1981) and are willing to make relatively large time commitments when there is the prospect of participation having a direct influence on decision-making (Dyson, 1999; Kathlene & Martin, 1991, p. 87).

The administrator may be able to pull stakeholders into participation by incentivizing participation. An invitation to participate and associating with active stakeholders are solidary incentives since they leverage affiliation. Being pulled into participation through promises of knowledge development or the direct provision of resources, such as child care (Gilman, 2016), are examples of material incentives. Issue salience and active venues are purposive incentives since the reward will be a perceived higher probability of success. Thus, it appears that all three of the incentives have the potential to be influential pull factors.

Direct influence on decisions has been found to explain the willingness of people to serve on boards, councils, or commissions (Franklin & Rickard, 2016; Schlupp & Franklin, 2014), suggesting it is an influential pull factor. Not only do these participation incentives increase the likelihood that a stakeholder's preferences will be served, but repeated interactions can also be analogous to the behaviorist's conclusions that association and reinforcement are powerful incentives (Towry, 2003). Another type of incentive is offering a role that is more than advisory. Irland (1975) cautions that giving advisory status to stakeholders participating in the decision process should be done only when they represent the broader constituency that could be impacted. It may be dangerous to suggest that input will be binding since stakeholder influence can be diluted when there are a more significant number of decision-makers or stakeholders providing input.

4.4.7 Pull Factor #7: Benefit-Cost Analysis of Pull Factors

Previously, I described the seventh push factor as benefit-cost analysis, noting the individual's tendency to value benefits and costs over time based on intrinsic motivation. As I noted above, the pull factors tend to be related more to extrinsic motivation; a successful outcome does not just serve the preferences of one person, but those of others with the same preferred outcome.

Behavioral economists remind us that people will analyze their prospects of a successful outcome as part of decision-making (Westheimer & Kahne, 2004). When they do this based solely on the push factors, they are likely adhering to individualistic characteristics of good citizenship – attempting to be the personally responsible citizen. When individual stakeholders consider others who are active on issues, especially those with high salience for the community, then they should be classified as acting more like the participatory citizen since they are exhibiting

Table 4.3 A model of stakeholder motivation and the participation decision

	Stakeholder Motivation $(_{t0})$	
Push factors (IV_{Push})		*Pull factors* (IV_{Pull})
Stakeholder profile		Stakeholder invitation
Demographics		Participant development
Efficacy		Active stakeholders
Group membership		Issue salience
Transaction/issue salience		Active venues
Resources		Incentives
Benefit-cost analysis		Benefit-cost analysis
	Stakeholder motivation$(IV_{(t1)})$	
	Participation decision$(DV_{(t1)})$ (yes, monitor, no)	

characteristics of altruism (in some combination with serving their interests) (Westheimer & Kahne, 2004, pp. 2–3).

Since the considerations of the participatory citizen are different from those of the good citizen, I include benefit-cost analysis as a pull factor. For the participatory citizen, the benefits associated with pull factors may include reputational effects, the prospect of repeated transactions or interactions at lower costs, and trust-based relationships. These benefits could be in addition to those associated with the push factors.

The costs associated with a decision to participate may differ as well. For example, affiliation with others may require a more significant time commitment since additional processing time will be required for group interactions, or there may be group membership requirements necessitating additional resources (such as a membership fee). Finally, a positive or negative affiliation status can have reputational effects.

In Table 4.3, I present a model that presents the push and pull factors for stakeholder motivation. The combined motivations lead to a decision at one point in time$(_{t1})$. The participation decision can be one of three outcomes: Yes, the stakeholder will participate. No, the stakeholder will not participate. Alternatively, the stakeholder is still undecided and will monitor the situation and decide about participation in the future.

4.5 Strategies for Incentivizing Interactions Based on Push Factors

In addition to a stakeholder monitoring the situation, the administrator will also need to monitor stakeholder input and determine when to pull specific stakeholders into interactions proactively. Armed with the knowledge about who is predictably likely to interact with the organization based on the seven push factors, the administrator's task for monitoring stakeholders under general operating conditions is minimal.

Much of the data needed to understand if stakeholder preferences are being met can be gathered from performance measures the organization already has in place about time and cost of service as well as satisfaction with routine transactions. Variance indicators that categorize non-routine transactions such as returned goods or service complaints can be another vital source of on-hand information about stakeholder relationships. Information external to the organization can be gathered passively by monitoring social media postings, reviews, and ratings/rankings. Another source of information is the regularized interactions with the usual suspects.

When combined, these three data sources can serve as an early warning detection method for changes in stakeholder satisfaction and preferences and added to a dashboard of performance indicators (Wholey, Hatry, & Newcomer, 2010) that is regularly updated and routinely analyzed to assure that the status quo is maintained or even improving. Reviewing each of the seven push factors, organizational administrators can also gain insight into the relative costs of capturing generalized stakeholder input versus the cost of direct interactions with purposefully selected stakeholders.

The stakeholders' profile is the first on the list of push factors (see Table 4.3). Recall that the left-hand column had the characteristics of those unlikely to participate when the activities of the organization are at the status quo. In this situation, the organization does not need to develop strategies to facilitate interactions and should instead look for opportunities for passive stakeholder monitoring. As I described in Chap. 2, stakeholder profiles can be created for the routine activities of the organization. Once the kinds of stakeholders already pushed into participation are identified, the organization can establish interactions and build relationships with any stakeholder categories not currently served, but that may be important for preserving the status quo in the organization's activities and transactions.

The second push factor considers the demographic characteristics of stakeholders. We might expect that demographics, as a moderating factor, provides a base level of likeliness to participate that is or is not sufficient to push someone into participating. The likelihood to participate may be determined by looking at the profile of the organization's clients. If the organization routinely gathers preference and satisfaction data passively or offers mechanisms such as customer satisfaction interfaces, then there is little need to develop facilitated interaction strategies for general stakeholder monitoring.

The remaining push factors, efficacy, group membership, transaction/issue salience, and resources, would tend to push someone into participation when they are already present. However, the effectiveness of these push factors may be diminishing over time. As described above, group membership has been on the decline (Putnam, 2000). Additionally, slack resources (especially time) are perceived by individuals as being stretched now more than in the past (Skocpol & Fiorina, 2004). Lastly, unless the organization is not satisfying current clients or is considering changes its activities, then there is no reason to expect that stakeholder engagement will rise due to changed levels of transaction or issue salience. The impact of this push factor will need to be reconsidered as contextual factors change.

Therefore, from the organization's perspective, when the organization's activities are at a status quo level, one can argue that typical participation activities will provide sufficient stakeholder input for monitoring purposes. No additional benefits will be gained if additional participation activities are offered by the organization, except perhaps for the goodwill that might come from perceptions of enhanced accessibility. To achieve these incremental benefits at low cost, the administrator tasked with stakeholder engagement can use the communication platforms that already exist for the organization to periodically remind stakeholders about the mechanisms that are continuously available to provide input into the organization activities. Communications offer the potential to increase net present value through new data that can supplement and allow triangulation of the data already being monitored in the organization's performance dashboard. Knowing when is the right time and condition for pulling stakeholders into participation is the next section's topic.

4.6 Participation Decision Calculus

When introducing the taxonomy of stakeholder motivation, I presented vectors of push and pull variables that can influence an individual's participation decision. In this section, I use these to develop a model of stakeholder motivation and reflect on the impact of the push and pull factors on a stakeholder's decision to participate.

In the proposed model, the stakeholder starts at the time $_{(0)}$ with a baseline level of motivation to participate, as shown in Eq. 4.1. The baseline level derives from the strength of the push factors that are mediating variables (such as demographics and efficacy) and assumes that the moderating factors at time $_{(0)}$ are zero. Then, at time $_{(1)}$, the stakeholder reconsiders participation and makes a decision based on the level of motivation she has at time $_{(0)}$ combined with the effects of the push and pull factors at time$_{(1)}$.

The participation decision at time$_{(1)}$ is modeled in Eq. 4.2. When a stakeholder considers participating, the model proposes three possible decisions, Yes, I will participate; No, I will not participate; or I am not deciding now, preferring to monitor the process and decide about participating later.

$$\text{Stakeholder Motivation}_{(t0)} = \alpha + \beta IV_{\text{Push(Moderating)}} + \varepsilon \tag{4.1}$$

$$\text{Participation Decision}_{(t1)} = \alpha + \beta IV_{\text{Motivation}(t0)} + \beta IV_{\text{Push}} + \beta IV_{\text{Pull}} + \varepsilon \tag{4.2}$$

This model of the participation decision is simplistic. However, I believe it parsimoniously incorporates the vectors of variables that could push or pull a stakeholder into participation in a specific, time-bound context. An argument can be made that, in practice, stakeholders may already replicate this simplicity. Downs (1957) writes of the shortcuts that a rational voter makes to manage the complexities of politics, choosing varying levels of participation based on the situation. Popkin (1991, p. 218) reached the same conclusion, claiming that voters use heuristics drawn from their daily life interactions and the media to construct an internal narrative that guides choices.

Decision theorists also recognize the value of shortcuts and heuristics when making decisions related to wicked problems (Head and Alford, 2015). For many decisions, individuals seldom have the luxury of rational and comprehensive decision analysis (Simon, 1965) and often suffer from cues fatigue when too many variables and alternatives are present, leading to ambivalence about the decision or even to no-decision. Lindblom (1959) addresses this likelihood and suggests that people employ a strategy of limited (mixed) scanning of variables and alternatives. They then adopt a strategy of satisficing or accepting the first alternative that yields a minimally acceptable outcome. Scholars in behavioral economics (Ariely, 2009; Kahneman & Tversky, 1979; Thaler & Sunstein, 2008) have described a situational decision calculus that considers anticipated costs in relation to the expected benefits of doing something.

Using the discussion about the push and pull factors related to stakeholder motivation, we can assume that when considerable benefits are expected relative to the anticipated costs, active participation is likely. In a study of four advanced western democracies, Dalton (1996, p. 31) reached a similar conclusion noting that: "Most citizens … find a means of balancing the costs and benefits of political activity." He finds that this is what drives the choice between various forms of active and passive participation. Passive participation seems likely in situations where there are few perceived benefits and low costs, but the opportunity cost is high. When small or moderate benefits are expected, or the stakeholder has already engaged in passive participation, the participation decision may be to monitor the environment and reconsider participation when there are changes in the push and pull factors causing changes in expected costs or benefits. If there is an expectation of high costs relative to benefits, then participation is not likely.

Parsimonious modeling of the factors that motivate participation sets the stage for a more in-depth analysis of how these factors could interact to motivate the participation decision. A typology is presented in the next section that argues for including interaction effects between variables and adding a variable for recursive decision-making as a means for capturing the dynamic nature of the participation decision to improve the predictive value of the stakeholder motivation model.

4.7 Dynamic Influences on Motivation to Participate

In the model of stakeholder motivation, I suggested that monitoring the situation could be one decision outcome. When a stakeholder decides to monitor rather than to participate, this suggests that they expect the push and pull factors to change in some way that may cause them to become motivated to participate in the future (Forss and Schwarz, 2011). If this expectation is accurate, then deciding to participate is not a one-shot, dichotomous decision; instead, it is a recursive process where new information for any of the push or pull variables may alter the participation decision (Rabin, 1998). It could also suggest that there are interactions between the vectors of push and pull factors in addition to interactions between individual variables in each of these vectors.

When considering these possibilities, I was stymied by a dearth of theoretical prescriptions or empirical findings addressed specifically to factors influencing a stakeholder's motivation to participate. While thinking about the relationships between the vectors of variables influencing one's motivation to participate and the dynamic nature of the participation decision, I wrestled not only with the difficulties of predicting the individual independent variables but also with the possibility of confirming suspected interaction effects between variables and vectors. I concluded that sufficient theoretical prescriptions or empirical knowledge to present the model authoritatively or to analyze the likelihood of interactive effects and recursive decision-making do not exist.

Realizing this, I looked outside the ivory tower of the academy to see what insights by analogy could be gleaned from the real world. The first possibility came from my nephew's third-grade science book. He was learning about reciprocal, symbiotic, and mutually dependent relationships in an ecosystem and how all types are necessary to preserve the health of the ecosystem. This concept speaks very well to the influence that other stakeholders and the organization can have on pulling the stakeholder into participation. I return to these relationships in Chap. 6. However, for this chapter, the nature of relationships active in a vector of pull factors, by itself, did not adequately capture the motivation decision.

After a week of wondering how to model a recursive stakeholder motivation to participation model, I realized the board game Monopoly was the answer. In the next few paragraphs, set up the analogy. Then, I apply what I learned from Monopoly to refine the model of stakeholder motivation. For readers who think this is the perfect metaphor, just skip ahead to the end of this subsection for my argument about how the predictive model is enhanced by the inclusion of dynamic effects between variables and vectors. For those who want more facts, please read on!

4.7.1 Monopoly as a Metaphor for Dynamic and Recursive Decisions

To start the Monopoly game, each player gets a certain amount of money (for the fast game, the players also get some properties). I would suggest that money and properties represent the push factors of resources, group membership (playing the game with others), and efficacy.

Then, the game begins, and players roll the dice, move their game pieces to the proper space, and start making decisions. The rolling of the dice represents the stochastic probability of success (as do the properties a player received at the start of the game – if applicable). The token's landing space determines the relevant push and pull variables for the first decision, which then establishes the status quo upon which future decisions are compared. Recursive decision-making occurs after each round of play. It includes consideration of how a player's decisions will influence and are influenced by what other players have done during their turns. The process is analogous to interaction salience about a policy or administrative decision.

The Monopoly board is set up so that the properties one first encounters are relatively cheap, but also have small paybacks. To me, looking at the net payback is analogous to the cost-benefit analysis comparing resources to outcome probabilities in the push factors. The decision about whether to purchase property also incorporates opportunity costs, such as choosing a venue or mechanism for participation, since the player must decide which properties to buy as well as on which properties to add houses and hotels (now or later).

The game also includes actions that emulate the pull factors. The organization and mixed stakeholders who are intermediaries and how they attempt to influence the stakeholder's decision are represented by the Community Chest and Chance cards, as well as by the board spaces that are not property-related [i.e., Income Tax, In Jail/Just Visiting, Free Parking, Go To Jail, and Go (Collect $200)].

The actions required on these spaces also provide feedback about the probability of success influencing recursive decision-making since 75% of the Community Chest cards have a benefit (only 25% have a benefit in the Chance cards) and 50% of the Chance cards direct the player to advance their token to a specific space, which may yield positive or negative benefits. There is a similar situation for the Free Parking space, which may yield a lottery-like win, and Go to Jail spaces, which require payment or forfeiture of a Get Out of Jail card. Both Community Chest and Chance have 25% of cards requiring payment by the player, which would represent a diminishment of resources related to participation.

The influence of other active stakeholders is analogous to the other Monopoly players and the decisions they make during their respective turns. The other players can also influence what a player does when they suggest side deals and exchanges (which could be equivalent to considering different venues, participation activities, and incentives). As the other players accumulate properties and money to purchase houses and hotels, or mortgage their properties, the salience of what is happening overall in the game rises since this can influence what a player does in his next turn, as will the relative location of all players' game pieces on the Monopoly board.

One take-away point from the Monopoly metaphor is that interaction effects between the independent variables in a specific vector as well as between the push and pull vectors should be expected. The push factors are intrinsic and determine if a player will participate in activities that are beyond what is required by the space on which he has landed. Push factors have moderating effects that can assist the

Table 4.4 Enhanced model of stakeholder motivation and the participation decision

	Stakeholder Motivation (DV_{t0}) (Baseline)	
Push factors (IV_{Push})		*Pull factors* (IV_{Pull})
Stakeholder profile	*Recursive cost-benefit analysis*	Stakeholder invitation
Demographics	*Based on*:	Participant development
Efficacy		Active stakeholders
Group membership		Issue salience
Transaction/issue salience	Variable interactions ($IV_{Interactive}$)	Active venues
Resources	Dynamic decision-making ($IV_{Recursive}$)	Incentives
Benefit-cost analysis	*Stakeholder motivation*$_{(t-1)}$	Benefit-cost analysis
	Participation decision ($DV_{(t+1...x)}$) (yes, monitor, no)	

player in predicting what other players will do and then influence choices for action. The pull factors are extrinsic and shape the form and venue of participation. Pull factors can be leveraged by other stakeholders to influence an individual's participation decision, making them intervening variables that have mediating effects on an individual's participation decision.

A second take-away is that stakeholders can be expected to engage in recursive decision-making about their participation because the push and pull vectors of motivation contain variables that have dynamic relationships. As more information becomes known (through monitoring, learning, or participant interactions), uncertainty elements that influence stakeholder participation are reduced, which may cause a re-evaluation of the participation decision. From these two take-away points, Table 4.4 presents the enhanced model of stakeholder motivation.

Including a variable to capture the interactive effects between variables and vectors can improve the model of stakeholder motivation. Also, the recursive nature of the cost-benefit calculus can be explicitly articulated in an enhanced predictive model (Eq. 4.3). Systems dynamics modeling could nicely accommodate the non-linearity and feedback between variables as well as endogenous behavior changes based on recursive simulations (System Dynamics Society, n.d.). Combining these ideas, stakeholder participation is like the board game Monopoly, which is an analogy that can be empirically tested.

$$\text{Participation Decision}_{(t+1...x)=}\alpha + \beta IV_{\text{Motivation}(t0)} + \beta IV_{\text{Push}} + \beta IV_{\text{Pull}} + \beta IV_{\text{Interactive}} + \beta IV_{\text{Recursive}} + \varepsilon \quad (4.3)$$

4.8 Strategic Use of the Push and Pull Factors

In this section, we systematically consider the push and pull factors from the perspective of the administrator tasked with stakeholder engagement. Table 4.5 identifies potential administrative actions for each of the seven push factors of participation motivation. These actions would be taken when a specific push factor is causing a lack of participation for some group of stakeholders whose preferences are not likely to be communicated voluntarily.

In the first row, the administrator communicates about negative externalities that stakeholders may be experiencing. Examples are public recall notices (faulty airbags or tainted food), class-action suit notifications for groups of clients (not disclosing charges for services before they are assessed), and public announcements about upcoming activities (like zoning changes for municipal planning boards). The last example would be a coercive incentive since without taking the advice or seeking the remedial action provided by the organization, the stakeholder suffers a penalty.

An administrative action that could leverage moral and natural incentives based on demographic characteristics is to communicate directly to stakeholders and describe the venues that exist to provide input. Also, the administrator tasked with stakeholder engagement can extend an invitation (general, selective, or recurring) or provide resources or incentives necessary to gain stakeholder participation.

The younger members of society may be a group of stakeholders that need an invitation to participate since they may not be aware of how organizational decisions could impact them. In a lecture given by Jennifer Hothschild (2007), she noted that people in this demographic claim that they do not participate because the issues under discussion are not of interest to them. If this is true, then administrators should seek to inform subgroups of the population about specific issues for which they do

Table 4.5 Administrative pull actions to incentivize participation

Stakeholder profile	The administrator can communicate directly to a broad group of stakeholders likely to suffer negative externalities and describe venues for providing input
Demographics	The administrator can invite stakeholders to participate
Efficacy	The administrator can inform about activities and identify other stakeholders with similar interests who are active or who can serve as representatives
Group membership	The administrator can make presentations at group meetings and regularly communicate by providing statements that can be published by the group (such as newsletters, emails, and website postings)
Resources	Administrator can provide supportive services to remove participation access barriers AND can provide incentives to participate in internal venues
Transaction/issue salience	Administrator can make more information available to make the issue salient and provide information about venues for participation
Benefits	The organization can incentivize participation by committing to use the input provided from participation or can signal openness to coproduction

or will have a direct interest in the future and take special care to invite them to participate in events focused on these issues.

As described above, stakeholder participation can be incentivized if there is an education function provided as part of the interaction. This type of incentive would work well for stakeholders who have not previously interacted with the organization and have low participation efficacy as a result. The education function can provide information about how to be a participant, thus increasing the transparency of the process. Administrators can also educate stakeholders about the range of mechanisms available to them to communicate their preferences making the input process more accessible.

When the administrator knows that members of a public or special interest group may want to provide input on a future decision, then the administrator can work with the leaders of the group to provide background information and details about mechanisms available for providing input. By communicating with the members, the group affiliation may become more potent, thus pulling in members who have not previously been active.

For the last push factor, a strong incentive for participation can be a commitment by the organization to adopting the preferences of the participating stakeholders. For example, the Citizens Participation Organizations that were created in the 1960s in Wichita were given the power to recommend the distribution of Community Development Block Grant funds with the understanding that city leaders would adopt their recommendations (Ebdon & Franklin, 2004). Participatory budgeting efforts in Chicago and New York City have followed a similar practice (Lerner, 2011, 2014). Elected officials guaranteed a specific dollar amount of capital funds to be allocated in their ward or district based upon the recommendations of a citizen's advisory board.

The push factors an individual considers in the participation decision are moderating variables. Moderating factors are not easily changed, but they can provide insight into who is most likely to participate. The pull factors may be more potent for influencing both the decision to participate and the choice of participation activity. This may be especially true when the administrator incentivizes participation by leveraging the mediating factors that may pull un(der)represented stakeholders into participation. The x-factor in predicting participation is that the administrator cannot control how the stakeholder calculates the costs and assigns benefits to the outcomes they prefer. However, the administrator can consider in what venues stakeholders prefer participating and if a change in venue would motivate participation. These possibilities are considered in the next section.

4.9 Venues and Stakeholder Engagement

From the organization's perspective, when compared to discovering preferences communicated by stakeholders in venues beyond the control of the organization, the costs of gathering preference information that confirms willingness to pay or willingness to share are decreased, and the benefits of learning sincere preferences are increased when there is direct interaction with stakeholders in the organization's preferred venue. Understanding stakeholder motivation and the factors associated with venue selection can be a means for anticipating who is, and who is not, likely to communicate preference information directly to the organization.

In Chap. 3, I described the venues, participation activities, and mechanisms through which a stakeholder can communicate their preferences. Additionally, in the description of venues as a pull factor in this chapter, I suggested that a stakeholder is likely to choose a venue where the probability that their preferences will be chosen is perceived to be relatively higher. There may be an interaction effect with the push factor for efficacy since a certain level of efficacy would be required to identify and understand the pros and cons of different venues. Stakeholders with higher levels of efficacy will generally not require resource support for participation, so the power of that pull factor may be muted in different venues. Therefore, it is likely that venue selection is also a recursive decision since the stakeholder may choose other venues if not satisfied with the interactions they have had with the organization in one venue; thus, the status quo is costly.

Venue selection may be a case of punctuated equilibrium (Baumgartner & Jones, 1993), where the changes could be outside the stakeholder's control. For example, there may be changes in the organization's environment, necessitating policy, or organizational activities changes that are unsatisfactory for the stakeholder. When this occurs, stakeholders may be more likely to reconsider which venue will be best for communicating their preferences. Walters (2004) found this to be the case when a city fire department was faced with cutbacks.

Venue shopping refers to activities of policy entrepreneurs who seek out a decision setting where they can air their grievances with current policies or pursue activities in support of their proposals (Pralle, 2003, p. 233). Theories about venue selection consider both the objective biases of organizations and venues and the subjective perceptions of the policy entrepreneurs themselves. In the case of venue shopping, such perceptions and thoughts affect whether to shop for another venue as well as the choice of venue. Strategic venue selection can be a means of attracting allies and shaping a stakeholder's public image, as well as a way to achieve substantive goals. The choice of particular venues can take into consideration goals beyond a particular decision and stakeholder preferences (Baumgartner & Jones, 1993).

Theoretical conclusions about venue shopping are based primarily on the study of advocacy groups or policymakers acting as policy entrepreneurs. Strategically minded policy entrepreneurs will target a venue that offers the best advantage over their opponents (Adams, 2007) or when a venue has already provided success. Thus, the choice of venue can be based on instrumental and learned behavior. Venue shopping that results from learning occurs when a stakeholder chooses a venue that supports a new, or more complex, definition of an issue requiring decisions on alternatives. The choice of the venue then shapes the definition and kinds of issues promoted, such that it becomes a self-reinforcing process.

Some issues may already be established in a particular venue, and it would be difficult to change the status quo without being able to argue persuasively that the problem must be defined differently. Frustrated by biases within organizational venues where decisions are made, entrepreneurs may seek a change in venue, especially when transaction costs are high (King, 2007).

Alternative venues give entrepreneurs who are on the losing side of a decision an opportunity to go to a different venue with more favorable decision rules or supportive stakeholders. If successful, the conflict moves from a venue where challengers compete with their opponents to an arena where opponents are not yet mobilized. Change often follows when alternative definitions of a problem are accepted and promoted in the new venue. Also, stakeholder participation can expand as a result of venue shifting or when new rules are articulated and enforced in the arena by new actors.

Taken together, the variables related to a stakeholder's efficacy, the need to change the status quo, the other stakeholders participating in a venue, and the potential to have successful outcomes can influence a stakeholder's venue selection. These variables and their expected relationships are modeled in Eq. 4.4.

The equation is a starting point for identifying factors that may represent variables that have the potential for elucidating how the choice of active venues occurs and why this may pull a stakeholder into participation. Specifically, they are efficacy, the status quo change cost, alternative problem definitions, other stakeholders, and the likelihood of success.

$$\begin{aligned}\text{Venue Selection}_{(\text{Stakeholder})} &= \alpha + \beta IV_{\text{Effic}} - \beta IV_{SQ\Delta\$} + \beta IV_{\text{AltDefin}} \\ &\quad -\beta IV_{\text{Others}} + \beta IV_{\text{Success}} + \varepsilon\end{aligned} \tag{4.4}$$

Extant literature suggests that stakeholders, alone or working as a member of an interested-based organization, are strategic in their selection of venues in which to pursue policy change. There is also anecdotal evidence that organizations are attentive to the costs and benefits of decision-making in different venues. In this section, I reflect on the factors that may influence venue selection by organizations as part of a stakeholder engagement strategy. The model and equations can help spur research examining how organizations can use pull factors to motivate or incentivize stakeholder participation in the venue the organization prefers.

4.9.1 Organizational Venue Selection

Just like the decision calculus of stakeholders for choosing the perceived best venue, participation activity, or mechanism for communicating their preferences, the organization can strategically manage the venues that are available for a stakeholder to reveal their preferences. When stakeholders' interactions are desired by (s)elected officials (Jiang, Ebdon, & Franklin, 2016), the administrator can make a recommendation about an appropriate venue for these interactions. In order to make the venue recommendation, administrators can analyze the costs and benefits of (1) doing nothing, (2) interacting with (dis)affected stakeholders, (3) sticking with current or offering new mechanisms for input, or (4) moving the decision to an external venue (but losing control over decision-making).

To choose between offering mechanisms for stakeholders to provide input through internal venues and relying on decisions made in external venues, the administrator can gather information about the relative level of influence participating stakeholders are expected to have in a particular venue, the likelihood that an alternate definition of the issue will be pursued in an external venue, the amount of change that would be required if the decision in the external venue is not what the organization prefers, and the presence of other stakeholders who are currently (or likely to be) motivated to communicate their preferences. Also, the recommendation for a venue should take into account the decision rules. For example, choosing a venue that operates like a court may remove the organization's control of the decision. Equation 4.5 identifies the factors that influence an organization's venue selection. It can be based on stakeholder influence, alternate problem definitions, changes to the status quo, other participating stakeholders, and the expected probability of success.

$$\begin{aligned}\text{Venue Selection}_{(\text{Orgzn})} &= \alpha + \beta IV_{\text{StkInfl}} - \beta IV_{\text{AltDefin}} - \beta IV_{SQ\Delta\$} \\ &\quad + \beta IV_{\text{Others}} - \beta IV_{\text{Success}} + \varepsilon\end{aligned} \tag{4.5}$$

Comparing the variables thought to influence stakeholders' venue selection with the variables influencing venue selection by the organization, each equation has one variable that is not in the other equation. For the stakeholders' venue selection equation, the decision may be influenced by stakeholder's sense of their efficacy. Organizations are less concerned with efficacy and more concerned with the influence that stakeholders operating in an external venue may have relative to the level of influence of the organization.

Both equations are concerned about alternate definitions of the problem that can provide the impetus for stakeholders to participate. Equation 4.4 and Eq. 4.5 are repeated for ease in comparison. The difference is that stakeholders are likely to shop for a new venue when they are dissatisfied with the status quo and think that a new definition is possible elsewhere. When the organization fears an alternate definition of a problem or an acceptable solution, it will resist selecting an outside venue. The status quo is a variable in both models; however, stakeholders are likely to select a new venue when they want to change the status quo, and organizations will be more concerned about how the status quo may be changed if they move the deliberation to an external venue.

$$\begin{aligned}\text{Venue Selection}_{(\text{Stakeholder})} &= \alpha + \beta IV_{\text{Effic}} - \beta IV_{SQ\Delta\$} + \beta IV_{\text{AltDefin}} \\ &\quad - \beta IV_{\text{Others}} + \beta IV_{\text{Success}} + \varepsilon\end{aligned} \tag{4.4}$$

$$\text{Venue Selection}_{(\text{Orgzn})} = \alpha + \beta IV_{\text{StkInfl}} - \beta IV_{SQ\Delta\$} - \beta IV_{\text{AltDefin}} + \beta IV_{\text{Others}} - \beta IV_{\text{Success}} + \varepsilon \quad (4.5)$$

Each model has a variable for other stakeholders. When there are fewer stakeholders who want competing problem definitions or policy outcomes, the likelihood of a stakeholder selecting a new venue goes up. However, the presence of other active stakeholders tends to increase the organization's likelihood of selecting an external venue to pursue policy preferences.

The models also each include a variable about the probability of success. The stakeholders select a venue they think will increase their perceived possibility of success. Organizations think about this as well but may prefer internal venues since they have more control over the decision and would often want to avoid venues where decisions are binding. For this reason, the relationship between the IV and DV is positive and negative, respectively.

Like the model of suspected push and pull factors that can motivate a stakeholder to participate, the variables in the equation for venue selection are based on weak empirical confirmation in extant literature. For this reason, the goal of the discussion about venue selection is to suggest that both stakeholders and organizations are strategic. Stakeholders will consider venues as one of the factors motivating participation. Administrators could use this knowledge to anticipate when stakeholders will use an external venue and to analyze the potential benefits and costs of venue shifting.

4.10 Summary

This chapter has explored the many variables that can influence stakeholder motivation to participate. I have arranged these variables into a taxonomy with two vectors, representing push and pull factors that may motivate stakeholder participation. The push factors are specific to an individual and determine whether there is sufficient motivation to participate. The pull factors are ways that organizations can influence stakeholder's motivation for participation. Combined, the push and pull factors result in a decision calculus that weighs the costs and benefits of an action and considers the probability of success and the net value of that action.

In the typology, I offered a model of stakeholder motivation that featured the push and pull factors as well as interaction effects between variables and a recursive decision-making process that takes into consideration dynamic changes in the participation environment as well as changes in push and pull factors.

Stakeholder motivation and the participation decision are difficult to model using variables and findings in the extant literature, but system dynamics literature offers some prospects for modeling stakeholder motivation. To do this, researchers need a better understanding of the significance of variables that push or pull motivation, which are mediating, which are moderating, and if bivariate relationships have stable temporal ordering. This suggests that future models need to account for dynamic relationships and recursive decision-making. To gain traction on stakeholder motivation, systematic testing of the variables identified in this chapter and the purposeful exploration of how the stakeholder and the organization select participation venues are needed.

A better understanding of how push and pull factors influence a stakeholder's motivation to participate can improve the representativeness of input gathered from stakeholder interactions. In the following chapter, we tackle the question of how an administrator can facilitate interactions with the stakeholders who are motivated to participate. The goal is to gather data that represent sincere preferences, which are more valuable for informing organizational decisions.

References

Aberbach, J. D., & Rockman, B. A. (1978). Administrators' beliefs about the role of the public: The case of American federal executives. *The Western Political Quarterly, 31*(4), 502–522. https://doi.org/10.2307/447232

Adams, B. E. (2007). *Citizen lobbyists: Local efforts to influence public policy*. Philadelphia, PA: Temple University Press.

Almond, G., & Verba, S. (1965). *The civic culture*. Boston, MA: Little, Brown and Company.

Ariely, D. (2009). *Predictably irrational: Hidden forces that shape our decisions*. New York, NY: HarperCollins.

Arnold, R. D. (1990). *The logic of congressional action*. New Haven, CT: Yale University Press.

Baumgartner, F., & Jones, B. D. (1993). *Agendas and instability in American politics*. Chicago, IL: University of Chicago Press.

Beatty, K. M., Doerksen, H., & Pierce, J. C. (1978). Water resources, politics and interest group tactics. *Water Resources Bulletin, 14*(2), 399.

Berry, J. M. (1977). *Lobbying for the people: The political behavior of public interest groups*. Princeton, NJ: Princeton University Press.

Buck, J. V. (1984). The impact of citizen participation programs and policy decisions on participants' opinions. *Western Political Quarterly, 37*(3), 468–482.

Campbell, A., Converse, P. E., Miller, W. E., & Stokes, D. E. (1960). *The american voter*. New York, NY: Wiley.

Chang, I.-C., Liu, C.-C., & Chen, K. (2014). The push, pull and mooring effects in virtual migration for social networking sites. *Information Systems Journal, 24*(4), 323–346. https://doi.org/10.1111/isj.12030

Ciociola, A. A., Karlstadt, R. G., Pambianco, D. J., Woods, K. L., Ehrenpreis, E. D., & FDA-Related Matters Committee of the American College of Gastroenterology. (2014). The Food and Drug Administration advisory committees and panels: How they are applied to the drug regulatory process. *The American Journal of Gastroenterology, 109*(10), 1508–1512.

Clark, P. B., & Wilson, J. Q. (1961). Incentive systems: A theory of organizations. *Administrative Science Quarterly, 6*(2), 129. https://doi.org/10.2307/2390752

Cole, C. R., He, E., McCullough, K. A., Semykina, A., & Sommer, D. W. (2011). An empirical examination of stakeholder groups as monitoring sources in corporate governance. *The Journal of Risk and Insurance, 78*(3), 703–730.

Coleman, E. A. (2014). Behavioral determinants of citizen involvement: Evidence from natural resource decentralization policy. *Public Administration Review, 74*(5), 642–654. https://doi.org/10.1111/puar.12249

Communities Scotland. (2014). *National standards for community engagement*. Edinburgh, Scotland.
Cooper, C. A., Nownes, A. J., & Roberts, S. (2005). Perceptions of power: Interest groups in local politics. *State & Local Government Review, 37*(3), 206–216.
Creighton, J. L. (1981). *The public involvement manual*. Cambridge, MA: ABT.
Dalton, R. J. (1996). *Citizens, politics: Public opinion and political parties in advanced western democracies* (2nd ed.). Chatham, NJ: Chatham House Publishers.
Dervitsiotis, K. N. (2003). Beyond stakeholder satisfaction: Aiming for a new frontier of sustainable stakeholder trust. *Total Quality Management, 15*(5), 511–524.
Donovan, T., & Bowler, S. (2004). *Reforming the republic: Democratic institutions for the new America*. Upper Saddle River, NJ: Pearson Prentice Hall.
Downs, A. (1957) An Economic Theory of Political Action in a Democracy. *Journal of Political Economy 65*(2):135–150
Dyson, L. L. (1999). Developing a university-school district partnership; researcher-district administrator collaboration for a special education initiative. *Canadian Journal of Education Revue Canadienne de l'Education, 24*(4), 411–425.
Ebdon, C., & Franklin, A. L. (2004). Searching for a role for citizens in the budget process. *Public Budgeting & Finance, 24*(1), 32–49.
Ekelund Jr., R. B. (1968). Jules Dupuit and the early theory of marginal cost pricing. *Journal of Political Economy, 76*(3), 462–471.
Folz, D. H. (1991). Recycling program design, management, and participation: A national survey of municipal experience. *Public Administration Review, 51*(3), 222–231.
Forss, K., & Schwartz, R. (2011). Introduction. In K. Forss, M. Marra, & R. Schwartz (Eds.), *Evaluating the complex: Attribution, contribution, and beyond* (pp. 12–13). New Brunswick, NJ: Transaction.
Franklin, A. L. (2001). Involving stakeholders in organizational processes. *International Journal of Public Administration, 24*(4), 385–403.
Franklin, A. L., Krane, D., & Ebdon, C. (2013). Multilevel governance processes–citizens & local budgeting: Comparing Brazil, China, & the United States. *International Review of Public Administration, 18*(1), 1–24.
Franklin, A. L., & Rickard, V. (2016). Civic engagement motivations of municipal board members. Special issue on empowering the public to fix our national fiscal crises. *Journal of Public Budgeting, Accounting and Financial Management, 28*(1), 49–71.
Fung, A. (2003). Recipes for public spheres: Eight institutional design choices and their consequences. *The Journal of Political Philosophy, 11*(3), 338–367.
Gilman, H. R. (2016). *Democracy reinvented: Participatory budgeting and civic innovation in America*. Washington, DC: Brookings Institution Press.
Gittell, M. (1980). *The decline of community organizations: Limits to citizen participation*. Beverly Hills, CA: Sage Publications.
Greenwald, C. S. (1977). *Group power lobbying and public policy*. New York, NY: Praeger.
Hausknect, M. (1962). *The joiners: A sociological description of voluntary association membership in the United States*. New York: Bedminster.
Head, B. W., & Alford, J. (2015). Wicked problems implications for public policy and management. *Administration & Society, 47*(6), 711–739. https://doi.org/10.1177/0095399713481601
Hirlinger, M. W. (1992). Citizen-initiated contacting of local government officials: A multivariate explanation. *The Journal of Politics, 54*(2), 553–564.
Hothschild, J. L. (2007). *Facts, politics, and democracy*. Rothbaum Lecture, Norman, OK: University of Oklahoma.
Hothschild, J. L., & Einstein, K. L. (2015). *Do facts matter?* Information and misinformation in american politics: Norman, OK: University of Oklahoma Press.
Irland, L. C. (1975). Citizen participation: A tool for conflict management on the public lands. *Public Administration Review*, 263–269.

Jiang, Y., Ebdon, C., & Franklin, A. L. (2016). Perceptions of public officials regarding democratic efficacy and the use of citizen participation. *Journal of Public Budgeting, Accounting and Financial Management, 28*(1), 103–124.

Johnson, N., & Ward, E. (1972). Citizen information systems: Using technology to extend the dialogue between citizens and their government. *Management Science, 19*(4), 21–34.

Jones, B. A. (2015, May). *Environmental air quality and wildfires*. Norman, OK: Center for Risk and Crisis Management.

Kahneman, D., & Tversky, A. (1979). Prospect theory: An analysis of decision under risk. *Econometrica, 47*(2), 263–291.

Kathlene, L., & Martin, J. A. (1991). Enhancing citizen participation: Panel designs, perspectives, and policy formation. *Journal of Policy Analysis and Management*, 46–63.

Khagram, S., Fung, A., & DeRenzio, P. (2013). *Open budgets: The political economy of transparency, participation, and accountability*. New York, NY: Brookings Institution Press.

King, A. (2007). Cooperation between corporations and environmental groups: A transaction cost perspective. *The Academy of Management Review, 32*(3), 889–900. https://doi.org/10.2307/20159340

King, S. M., Chilton, B. S., & Roberts, G. E. (2010). Reflections on defining the public interest. *Administration and Society, 41*(8), 954–978.

Kirlin, M. (2005). Understanding the relationship between civic skills and civic participation: Educating future public managers. *Journal of Public Affairs Education, 11*(4), 305–314.

Kohlmeier, L. (1969). *The regulators: Watchdog agencies and the public interest*. New York, NY: Harper and Row.

Kweit, R. W., & Kweit, M. G. (1980). Bureaucratic decision-making impediments to citizen participation. *Polity*, 647–666.

Lawrence, D. G. (1981). Towards an attitudinal theory of political participation. *Polity, 14*(2), 332–346. https://doi.org/10.2307/3234551

Lerner, J. (2011). Participatory budgeting: Building community agreement around tough budget decisions. *National Civic Review, 100*(2), 30–35. https://doi.org/10.1002/ncr.20059

Lerner, J. (2014). *Everyone counts: Could "participatory budgeting" change democracy?* Ithaca, NY: Cornell Selects.

Levin, D. Z., & Cross, R. (2004). The strength of weak ties you can trust: The mediating role of trust in effective knowledge transfer. *Management Science, 50*(11), 1477–1490.

Lindblom, C. E. (1959). The science of "muddling through". *Public Administration Review*, 79–88.

Milbraith, L. (1965). *Political participation: How and why do people get involved in politics?* Chicago, IL: Rand McNally.

Moe, T. M. (1980). *The organization of interests*. Chicago, IL: University of Chicago Press.

Moyser, G., & Parry, G. (1989). Participation and non-participation in an english town. In A. Mabileau, G. Moyser, G. Parry, & P. Quantin (Eds.), *Local politics and participation in Britain and France*. Cambridge, MA: Cambridge University Press.

Nagel, J. H. (1987). *Participation*. Englewood Cliffs, NJ: Prentice-Hall.

Narayan-Parker, D. (2002). *Empowerment and poverty reduction: A sourcebook*. Washington, DC: World Bank.

Olsen, A. L. (2015). Citizen (dis)satisfaction: An experimental equivalence framing study. *Public Administration Review*. https://doi.org/10.1111/puar.12337

Pateman, C. (1970). *Participation and democratic theory*. London, UK: Cambridge University Press.

Pavlov (1927), P. I. (2010). Conditioned reflexes: An investigation of the physiological activity of the cerebral cortex. *Annals of Neurosciences, 17*(3), 136–141. https://doi.org/10.5214/ans.0972-7531.1017309

Pierce, J. C., Lovrich, N. P., & Matsuoka, M. (1989). Support for citizen participation; A comparison of American and Japanese citizens' activities and elites. *The Western Political Quarterly, 43*, 39–59.

Popkin, S. (1991). *The reasoning voter*. University of Chicago Press.

Porumbescu, G. A. (2013). Assessing the link between online mass media and trust in government: Evidence from Seoul, South Korea. *Policy & Internet, 5*(4), 1944–2866.
Pralle, S. B. (2003). Venue shopping, political strategy, and policy change: The internationalization of Canadian forest advocacy. *Journal of Public Policy, 23*(3), 233–260. https://doi.org/10.1017/S0143814X03003118
Prayag, G., & Ryan, C. (2012). Antecedents of tourists' loyalty to Mauritius: The role and influence of destination image, place attachment, personal involvement, and satisfaction. *Journal of Travel Research, 51*(3), 342–356. https://doi.org/10.1177/0047287511410321
Putnam, R. D. (2000). *Bowling alone: The collapse and revival of American community*. New York, NY: Touchstone/Simon & Schuster.
Pye, L. W. (1958). Administrators, agitators and brokers. *The Public Opinion Quarterly, 22*(3), 342–348.
Rabin, M. (1998). Psychology and economics. *Journal of Economic Literature, 36*(1), 11–46.
Reed, D. (2002). Employing normative stakeholder theory in developing countries a critical theory perspective. *Business & Society, 41*(2), 166–207. https://doi.org/10.1177/0007650302041002003
Reidel, J. A. (1972). Citizen participation myths and realities. *Public Administration Review*, 211–220.
Rice, T. W. (2001). Social capital and government performance in Iowa communities. *Journal of Urban Affairs, 23*(3–4), 375–389.
Rowley, T. J. (1997). Moving beyond dyadic ties: A network theory of stakeholder influences. *The Academy of Management Review, 22*(4), 887. https://doi.org/10.2307/259248
Rowley, T. J., & Moldoveanu, M. (2003). When will stakeholder groups act? An interest- and identity-based model of stakeholder group mobilization. *The Academy of Management Review, 28*(2), 204. https://doi.org/10.2307/30040709
Rudder, C. E. W. (2008). Private governance as public policy: A paradigmatic shift. *The Journal of Politics, 70*(4), 899–913.
Ryan, R. M., & Deci, E. L. (2000). Self-determination theory and the facilitation of intrinsic motivation, social development, and well-being. *American Psychologist, 55*(1), 68–78. https://doi.org/10.1037/0003-066X.55.1.68
Schatteman, A. M. (2012). Online citizen participation: A case study of Illinois nonprofit organizations. In H. Schachter & Yang (Eds.), *The state of citizen participation* (pp. 225–238). Charlotte, NC: Information Age Publishing.
Schlupp, J., & Franklin, A. L. (2014). Civic engagement motivations: Understanding why some do and some don't. *Oklahoma Politics, 24*, 21–44.
Schmid, A. A. (1971). *Federal decision-making for water resources development*. Springfield, VA: National Technical Information Center.
Shingles, R. D. (1981). Black consciousness and political participation. *American Political Science Review, 75*(1), 76–91.
Simon, H. A. (1965). *Administrative behavior* (4th ed.). New York, NY: Free Press.
Skocpol, T. (2000). A nation of organizers: The institutional origins of civic voluntarism in the United States. *American Political Science Review, 94*(3), 527–546.
Skocpol, T., & Fiorina, M. P. (2004). *Civic engagement in american democracy*. Brookings Institution Press. http://www.brookings.edu/research/books/1999/civicameric
Smith, Z. A. (1985). *Interest group interaction and groundwater policy formation in the southwest*. Lanham, MD: University Press of America.
Souza, C. (2001). Participatory budgeting in Brazilian cities: Limits and possibilities in building democratic institutions. *Environment and Urbanization, 13*(1), 159–184.
Stecklein, K. (2014). Voting with a purpose. *Norman Transcript, 1*, 6.
System Dynamics Society. (n.d.) *Introduction to systems dynamics*. Retrieved June 25, 2015, from http://www.systemdynamics.org/what-is-s/
Tao, J. (2013). Structuring citizen–government relationships: Regimes, regulators, media, and citizen discourse online. *Policy & Internet, 5*(4), 365–369.

Thaler, R. H., & Sunstein, C. R. (2008). *Nudge: Improving decision about health, wealth, and happiness*. New Haven, CT: Yale University Press.

Theiss-Morse, E., & Hibbing, J. R. (2005). Citizenship and civic engagement. *Annual Review of Political Science, 8*(1), 227–249. https://doi.org/10.1146/annurev.polisci.8.082103.104829

Thomas, J. C. (1982) Citizen-initiated Contacts with Government Agencies: A Test of Three Theories. *American Journal of Political Science 26*(3):504

Thurmaier, K., & Ceka, E. (2019). Nattering nabobs of negativism are no match for participatory budgeting. *Local Government Review*, July, 3–7.

Towry, K. L. (2003). Control in a teamwork environment-the impact of social ties on the effectiveness of mutual monitoring contracts. *The Accounting Review, 78*(4), 1069–1095.

Uslaner, E. M. (2005). Inequality, trust, and civic engagement. *American Politics Research, 33*(6), 868–894. https://doi.org/10.1177/1532673X04271903

Van Ryzin, G. G. (2013). An experimental test of the expectancy-disconfirmation theory of citizen satisfaction. *Journal of Policy Analysis and Management, 32*(3), 597–614.

Verba, S., & Nie, N. H. (1972). *Participation in America: Political democracy and social equity*. New Haven, CT: Harper and Row.

Verba, S., Schlozman, K. L., & Brady, H. E. (1995). *Voice and equality: Civic volunteerism in American politics*. Harvard University Press.

Vogel, D. (1980). The public interest movement and the american reform tradition. *Political Science Quarterly, 95*(4), 607–627.

Vygotsky, L. S. (1978). *Mind in society: The development of higher mental process*. Cambridge, MA: Harvard University Press.

Walters, P. (2004, September 22). Fire departments turn to courts to stave off cutbacks. *The Norman Transcript*, 8.

Wang, X. (2001). Assessing public participation in U.S. cities. *Public Performance and Management Review, 24*(4), 322–336.

Weimer, D. L. (2005). Institutionalizing neutrally competent policy analysis. Resources for promoting objectivity and balance in consolidating democracies. *Policy Studies Journal, 33*(2), 131–146.

Westheimer, J., & Kahne, J. (2004). Educating the "good" citizen: Political choices and pedagogical goals. *PS Online*, 1–7.

Wholey, J. S., Hatry, H. P., & Newcomer, K. E. (2010). *Handbook of practical program evaluation* (3rd ed.). Jossey-Bass.

Yackee, S. W. (2006). Sweet-talking the fourth branch. The influence of interest group comments on federal agency rulemaking. *Journal of Public Administration Research and Theory, 16*(1), 103–124.

Yang, K., & Callahan, K. (2007). Citizen involvement efforts and bureaucratic responsiveness. Participatory values, stakeholder pressures and administrative practicality. *Public Administration Review, 67*(2), 249–264.

Chapter 5
Facilitating Stakeholder Participation

Abstract Few organizations purposefully design processes for facilitating stakeholder interactions. Doing this requires knowledge of stakeholders who are and who are not likely to participate as well as the strengths, weaknesses, and limitations of different participation activities for gathering stakeholders' preferences. Systematic analysis can lead to tailored opportunities for the facilitation of stakeholder interactions and the development of routines for the transmission of preference information from administrators to decision-makers. The challenges of facilitated interactions are primarily in structuring the process so that the perspectives of non-participants are represented and perceptions of undue influence are lowered. By carefully designing a facilitated process for stakeholder interactions, administrators can expand the quantity and quality of stakeholder preference data available for decisions. Then, they can routinely communicate this information to decision-makers. The value expected to be produced by facilitated participation is improvement in the stakeholders' perception of organizational responsiveness.

5.1 Introduction

The value of responsiveness is the topic for this chapter. I argue that facilitated participation that is purposefully designed by an organizational administrator can enhance the responsiveness of an organization. When an organization purposefully and regularly interacts with stakeholders, a tighter link between what the stakeholders wants and the goods, services and activities the organization provides is created (Thurmaier & Ceka, 2019).

From the organization's perspective, there are three outputs desired from facilitated participation: (1) to gather information about what stakeholders want the organization to do, (2) to understand the magnitude and sincerity of stakeholders' preferences, and (3) to learn about a stakeholders' willingness to pay for preferences that change organization activities or their willingness to share resources to reduce the costs of change in order to obtain enhanced benefits that better satisfy their preferences.

Magnitude is defined as the relative strength of preferences stakeholders have for a proposed course of action. The organization can measure the magnitude of stakeholders' preferences in two ways – passively and actively. Passive measurement of

A. L. Franklin, *Stakeholder Engagement*,
https://doi.org/10.1007/978-3-030-47519-2_5

preferences occurs by synthesizing preferences from existing data that stakeholders share but do not communicate directly to the organization. Active measurement occurs when the organization offers mechanisms for stakeholders to provide input directly to the organization.

Sincere preferences are an individual's comparative ranking when presented with a variety of options. Gathering stakeholders' input about a specific list of options to gauge sincere preferences is preferred over asking about broad preferences. The reason why this is preferred is that ranked preferences for a range of options being considered convey what is most important to the stakeholder in a specific decision context.

Willingness to pay is discovered when stakeholders indicate the amount of additional cost they would be willing to pay if the organization makes the decision they desire. Willingness to share identifies where mutually beneficial partnerships are possible so that resources to achieve an outcome that cannot be obtained by one partner acting alone are available. Knowing the magnitude and sincerity of preferences and establishing that there is a willingness to pay or a willingness to share resources informs decisions in ways that can better align what the stakeholders want with what the organization offers. When this occurs, transaction costs can be lower, ongoing relationships can be established, and organizational sustainability is enhanced.

Facilitated participation has as its overarching purpose the gathering of stakeholder input from a representative sample of stakeholders. The input then informs decision-making. Participation facilitated by the organization signals that the invited stakeholder's input is valuable enough to extend additional efforts for interactions. It can also create an expectation that the input will be considered as part of the policy and administrative decision-making processes of the organization. Participation can create positive perceptions of responsiveness. In the next section, we explore the components of being responsive to stakeholders.

5.2 The Components of Stakeholder Responsiveness

The stakeholders who proactively provide preference data to organizations are generally a small proportion of all stakeholders. This challenges the administrator responsible for gathering preference data to understand the degree to which voluntarily provided input is representative. Knowing this, the administrator can consider what stakeholder perspectives are missing. The missing perspectives could mean the difference between an organization offering goods and services that are valued by current as well as future stakeholders versus an organization perceived as unresponsive and in danger of losing clients, constituents, and partners.

A first step to being responsive to a wide range of stakeholder perspectives is to anticipate who is likely to be motivated to participate without any organizational action. The task of predicting participation is not as difficult as it may seem. The previous chapters have identified three inputs (stakeholders, participation activities, and motivation to participate) and considered potential administrator actions to enhance representation, transparency, and accessibility.

Recall from Chap. 2; I argued that the stakeholders most likely to participate are those who engage in voluntary transactions with the organization. Alternatively, those who have a mixed stake in organization activities (such as intermediaries, or those with interlocking or interpenetrating relationships) or have overlapping interests from the internal or the external column and the mixed stakeholder column (suggesting delegated, mediating, or compensated relationships) are likely to participate. Additionally, those who experience direct impacts or have influence based on their individual or organizational interests are likely to participate. Stakeholders are also more likely to participate in administrative decision-making, especially if they will directly experience a negative or mixture of positive and negative externalities.

These suppositions are partially supported by empirical evidence. When stakeholders do become participants, it is likely because of dissatisfaction with a proposed policy, current service delivery, a desire for new programs or services, or a reallocation of existing resources to an activity that they prefer (Kweit & Kweit, 1980, p. 654). I learned that input from clients and rank and file employees was gathered by less than one-half of the 20 federal agencies I studied (Franklin, 2001), suggesting that direct interests are not a reliable predictor of input into the decision process. Also, Buckwalter (2014) found that those with strong personal agendas tend to leave the participatory processes earlier and at a higher frequency to seek a different venue to pursue their interests.

Venue selection is a double-edged sword for predicting the representativeness of participation based on interests. It is not that individuals are only self-interested; they may also have preferences that are valuable for the collective. However, rigidity in their expectation that participation will yield personal rewards may be a stronger predictor of participation. Once the administrator has a sense of who will be self-motivated to participate, then a strategy to facilitate the participation for those less likely to participate can be designed to ensure representation. Doing so can minimize claims that the organization is responsive to some but not all stakeholders whom it influences.

In Chap. 3, I described how the stakeholder could passively provide preference data through activities that do not require interaction with the organization. In this case, the organization must find this preference information and interpret it. Stakeholders who know how to communicate their preferences directly to the organization can use passive (one-way) mechanisms to make requests, such as those submitted through websites. They can also use mechanisms that promote interactions that provide the opportunity for two-way discussion and resolution of issues related to specific transactions or the organization's activities.

Increased accessibility benefits stakeholders since it enhances the likelihood that the organization will deliberately consider a wider range of stakeholder preferences. The organization also benefits from increased accessibility since direct communication with stakeholders allows the organization to gather additional information to clarify preference data that has been received as well as to communicate the decision outcomes arising from these direct interactions.

Chapter 4 examined the push and pull factors that individuals may consider when they are deciding if and how they would like to provide input about an organization's activities. Knowing these factors provides insights into who is most likely to participate in order to establish the kinds of stakeholders least likely to participate.

Armed with this prediction, the administrator can design participation processes that enhance accessibility for specific stakeholders. This can be done by identifying incentives that may persuade a stakeholder to use available participation activities to provide input voluntarily. Should this strategy be successful, the administrative costs of data collection could be lower than purposefully designing and carrying out facilitated participation.

Administrators can combine results from the identification of stakeholders and learning the range of participation activities currently being used with knowledge of the factors that influence participation motivation to predict who is likely to participate at no or low additional costs to the organization. In this chapter, we consider challenges that may be negatively impacting current levels of participation and how these can be overcome by purposefully inviting stakeholders to interact with the organization and provide input through facilitated participation. We combine what has been learned in previous chapters, and now in this chapter, to construct a matrix of ten kinds of participation activities for gathering input that meets four criteria: representative, transparent, accessible, and responsive.

5.3 Challenges to Responsiveness

The literature identifies two challenges that have been encountered when attempting to gather representative stakeholder input to guide decision-making. The first is identifying the preferences of nonparticipating stakeholders and avoiding perceptions that some stakeholders, especially external stakeholders, have more influence on decision-making than do others. The second challenge is to offer a combination of participation mechanisms that can foster congenial interactions and provide usable information about a broader range of stakeholders' preferences. In the following subsection, we address the challenge of nonparticipants.

5.3.1 Nonparticipating Stakeholders

Extant literature offers guidance about the types of stakeholders who are unlikely to participate without an invitation or incentives, such as resources from the organization. From the political science and public policy/administration literatures, we know that disadvantaged groups, and in particular program clients, are among the least likely to participate. The lack of resources and lower individual efficacy, commonly found in disadvantaged client groups, are significant predictors of nonparticipation (Prohl, 1997 p. 78). Coleman (2014) found that elites tend to dominate the stakeholder input processes since they have better access to resources, high socioeconomic status, more leisure time, and civic skills/political efficacy.

Drawing from this literature, the administrator tasked with facilitating participation should identify groups of stakeholders who face barriers to participation. Participation can be structured so that underrepresented groups are purposefully included to assure broad representation (Schattschneider, 1960). The participatory budgeting literature has demonstrated that training and the provision of resources such as child care and transportation dramatically increase the participation of disadvantaged groups (Gilman, 2016). These resources have the added benefit of building efficacy and making participants more effective in future participation activities.

As I noted in Chap. 2, it is not necessary to gather input from every kind of stakeholder. When a stakeholder interacts with the organization, the interests that are represented, whether they are specific to the individual or whether they are as an agent representing an organization, group, or collective, should be considered. The categories are not mutually exclusive and can be served simultaneously.

For example, the University of Oklahoma President can communicate concerns and preferences about the condition of higher education funding as (1) the head of the University, (2) a powerful political actor in Oklahoma, or (3) a private citizen. When this individual communicates preferences, the organization receiving the input needs to assess what role the stakeholder is assuming and determine how this contributes to the representativeness of the input received from different kinds of stakeholders who can influence or are influenced by the organization's decisions and activities. Knowing the stakeholder's role when providing input helps to understand how representative the input is that the organization receives.

Recall from Chap. 2; stakeholders can be analyzed based on the types of interactions they have with the organization, ranging from nonparticipating to casework. These interactions could be related to policy or administrative decisions and range from episodic to nearly continuous. Within this framing of external, mixed, and internal stakeholders were two groupings of stakeholders who have delegated responsibilities or who represent a mediating institution. Since people in both groupings have agency relationships for a variety of stakeholders, they could provide valuable preference data that is representative of nonparticipating stakeholders.

Another possible solution is for the administrator to gather input from proxy stakeholders, meaning those who share the same attributes as the unrepresented stakeholders. This can be done by using a sampling protocol where the attributes of potential samples are compared to the critical natural or learned attributes of the target population to judge the suitability of using a similar population sample or a subpopulation (Lu & Franklin, 2018).

One example of how proxy sampling can be worthwhile is to include people who regularly provide input and who also share the preferences of a cross-section of society, called descriptive representation (Donovan & Bowler, 2004, p. 53). The value of this form of passive representation is documented for nonprofit or governmental organizations that provide services to nearly all persons in the general population (Goodsell, 2013; Selden, 1997). Active representation occurs when members of a group serve as advocates for all members when they provide input concerning an organization's activities. This is another avenue for leveraging the participation of a proxy population to act as agents when they provide inputs (Selden, Brudney, & Kellough, 1998).

5.3.2 Stakeholders with Undue Influence

For many organizations, the process of gathering stakeholder input is mostly ad hoc and seldom institutionalized (Ebdon & Franklin, 2006). The lack of institutionalized expectations for stakeholder engagement can create perceptions that the squeaky wheel gets the grease, or put another way, that some stakeholders have a more significant amount of influence than do others. Fenno (2003 reprint) describes concentric circles of constituents for elected officials in which higher weight is given to these stakeholders (in the order presented): original supporters, trusted advisors, and those with whom the elected official identifies through group membership like a political party, church, family, and voluntary associations.

Interest groups have received much attention regarding undue influence between stakeholders. The so-called cozy relationships that interest groups form with organizational decision-makers and administrators have long been a source of concern because there is a danger that one or a few stakeholders can have better access to decision-makers and capture their attention (Golden, 1998). The unique position of interest groups and their ability to use their relatively superior power and resources for undue influence is a concern. Aberbach and Rockman (1978, p. 503) found that 93 percent of federal executives in their study indicated regular and frequent face-to-face contact with representatives of organized interest groups. Why is this a concern? Like the people in the inner circles of decision-making, when interest groups are involved, they tend to be concerned more with particularized self-interests rather than the organization's or collective interests (Kathlene & Martin, 1991, p. 59). While these perceptions may not be accurate, the suspicions and whispers caused by faulty perceptions damage the legitimacy of an organization.

Many scholars claim that nonrepresentative participation processes are suspect because they protect the status quo when participants are drawn from (s)elected and administrative decision-makers and policy elites such as those in iron triangles or issue networks (Heclo, 1978). Alliances such as this present a danger of control by minority interests (often representing industry rather than the ordinary person or consumer) (Cupps, 1977, p. 480). When this occurs, there may be a mobilization of bias (Majone, 1989, p. 204; Schattschneider, 1960, p. 103).

Johnson and Ward (1972, p. 22) urge special efforts to avoid the perception that participation is exclusive, or limited to the few, mainly those who have resources and political efficacy. The frequent and favored access to cozy relationships is a concern because of the disproportionate influence these stakeholders may have, allowing them to influence organizational decision-making unless the organization takes deliberate action to avoid this. The formation of cozy relationships was a concern for the Nixon and Reagan administrations which were more business and economically minded (Berry, 1990). As a countermeasure, the presidents enacted limitations on the number and form of citizen interest groups with which an agency could work. In 1993, Berry (p. 31) concluded that the efforts to include citizens and groups representing vulnerable populations have made the policymaking process more open and participatory. Other strategies to mitigate undue influence can be found in the Federal Advisory Committee Act and President Clinton's Executive Order 12838, each of which describes expectations and processes for transparency and accessibility (Koontz, 1999, p. 260).

For some mechanisms, participants with strong opinions may unduly influence the input that is received (Ebdon & Franklin, 2006). To overcome this challenge, mechanisms that encourage two-way dialogue, such as collaboration or co-production, decrease the likelihood that some actors will be perceived as controlling the process since there is a sharing of ideas and search for solutions that benefit all.

Culhane (1981) suggests that the perceived neutrality of the organization is strengthened when interactions occur with a diversity of stakeholders. However, expanding participation to include not currently participating stakeholders, or their agents, may challenge the status quo by destabilizing existing relationships (Aberbach & Rockman, 1978, p. 555). Cupps (1977, p. 481) maintains that administrators are tasked with balancing conflicting interests and "… must take pains not to allow the public interest claims of citizen groups to mislead them into thinking that those views should be weighed more heavily than any others in the process."

Another possible strategy to overcome perceptions of undue influence is for administrators to reduce the proximal and qualitative distance between the parties. In psychology, the zone of proximal development is the distance between what a learner can do with and without help. Spatial theorists describe qualitative distances that are shortened by creating a standard frame of reference and using articulation rules to mediate between the different frames of reference of participants.

The distance of and connections between stakeholders are the focus of network theory. Facilitated participation can reduce the distance between parties by positioning the administrator at the center of the interaction nodes to foster the flow of information, creating favorable conditions for dialogue and the discovery of shared preferences (Rethemeyer, 2007). It can also strengthen the connections between stakeholders in the network and with the organization.

Perceptions of neutrality can also be influenced by the mechanisms used during the interaction process. Arnstein (1969) cautioned that citizen involvement usually starts with one-way communication forms that can be manipulative, can co-opt people, or lead to token or pseudo-empowered participation. When there is a perception that stakeholders have been co-opted or that the organization has been captured through undue influence, other stakeholders may choose to participate through other activities, participation mechanisms and venues or use more adversarial approaches (Kohlmeier, 1969). The next section addresses considerations related to neutrality.

5.4 Considerations When Designing Facilitated Interactions

As described in Chap. 3, a broad spectrum of participation activities and mechanisms exist from which the organization can select for gathering stakeholders' input. Some of these are passive, which lowers administrative costs. Although more costly, there is a wide range of active participation mechanisms from which the administrator can choose. Some can rapidly provide low-cost data from large numbers of stakeholders in a way that includes details about the degree of representativeness. Others can gather input from groups of stakeholders who are least likely to participate and for whom incentives may be necessary. In this situation, the increased costs of data gathering should be offset by the net value of learning the unrepresented perspectives of stakeholders profoundly impacted by organizational activities. The challenge for the administrator tasked with designing data collection and facilitated interaction is to determine to what extent a combination of data collection activities enhances representation, transparency, and accessibility while also efficiently gathering usable preference data that can inform decisions.

5.4.1 Design Considerations Related to Stakeholders

Time is an essential consideration for stakeholders when deciding if they will participate. Extant literature identifies three factors related to time. First, the time required from participants is a consideration for administrators to weigh when designing facilitated interactions. A lower time commitment generally correlates with less information gathered. For example, indicating preferences on a survey entails a minimal time commitment when compared with participation in a focus group. Also important is the timing of interaction opportunities and the location (website, office building, community center) for providing input. If interactions must occur in real time rather than asynchronously, or if they occur at inconvenient locations that require transportation access, then participation levels will be dampened (Wondolleck, Manning, & Crowfoot, 1996, p. 252). An example is when public hearings are conducted only at the city hall in the mornings or afternoons. Not only is this time inconvenient for most people, but it may impose additional costs for disadvantaged groups who may not live close to the city hall (Schaller, 1964, p. 178).

The time issue has another dimension. Meeting time will need to be structured to allow sufficient time to move beyond initial posturing to clarifying and identifying shared interests and making progress on the more difficult issues (Wondolleck et al., 1996, p. 255). This challenge could be overcome by using the development model of Tuckman (1965) that suggest group processes occur in four stages: forming and norming before storming and performing.

Another administrative concern related to time is how to assure the timeliness of gathering the preference data so that there is an enhanced likelihood that it will inform decisions (Van Meter, 1975, p. 808). Even though stakeholder interactions take up time and may delay action, they may yield huge returns if legal challenges are avoided through these actions (Van Meter, 1975, p. 811). The ability of an organization to ensure representation depends mainly on the amount of time and resources the organization is willing to devote to getting this preference data.

A second consideration is getting participants to think about stakeholders other than themselves. Interactions can be self-initiated by the stakeholder, often in response to dissatisfaction with organizational activities. When this occurs, it may also tend to be more self-interested. Individuals who provide input on policy decisions, or who are also involved in a special interest group or serve on a board or commission, are more likely to consider group, organization, or collective interests.

When stakeholders consider both self and collective interests, their input will have higher utility since decisions using this input will benefit a wider range of stakeholder perspectives. Fortunately, most participation mechanisms can be structured to accommodate the involvement of collective and self-interested stakeholders and to encourage participants to consider the preferences of others and weight their rankings.

A third consideration when inviting interactions is the varying levels of efficacy that stakeholders may have. Pierce, Lovrich, and Matsuoka (1989, p. 39) argue that administrators need to avoid using participation mechanisms that do not mitigate the knowledge gap, where technical and complex issues limit the involvement of the general public in favor of a narrow stratum of activists and experts in organized groups. The administrator can use predictions about which stakeholders will be self-motivated to participate to guide mechanism selection so that the anticipated number of participants can be accommodated, plus the activities can be appropriate to the stakeholders' efficacy levels.

5.4.2 Design Considerations Related to Mechanisms

The decision about which mechanisms to use should be guided by the strengths or weaknesses of a mechanism. Ebdon (2002) suggests choosing mechanisms that combine education with data gathering. When decisions could cause a significant change to the status quo, it may be necessary to develop FAQs or other information materials or offer interactive mechanisms. This can assure that sufficient information is available for stakeholders to communicate their sincere preferences. It may also be possible to use relatively low cost, asynchronous, or automated data collection techniques such as internet-based surveys if stakeholders are expected to have sufficient knowledge and resources.

Simulations are another technology-assisted participation activity that provides education alongside data gathering. However, simulations take a substantial amount of time for staff to develop because of the background information about the pros and cons of different alternatives, especially if the simulation covers the entirety of an organization's activities. For this reason, it is common to ask stakeholders about a few key issues; however, this can lead to perceptions of the simulation process as being artificial (Ebdon & Franklin, 2004). There is a similar concern for surveys when participants are often forced to comment on a reality constructed by city officials (Thomas, 1995). Carefully worded data collection prompts are necessary for gathering preference data with high utility (Hatry & Blair, 1976).

The choice of mechanisms should take into consideration whether passive or one-way communication of preferences is sufficient to inform decisions. Or, is a two-way dialogue more beneficial for gauging sincere preferences as well as willingness to pay or willingness to share resources? Through an interactive exchange, rationales behind positions and preferences are shared. Through facilitated interactions, stakeholders can identify where there is dis-/agreement and where there may be space for bargaining and compromise. Additionally, this allows stakeholders to find out how well aligned their perceptions of a situation are with those of others and where and why differences exist. With this enhanced understanding, individual preferences may be softened, and new approaches or the willingness to compromise or to share resources might be discovered.

Another challenge to consider is the ability of a mechanism to foster accessibility. This could mean that the organization must design a data collection process that features multiple mechanisms to assure that input can be provided at a time, in a place, and in a format convenient for most stakeholders at a reasonable cost. Ultimately, there will be trade-offs between the quantity and quality of input an organization gathers; meeting both criteria may not be possible at a reasonable cost (Prohl, 1997).

What are the minimal conditions to make facilitated interactions valuable for all kinds of stakeholders? For external stakeholders, the topic of the interaction has to be something that they care enough about to participate. This is assured through education-focused communications explaining why the topic is relevant to them. Second, the form of participation has to be convenient enough that they will prioritize this activity over other competing activities. This may be a factor for mixed stakeholders who have obligations to satisfy inside and outside the organization. For internal and mixed stakeholders, facilitated interactions would provide information about potential negative impacts relevant to external stakeholders.

However, the real value derived from purposefully gathering internal and mixed stakeholders' perspectives comes from establishing the broadest range of perspectives and then comparing these perspectives in order to find similarities and differences. The similarities can help with the identification of low-hanging fruit, or areas where proposed alternatives would be favored by many stakeholders. The differences can suggest areas where more intensive interactions may be necessary to identify the best alternative to a negotiated agreement or avoid mutually assured destruction. Either of these outcomes increases the cost of proposed changes in the organization's activities.

Finally, for all types of stakeholders, the facilitated interactions should result in a perception that their input will be considered alongside other stakeholders' input. When administrators provide feedback showing that the input was considered, even though an individual's preferences may not have been adopted, participants are more satisfied with their involvement (King, Feltey, & Susel, 1998). Stakeholders pragmatically realize that their voice is just one of many. Even if their preferences are not chosen, having their say is enough to make them satisfied with the decision-making process (Ebdon & Franklin, 2004).

Ultimately, it is desirable to match mechanisms so that the strengths of one overcome the weaknesses of another and so that the preference data is gathered at a low cost but has a high utility. When the administrator strategically selects and designs participation mechanisms to overcome these challenges, it is more likely that the sincerity of stakeholders' preferences can be discovered. Other administrative considerations related to the design of the participation process are the topic of the next section.

5.4.3 Design Considerations Related to Administrative Efforts

There is some evidence that organizations have a better representation of stakeholders' when they purposefully select a combination of activities for gathering input. Even better is when data gathering activities have reasonable administration costs and yield data that are useful for decisions. When reviewing federal NEPA requirements, Irland (1975, p. 266) found that federal agencies engage in the matching of mechanisms based on the ease with which missing stakeholder perspectives can be gathered and if the information will be available in time for the information to be useful in guiding decision-making. Ebdon (2000, p. 390) found that larger cities are more likely to use multiple methods simultaneously, suggesting an awareness of the need for complementary activities.

Inviting stakeholders to provide input through facilitated interactions requires a planned communication strategy. Details about the interaction process, the mechanisms for providing input, the timing, and what will be done with the data must be clearly articulated. The management of expectations for the use of inputs is vital since the input could be purely advisory, meaning that organizational officials are not bound to adopt what has been proposed, or it could be binding, such as in participatory budgeting processes. Even though the administrator can communicate that the input is only advisory, it is important to signal that stakeholders' preferences were considered. Participants can become disenfranchised if they perceive that their input is not considered during the budgetary process (Ebdon, 2003; Thomas, 1995).

The combined considerations related to stakeholders can inform the design of the facilitated interaction process. If the number of participants is relatively low when compared to who will be impacted, then additional passive or one-way mechanisms to gather input may be needed. Also, it may be wise to avoid using two-way and face-to-face mechanisms with large groups of participants if there are contentious issues. Increases in the time required to provide input will shrink the pool of participants as well. If the preferred mechanisms require an intensive time commitment, then the administrator may have to be more selective about who can participate.

Plus, the administrator may have to recruit participants to improve representativeness (and perhaps offer incentives) in order to gather representative input.

In this section, we identified considerations for designing facilitated interactions. The first group was based on assuring the representativeness of the stakeholders providing input. The second set of considerations included the selection of activities based on the information needed and the ability of a mechanism to foster transparency. The third set of considerations was related to administrative costs and how they compare to the value of the input gathered. Providing accessibility to organizational input processes may involve trade-offs between low-cost activities and highly useful results. In the next section, we identify ten different purposes for facilitated interactions from which these different considerations can be addressed.

5.5 Purposes for Facilitated Interactions

Let us assume that the administrator can design processes to overcome the challenges of nonparticipation and undue influence and also understand the design considerations described in the previous section. The next challenge for administrators is to make sure the design of facilitated interactions will provide the outputs desired by the organization. Yates (1972) found that stakeholders believe that participation will increase an organization's attentiveness and responsiveness to their particular needs. It can also decrease the likelihood that dissatisfied stakeholders will express their grievances (Cole, 1975, p. 770; Cupps, 1977, p. 479). Rossi (1969) suggests that stakeholder participation can lead to meaningful improvements in service delivery. My argument is that facilitated participation is an essential way to gather stakeholder preference data to inform decisions that increase the value the organization produces and promote sustainability.

Empirical evidence confirms that participation (De Dreu & West, 2002; Irvin & Stansbury, 2004; Renn, Webler, Rakel, Dienel, & Johnson, 1993), deliberation (Chaskin, Khare, & Joseph, 2012; Morrell, 2005), and equality (Messick & Schell, 1992; Nielsen & Huse, 2010) lead to better decision-making. The first characteristic, participation, results from stakeholders, an input analyzed in Chap. 2. Participation activities that can encourage deliberation were presented in Chap. 3. In this chapter, the characteristic of equality, through the inclusion of the perspectives of nonparticipating stakeholders and attention to avoiding undue influence, is addressed as a challenge. The typology for this chapter combines the findings about stakeholders and participation activities as inputs as well as motivations that push a stakeholder to participate and an organization's efforts to pull stakeholders into providing input to consider ten purposes for an organization to consider facilitated interactions.

Starting with the top row of Table 5.1, the combination of six characteristics of a stakeholder's profile from Chap. 4 and how these conditions influence motivation to voluntarily provide preference data are presented. In the second row, I have placed the six different activities and how preferences are communicated from Chap. 3.

Table 5.1 A matrix of facilitated interactions

Ch 2: Stakeholder Profile **and** **Ch 4: *Motivation to Participate* →**		***Unlikely*** Involuntary Indirect External/internal Collective, group Policy Positive		**SH Profile** #1: Relationship to org #2:SH interests #3:Location of SH #4: Interests repr'd #5: Org's action #6: Impact of action		***Likely*** Voluntary Direct Mixed, overlapping Individual, org Administrative Negative, mixed	
Ch3: Activities ↓	*Activity and direction* →	Info/data (1-way)	Advise (1-way) Org -> SH	Request (1-way) SH -> Org	Ask/consult (2-way)	Discuss (2-way)	Resolve (2-way)
Time Preferences revealed ↓	*Required→*	**Ch 5: Purposes of Facilitated Interactions** (# in Superscript) ↓					
Passively	One-shot	[1]Educate	[2]Persuade (tell or sell)				
	None						
Actively	Multiple over time clustered		[3]Notify of change request comment	[4]Rank and suggest actions	[5]Discover shared preferences	[6]Review or protest actions	
	Continuous	[7]Gatherinformation	[8]Explore options		[9]Collaborate	[10]Co-produce	
		Ch 4: Incentivize Participants →			**Ch 5: Facilitate Interactions ↑**		

Org organization, *SH* stakeholder, Repr'd represented

In the third row, starting with the left-hand column, the way stakeholders reveal preferences and the amount of time required for interactions are noted. At the bottom of the table is a box for incentivizing participants in an attempt to motivate participation from a representative group of stakeholders. There is also a box for facilitating interactions. In the discussion that follows, I describe the processes inside this box from which the administrator can design stakeholder interactions. Then, I categorize the nature of the interactions and suggest roles and skills required from the administrator to gather preference data to inform decisions.

The inner boxes of the table identify ten potential purposes for stakeholder interaction. As I have cautioned when presenting typologies in the other chapters, there are some important caveats for this typology. The categories are suggestive, and the boundaries are positioned for illustration and analysis. In reality, the categories seldom occur in isolation, and the boundaries undoubtedly differ from what is presented. I discuss the typology as if there is a linear flow, but the facilitated interaction process can start and stop anywhere within the grid.

In the narrative describing the purposes of stakeholder interaction, it may be appropriate to think of the purposes for different participation activities as being layered one upon the other or partially overlapping like a Venn diagram, rather than outputs occupying discrete spaces within the typology. For example, education can occur across all types of participation activities, but there is empirical evidence suggesting that the achievement of other purposes is dramatically improved when education occurs first (Franklin & Ebdon, 2004). Further, I describe the output of discovering shared preferences as occurring in a situation where there is a series of meetings. Multiple meetings could allow time for education, participant development, and the building of trust through facilitated interactions. While this may be an ideal situation, shared preferences could also be discovered by the use of one-shot mechanisms such as simulations. The placement as a clustered or multi-stage activity assumes that outputs achieved with this configuration of stakeholders, mechanisms, and active discovery of preferences will be superior to any other placement.

Starting in the left column, below the box titled Purpose of Facilitated Interactions is the education purpose. When facilitating interactions, education activities (#1) are designed and conducted by the administrator to inform all stakeholders about organizational activities or decision processes. The education function can range from requiring no time to a continuous time commitment from stakeholders (as can be seen in the inform column). However, it is generally limited to no time commitment activities that rely on public relations and public outreach mechanisms. The direction of education activities is typically one way, with administrators providing information to the public at large. In this activity, the nature of the interaction activity is neutral. The role of the administrator in education is a communicator.

All stakeholders are assumed to be pursuing the second purpose, persuasion (#2) when preference information is communicated using any mechanism. Participants in these kinds of interactions are more likely to be self-interested individuals. Persuasive communication strategies could result in cooperative or adversarial relations, depending on the position of the information recipient. The communicator role for administrators would be most helpful for this output, and facilitation would ensure that external stakeholders have access to the organization and communicate their preferences.

Interaction purposes three through six, occurring in the middle level of the typology, rely on one- and two-way mechanisms and require a more significant time commitment and active participation. When stakeholders communicate their preferences, their motivation for interacting is generally self-interest. It is up to the administrator to structure facilitated interactions so that other interests are considered if adversarial relationships are expected to develop. If stakeholders have traditionally been excluded from this activity, then the administrators could act as an advocate based on passive representation theories.

Notifications of changes or requests for comments (#3) are neutral activities that require a time commitment from stakeholders only when they decide to provide comments about their preferences. The role of the administrator is primarily communicator for the third purpose. Suggesting actions (#4) is more organization-interested and can be either an adversarial or cooperative activity. For this fourth purpose, administrators skilled in facilitation would be most important.

When mechanisms are employed that require participants to rank alternatives or suggest changes, stakeholders and the administrator can discover shared preferences (#5). Ideally, this would occur in a discussion format that features a two-way information exchange and would require the administrator to have excellent organizational and interpersonal skills. These interactions should be cooperative. The purpose on the right-hand side of the table, review, or protest actions (#6), focuses more on the resolution of dissatisfaction with existing organizational activities and tends to take place in an adversarial setting. Since these interactions usually are adversarial, a vital role for the administrator would be a mediator.

The row at the bottom of the table features purposes in the facilitated interaction typology that can occur with any level of frequency. To gather information to inform decision-making (#7) is the seventh purpose, and it generically represents all data that is communicated passively or actively and gathered by the organization directly through facilitated interactions or indirectly through secondary data monitoring. For this purpose, the administrator's role is one of a research analyst as well as a conduit for communicating preference data to (s)elected officials, and the relationship is cooperative. Exploring options (#8) can be achieved through one- or two-way interaction and can be based on self, group, organization, or collective interests. Since this process is non-binding, it can foster neutral or collaborative relationships. Administrators who are knowledgeable about a variety of mechanisms will be well equipped to facilitate interactions for this purpose.

When collaboration (#9) is the expected output, two-way interaction between stakeholders who have direct interests is preferable. In this cooperative activity, administrators with excellent interpersonal skills are most likely to succeed. Finally, co-production (#10) is a valuable output when facilitated interactions enable stakeholders to work together to resolve operational issues. Administrators with proper planning and organizational skills can make co-production more productive and ensure cooperative relationships.

5.6 Costs and Benefits of Facilitated Interactions

With this description of the ten different types of outputs from facilitated interactions, our attention now turns to analysis of the relative costs and benefits of each. To do this I draw from an expansive literature on the net value to the organization for stakeholder engagement (Graversgaard, Jacobsen, Kjeldsen, & Dalgaard, 2017; Henisz, Dorobantu, & Nartey, 2014; Holcombe & Anderson, 2010; Jeffery, 2009; Wickert, Scherer, & Spence, 2016).

I limit the analysis to three types of costs the organization may experience. First are the tangible costs. These include the time spent and resources needed to incentivize stakeholder participation. The second type of cost is intangible costs. The intangible costs include the dissatisfaction and distrust that may arise when an organization resists stakeholder interactions or does not commit to considering stakeholder input; each response can lead to a perceived lack of accountability. Should this occur, the organization's reputation and the prospect of repeated transactions can suffer. Facilitated interactions can lower intangible costs since participants do place value on the opportunity to be heard and feel better about the organization when the input process is perceived as legitimate. Another intangible cost is the opportunity cost of selecting one participation activity. When administrators devote time and attention to one type of participation activity in an attempt to achieve a specific output, their time is taken away from any other stakeholder interactions. Since intangible costs would apply nearly equally to all of the ten facilitated interaction outputs, I do not explicitly identify them in the analysis.

Third are the marginal costs for administrative support that arise when adding one additional participant to the facilitated interaction activities. As shown in Table 5.2, there are negligible costs associated with notifying stakeholders of proposed actions; however, when another stakeholder comments, there are some costs

Table 5.2 Costs and benefits of facilitated interactions

	Costs		Benefits	
Participation output	Tangible	Marginal	Short-term	Long-term
[1]Educate	Low	None	Transparency	Efficacy
[2]Persuade	Low	Low	Transparency	Efficiency
[3]Request comment	Lowest	Lowest	Transparency	Permeable
[4]Suggest, rank actions	Medium	Low	Learn preferences	Accessible
[5]Shared preferences	Medium	Medium	Learn WTP/WTS	Dialogue
[6]Review/protest actions	Highest	Highest	Lower transaction costs	Accountability
[7]Inform	Low	Low	Transparency	Accountability
[8]Explore options	High	High	Deliberation	Viability
[9]Collaborate	High	High	Shared resources	Partnerships
[10]Co-produce	Reduced	Reduced	Cost efficiency	Foster shared interests

Note: WTP is a willingness to pay. WTS is a willingness to share associated with integrating these new preferences into the aggregated data. Marginal costs are highest when another dissatisfied stakeholder becomes involved in adversarial deliberations protesting the status quo. This is based on the assumption that the newest stakeholder is becoming engaged since they feel that currently participating stakeholders are not adequately representing their preferences.

Potential benefits are divided into two categories, short-term and long-term. These benefits are presented from the perspective of how stakeholders perceive organizational actions after participating in facilitated interactions. Short-term benefits may disproportionately accrue to active stakeholders who have a direct interest, but all stakeholders can experience long-term benefits at relatively the same level.

When comparing the costs and benefits in this table, tangible costs start at a low level for inform, educate, and persuade and are lowest for requesting comments. This assumes that these activities are already a normal part of the administrator's duties, and administrative systems exist that promote efficiency. Costs are slightly higher for ranking actions and discovering shared preferences. The highest administrative costs occur when there are review or protest activities because time is necessary to develop the dialogue required for deliberation about potential decisions that improve the status quo. According to Mansbridge (2018), when conflict and distrust are high, and confidence is low, organizations can easily miss the subtle practical payoffs of deliberative discussion. Tangible costs are reduced when co-production occurs since the stakeholder agrees to do some of the work assigned to the organization's employees.

The benefits achieved from the different outputs gained through facilitated interactions start with the transparency that comes from educational activities that can enhance stakeholder efficacy over the long term. When stakeholder interactions are designed to persuade, transparency is increased, and efficiency in transactions and interactions is achieved.

Moving to the next level in the typology, we find more interactive participation activities, such as notifying stakeholders of proposed changes and requesting comments. With these, transparency is increased. The invitation to comment also increases permeability in the long term. When the input is used to rank actions, the organization can compare preferences and provide more accessibility in the long-term. The discovery of shared preferences yields the short-term benefit of learning stakeholders' willingness to pay and adjusting transactions accordingly. In the long-term, dialogue about preferences reduces transaction costs. When stakeholder interactions include a review of organizational policies or address protests about organizational activities, the activities of the organization that are modified based on stakeholder input will lower the transaction costs associated with dissatisfied clients. Over the long term, this can enhance the level of accountability of the organization.

At the highest level of participation purposes, we see the highest frequency of involvement and find short-term benefits ranging from transparency to facilitating deliberation, sharing vital resources, lowering the cost of organizational transactions, and creating efficiencies, respectively. Over time, these activities should yield a higher perception of accountability, enhance organization viability, foster interactive relationships, and encourage stakeholders to consider organizational as well as self-interests and collective interests.

Deliberative participation theory from the planning literature emphasizes the importance of long-term benefits from stakeholder interactions. Hoch, 1994, recommends rethinking the relationships between the adversarial and deliberative aspects of practice. Forcing an either-or choice is not mutually value-producing. Instead, one can look for integrative and mutual gain possibilities within apparently distributive or zero-sum disputes (Susskind & Cruickshank, 1987). Administrators can guide the search for transformative possibilities within what seems at first to be only occasions for simple bargaining (Forester, 1999, p. 89) as participants learn about one another and their preferences. Participants can change in the process. This change can create new, more deliberative working relationships and a basis for working together (Forester, 1999, p. 110).

Facilitated participation encourages stakeholders to take advantage of the transparency and accessibility of the organization to register their preferences. The interactions also provide an additional modality for organizations to communicate the choices that were considered, hopefully resulting in decisions supported not just by clients but also by stakeholders overall. In this respect, these activities can be an end in themselves or a means to an end, which is organizational sustainability.

Theory acknowledges the costs and benefits of gathering stakeholder data but offers no guidance on whether the costs of gathering stakeholder preference data are exceeded by the benefits of facilitated interactions. As suggested above, scholars and practitioners alike provide anecdotal evidence that this process improves stakeholder relations and does inform decisions. However, the impacts are intangible. Part of the reason for a lack of definitive evidence is there are so many sources of data that inform decisions. In addition to the input from stakeholders, decision-makers have to make decisions that reflect fiscal and operational realities or legal restrictions. Moreover, they may be influenced by their own personal preferences or may view one decision in light of many sequential decisions. Plus, bargaining, coalition building, and vote trading may occur which may also influence the decision. The purposes in the typology of facilitated participation have the potential to yield outputs useful to the organization and increasing perceptions of responsiveness.

The stakeholder facilitation processes of inviting and perhaps even incentivizing interactions to fulfill any of the ten interaction purposes may require dedication or redirection of organizational resources. Both the benefits expected and the costs of the resources necessary for facilitated participation must be considered (Roberts, 1997). The bottom line is that no participation activity is free (Wondolleck et al., 1996, p. 252). The trick is to evaluate the costs and benefits of different participation activities to find the ones with the highest net value based on the type of preference data the organization desires.

5.7 Achieving the Promise of Facilitated Interactions

The administrator can design facilitated interactions that encourage stakeholders to interact in ways that can lead to the desired outputs. It seems reasonable to expect that outputs like education, articulating needs and desires, suggesting goals and alternatives, and exploring options would be most likely when the problem is being defined. Alternatives can be generated for consideration by organizational decision-makers. At this stage, it is also likely that mechanisms that can persuade would be appropriate. These kinds of activities are expected to occur when decisions are being made. The decision process is a time when it would be appropriate to engage in activities that would discover sincere preferences and willingness to pay or share resources or identify areas for collaboration between the organization and other organizations. The implementation process would likely be the most appropriate stage for participation activities that feature review or protest activities as well as co-production of organizational programs.

Even though it is inaccurate to present the facilitated interaction process as one that is linear and can be divided into discrete stages (such as identifying missing perspectives, designing a facilitated participation process, purposefully inviting stakeholders, facilitating interactions, sharing the input with decision-makers, implementing the action which has been selected and notifying stakeholders), there is value in considering when the input will be gathered. This can be compared to when information is needed and the types of outputs that are useful to organizational officials. Doing this can indicate the types of stakeholders who should be invited to participate as well as the mechanisms that would be appropriate based on an estimate of the time commitment that will be expected from those who do ultimately decide to join facilitated interactions.

Traditionally, the administrator's roles focused on managing the internal operations of the organization. Facilitated interactions task administrators with deliberately structuring opportunities for gathering stakeholder preferences as well as sharing the preference data they gather with decision-makers and reporting the decisions back to stakeholders. In addition to facilitating interactions, administrators will be more active boundary spanners who pay attention to the external environment as much as to the internal operations (Waldman & Yammarino, 1999). Boundary spanning and facilitation activities are vital in an environment emphasizing increasing levels of collaboration between stakeholders and organizations in all sectors.

For many organizations, this may require changing administrative role expectations from responding to stakeholders on a case-by-case basis or during periods of crisis to the strategic management of stakeholder relations on an ongoing basis. Within the ten purposes of facilitated interactions in the typology, administrators may experience more than eight role expectations (administrator, communicator, representative advocate, facilitator, planning and organizer, promoter of interpersonal relationships, mediator, researcher, and subject matter expert).

In general, we can conclude that organizations need purposeful administrators willing to rethink historical roles and overcome structural barriers to better work with a wide ranging sample of stakeholders whose preferences the organization wishes to consider (O'Toole Jr. & Hanf, 2002, pp. 158–169). Poorly designed interactions can lead to dissatisfaction if the purpose is not relevant, the input is not considered during decision-making, implementation is not emphasized, or the short- and long-term outcomes for stakeholders are not considered (Elwyn & Miron-Shatz, 2010).

Extant literature is quite emphatic about the importance of high-level organizational support for administrators tasked with facilitating stakeholder interactions. As Strange concludes, "Citizens need staff assistance to be competent participants." (1972, p. 460). Stenberg (1972, p. 197) concurs and uses the label of advocate bureaucrats for those who work to empower community groups. Kathlene and Martin (1991) take this idea farther, suggesting a need for proactive and advocacy roles for administrators. They also suggest administrators should become facilitators as well as interpretive mediators. This is critical for authentic participation with active and shared accountability (Stivers, 1990). Wondolleck, Manning, and Crowfoot (1996, p. 253) concur with the facilitator role and extend it to include a role as a skilled mediator. According to Reich (2002, 170), administrators have two related but conceptually distinct procedural responsibilities. The first entails intermediating among interest groups and the second maximizing net benefits. This suggests the merging of pluralist political theory with decision and microeconomic theories. Although this quote was directed to planners, it is also applicable to those tasked with facilitating interactions with stakeholders. Hoch (1994: 315–316) finds they "... are not only gatekeepers, but path-breakers; not simply visionaries, but counselors; not just powerbrokers, but public servants; not only experts but teachers."

5.8 Summary

Few organizations purposefully design a strategy that guides the choice of mechanisms for interacting with specific stakeholders and facilitating the process. Prior research has found that most participation activities occur on an ad hoc basis and are not institutionalized (Franklin, Ho, & Ebdon, 2009). This limits the amount of comparable data available for long-term trend analysis and makes it challenging to assess the positive and negative stakeholder responses that may result from changes in the organization's activities. Facilitated interactions allow the organization to develop a baseline of stakeholder preferences for regular activities, which can be periodically monitored with minimal efforts. Additionally, facilitated interactions can be useful for enhancing the values of representativeness, transparency, accessibility, and responsiveness. From the organization's as well as the stakeholders' perspectives, facilitating interactions can also be a mutually value-producing experience that can encourage voluntary participation and continue engagement over the long term.

The challenges of facilitated interactions are primarily in structuring the process so that the perspectives of nonparticipants are representative and perceptions of undue influence are lowered. Selecting participation mechanisms can overcome some of these challenges. However, each has strengths and weaknesses that must be considered. There is also a need to understand the benefits and costs related to facilitating participation.

Designing participation processes can take considerable administrative time and effort, as well as financial resources. Gaining a commitment of financial resources can be challenging in times of fiscal scarcity. Technological advances can reduce costs since the process of gathering information can be automated to a more considerable extent than ever before (Kathlene & Martin, 1991, p. 58). Nevertheless, there are times when more intensive interaction is necessary.

By carefully designing a facilitated process for stakeholder interactions that strategically integrates considerations about stakeholders, participation activities, and administrative burdens, administrators can expand the quantity and quality of stakeholder preference data available for decisions and can routinely communicate this information to decision-makers to assure utilization of the data.

The value expected to be produced by facilitated participation is improvement in the stakeholders' perception of organizational responsiveness. When an organization devotes resources to facilitated interaction, this communicates a commitment to transparency about decision-making processes and formalizes the expectation for responsiveness to stakeholders who communicate their preferences. By adopting the expectation of facilitated interaction, (s)elected officials can reframe the relationship between an organization and its stakeholders to make it mutually value-producing. Actions, like incentivizing participation, facilitating the communication of stakeholder preferences, and then working to assure utilization of stakeholder inputs, require extra resources and new roles for administrators.

Systematic analysis by administrators of the stakeholder inputs the organization typically receives can lead to tailored opportunities for the facilitation of stakeholder interactions and the development of routines for the transmission of preference information from administrators to decision-makers. Administrators can identify low cost-high yield participation mechanisms that will gather preference data specific for a decision to assure high usability. They can also select mechanisms that will gather sincere preferences from a representative sampling of stakeholders or can consider using a panel of stakeholders to track trends over time.

However, the reality is that organizations seldom view this as a strategic management function (similar to the public relations function), causing one to ask, "What would be the conditions under which a strategy for gathering preference data would be institutionalized?" This is a question taken up in the next chapter on stakeholder engagement outputs.

References

Aberbach, J. D., & Rockman, B. A. (1978). Administrators' beliefs about the role of the public: The case of American federal executives. *The Western Political Quarterly, 31*(4), 502–522. https://doi.org/10.2307/447232

Arnstein, S. A. (1969). A ladder of citizen participation. *American Institution of Planners Journal, 35*(7), 216–224.

Berry, J. M. (1990). Citizen groups and the changing nature of interest group politics In America. *Annals of the American Academy of Political and Social Science, 538*, 30–41.

Buckwalter, N. D. (2014). *The potential for public empowerment through government-organized participation* (Vol. *74*, p. *573*). Public Administration Review.

Chaskin, R., Khare, A., & Joseph, M. (2012). Participation, deliberation, and decision making: The dynamics of inclusion and exclusion in mixed-income developments. *Urban Affairs Review, 48*(6), 863–906. https://doi.org/10.1177/1078087412450151

Cole, R. L. (1975). Citizen participation in municipal politics. *American Journal of Political Science, 19*(4), 761–781.

Coleman, E. A. (2014). Behavioral determinants of citizen involvement: Evidence from natural resource decentralization policy. *Public Administration Review, 74*(5), 642–654. https://doi.org/10.1111/puar.12249

Culhane, P. (1981). *Public Lands Politics: Interest Group Influence on the Forest Service and the Bureau of Land Management*. Baltimore, MD Johns Hopkins University Press.

Cupps, D. S. (1977). Emerging problems of citizen participation. *Public Administration Review, 37*(5), 478–487.

De Dreu, C., & West, M. (2002). Minority dissent and team innovation: The importance of participation in decision making. *The Journal of Applied Psychology, 86*, 1191–1201. https://doi.org/10.1037/0021-9010.86.6.1191

Donovan, T., & Bowler, S. (2004). *Reforming the Republic: Democratic institutions for the new America*. Upper Saddle River, NJ: Pearson Prentice Hall.

Ebdon, C. (2000). The relationship between citizen involvement in the budget process and city structure and culture. *Public Productivity and Management Review, 23*(3), 383–393.

Ebdon, C. (2002). *Interactive Surveys as Tools to Combine Citizen Education and Preference Revelation* [Working Paper].

Ebdon, C. (2003). Citizen participation in the budget process: Exit, voice and loyalty. In *Encyclopedia of public administration and public policy*. New York, NY: Marcel Dekker.

Ebdon, C., & Franklin, A. L. (2004). Searching for a role for citizens in the budget process. *Public Budgeting & Finance, 24*(1), 32–49.

Ebdon, C., & Franklin, A. L. (2006). Citizen participation in budget theory. *Public Administration Review, 66*(3), 437–447.

Elwyn, G., & Miron-Shatz, T. (2010). Deliberation before determination: The definition and evaluation of good decision making. *Health Expectations: An International Journal of Public Participation in Health Care and Health Policy, 13*(2), 139–147. https://doi.org/10.1111/j.1369-7625.2009.00572.x

Fenno, Jr., R. A. (2003). *Home Style: House Members in Their Districts*. New York, NY: Longman Publishers.

Forester, J. (1999). *The deliberative practitioner*. The MIT Press. https://mitpress.mit.edu/books/deliberative-practitioner

Franklin, A. L. (2001). Serving the public interest: Federal experience with participation in strategic planning. *American Review of Public Administration, 31*(2), 126–138.

Franklin, A. L., & Ebdon, C. (2004). Aligning priorities in local budgeting processes. *Journal of Public Budgeting, Accounting and Financial Management, 16*(2), 210–227.

Franklin, A. L., Ho, A. T., & Ebdon, C. (2009). Participatory budgeting in midwestern states: Democratic connection or citizen disconnection? *Public Budgeting & Finance, 29*, 52–73.

Gilman, H. R. (2016). *Democracy reinvented: Participatory budgeting and civic innovation in America*. Washington, DC: Brookings Institution Press.

Golden, M. M. (1998). Interest Groups in the Rule-making Process: Who Participates? Whose Voices Get Heard? *Journal of Public Administration Research and Theory, 8*(2), 245–270.

Goodsell, C. T. (2013). Public Administration as Its Own Steward in Times of Partisan Deadlock and Fiscal Stress. *Public Administration Review, 73*(1), 10–11. https://doi.org/10.1111/puar.12023

Graversgaard, M., Jacobsen, B. H., Kjeldsen, C., & Dalgaard, T. (2017). Stakeholder engagement and knowledge co-creation in water planning: Can public participation increase cost-effectiveness? *Water, 9*(3), 191. https://doi.org/10.3390/w9030191

Hatry, H. P., & Blair, L. H. (1976). Citizen surveys for local governments: A cop-out, manipulative tool, or a policy guidance and analysis aid? In T. N. Clark (Ed.), *Citizen preferences and urban public policy*. Beverly Hills, CA: Sage Publications.

Heclo, H. (1978). *Issue networks and the executive establishment*. In A. King (Ed.), The new American political system. Washington, DC: American Enterprise Institute.

Henisz, W. J., Dorobantu, S., & Nartey, L. J. (2014). Spinning gold: The financial returns to stakeholder engagement: Financial returns to stakeholder engagement. *Strategic Management Journal, 35*(12), 1727–1748. https://doi.org/10.1002/smj.2180

Hoch, C. (1994). *What planners do: Politics, power and persuasion*. Abingdon, Oxfordshire: Routledge.

Holcombe, E. A., & Anderson, M. G. (2010). Implementation of community-based landslide hazard mitigation measures: The role of stakeholder engagement in 'sustainable' project scale-up. *Sustainable Development, 18*(6), 331–349. https://doi.org/10.1002/sd.409

Irland, L. C. (1975). Citizen participation: A tool for conflict management on the public lands. *Public Administration Review, 35*, 263–269.

Irvin, R. A., & Stansbury, J. (2004). Citizen participation in decision making: Is it worth the effort. *Public Administration Review, 64*(1), 55–65.

Jeffery, N. (2009). *Stakeholder engagement: A road map to meaningful engagement*. Bedfordshire, UK: Doughty Centre for Corporate Responsibility, Cranfield University.

Johnson, N., & Ward, E. (1972). Citizen information systems: Using technology to extend the dialogue between citizens and their government. *Management Science, 19*(4), 21–34.

Kathlene, L., & Martin, J. A. (1991). Enhancing citizen participation: Panel designs, perspectives, and policy formation. *Journal of Policy Analysis and Management*, 46–63.

King, C. S., Feltey, K. M., & Susel, B. O. (1998). The question of participation; toward authentic public participation in public administration. *Public Administration Review, 58*(4), 317–326.

Kohlmeier, L. (1969). *The regulators: Watchdog agencies and the public interest*. New York, NY: Harper and Row.

Koontz, T. M. (1999). Administrators and citizens: Measuring agency officials' efforts to foster and use public input in forest policy. *Journal of Public Administration Research and Theory, 9*(2), 251–280.

Kweit, R. W., & Kweit, M. G. (1980). Bureaucratic decision-making impediments to citizen participation. *Polity, 12*, 647–666.

Lu, T., & Franklin, A. L. (2018). Selection protocol for identifying and sampling from proxy populations. *Social Science Quarterly, 99*, 1535. https://doi.org/10.1111/ssqu.12519

Majone, G. (1989). *Evidence, argument, and persuasion in the policy process*. Yale University Press.

Mansbridge, J. J. (2018, February 19). A deliberative theory of interest representation. *The Politics Of Interests*. https://doi.org/10.4324/9780429495984-2

Messick, D. M., & Schell, T. (1992). Evidence for an equality heuristic in social decision making. *Acta Psychologica, 80*(1–3), 311–323. https://doi.org/10.1016/0001-6918(92)90053-G

Morrell, M. E. (2005). Deliberation, democratic decision-making and internal political efficacy. *Political Behavior, 27*(1), 49–69. JSTOR.

Nielsen, S., & Huse, M. (2010). Women directors' contribution to board decision-making and strategic involvement: The role of equality perception. *European Management Review, 7*(1), 16–29. https://doi.org/10.1057/emr.2009.27

O'Toole Jr., L. J., & Hanf, K. I. (2002). American public administration and impacts of international governance. *Public Administration Review, 62*, 158–169.

Pierce, J. C., Lovrich, N. P., & Matsuoka, M. (1989). Support for citizen participation; A comparison of American and Japanese citizens' activities and elites. *The Western Political Quarterly*, 39–59.

Prohl, M. (1997). *International strategies and techniques for future local government. Practical aspects towards innovation and reform*. Gutersloh, Germany: Bertelsmann Foundation Publishers.

Reich, R. B. (2002). *Policy making in a democracy*. In P. Kobrak (Ed.), The Political Environment of Public Management (pp. 122–149). New York, NY: AB Longman.

Rethemeyer, R. K. (2007). The empire strikes back: Is the internet corporatizing rather than democratizing policy processes? *Public Administration Review, 67*(2), 199–215.

Renn, O., Webler, T., Rakel, H., Dienel, P., & Johnson, B. (1993). Public participation in decision making: A three-step procedure. *Policy Sciences, 26*(3), 189–214. https://doi.org/10.1007/BF00999716

Roberts, N. (1997). Public deliberation: An alternative approach to crafting policy and setting direction. *Public Administration Review, 57*(2), 124–130.

Rossi, P. H. (1969). No good idea goes unpunished. *Social Science Quarterly*, 469–480.

Schaller, L. E. (1964). Is the citizen advisory committee a threat to representative government? *Public Administration Review, 24*, 175–179.

Schattschneider, E. E. (1960). *The semisovereign people*. New York, NY: Rinehart and Winston.

Selden, S. C. (1997). *The Promise of Representative Bureaucracy*. Armond, NY: M. E. Sharpe, Inc.

Selden, S. C., Brudney, J. L., & Kellough, J. E. (1998). Bureaucracy as a Representative Institution: Toward a Reconciliation of Bureaucratic Government and Democratic Theory. *American Journal of Political Science, 42*, 717–744.

Stenberg, C. W. (1972). Citizens and the administrative state. *Public Administration Review*, 190–198.

Stivers, C. (1990). The public agency as polis: Active citizenship in the administrative state. *Administration and Society, 22*(1), 86–105.

Strange, J. H. (1972). The impact of citizen participation on public administration. *Public Administration Review, 32*(Special), 457–470.

Susskind, L., & Cruikshank, J. (1987). *Breaking the Impasse: Consensual Approaches to Resolving Public Disputes*. New York, NY: Basic Books.

Thomas, J. C. (1995). *Public participation in public decisions*. San Francisco, CA: Jossey-Bass.

Thurmaier, K., & Ceka, E. (2019, July). Nattering nabobs of negativism are no match for participatory budgeting. *Local Government Review, 100*(6), 3–7.

Tuckman, B. (1965). Developmental sequence in small groups. *Psychological Bulletin, 63*, 384–399.

Van Meter, E. C. (1975). Citizen participation in the policy management process. *Public Administration Review, 35*, 804–812.

Waldman, D. A., & Yammanno, F. J. (1999). CEO Charismatic Leadership. Levels of Management and Levels of Analysis Effects. *Academy of Management Review, 24*(2), 266–285.

Wickert, C., Scherer, A. G., & Spence, L. J. (2016). Walking and talking corporate social responsibility: Implications of firm size and organizational cost. *Journal of Management Studies, 53*(7), 1169–1196. https://doi.org/10.1111/joms.12209

Wondolleck, J. M., Manning, N. J., & Crowfoot, J. W. (1996). Teetering at the top of the ladder: The experience of citizen group participants in alternative dispute resolution processes. *Sociological Perspectives, 39*(2), 249–262.

Yates, D. (1972). Neighborhood Government. *Policy Sciences, 3*(2), 209–219.

Chapter 6
Institutionalizing Stakeholder Engagement

Abstract Processes for gathering representative inputs about organizational activities or preferences related to decisions are seldom institutionalized. After reviewing the inputs of stakeholders, participation activities, and participant motivations in the earlier chapters, this statement may not seem surprising. There are almost as many types and groupings of stakeholders as there are active and passive participation activities. The number and variety of both have been continuously growing alongside globalization and technological advances, which, when combined, increase the geographic reach of stakeholders and organizations. Motivations can push and pull people into participation. Making an organizational commitment to a stakeholder engagement regime signals that an organization desires to be proactively responsive to stakeholders through their decisions as well as in the everyday activities of providing goods and services. Stakeholder engagement practices promote and evaluate relationships and design strategies for relationship management that can enhance value creation related to the organization's economic and social performance goals.

6.1 Introduction

In Chap. 5, we explored the prospects for an organizational administrator to facilitate interactions with stakeholders to improve perceptions of stakeholder responsiveness. In this chapter, I continue the examination of what can be gained when the organization purposefully commits to stakeholder engagement.

A commitment to stakeholder engagement means that the organization views stakeholders as a resource to be managed in ways that enhance accountability. This can be accomplished by allocating resources and assigning responsibility to a staff function charged with gathering data on stakeholder preferences and presenting that information in a form that can be used for strategic decisions about the organization's policies and activities. A commitment to stakeholder engagement is similar to the commitment an organization makes for human resource management and financial resource management. It is part of a strategic management regime that integrates all internal management functions to focus on results and accountability.

A. L. Franklin, *Stakeholder Engagement*,
https://doi.org/10.1007/978-3-030-47519-2_6

6.2 Components of a Stakeholder Engagement Regime

There are many different components of a strategic management regime. Previously we focused on transactions and interactions between stakeholders. Transactions are the exchanges that occur for stakeholders to acquire goods and services from the organization. The term interactions refers to what stakeholders are doing together that reveals preferences for organization activities and decisions. In the review of the participation activities, we determined that there is no causal ordering for interactions. They can be multi-directional and multi-channel communications with feedback loops and learning.

These interactions can be evaluated across three dimensions. The first is content – referring to the topic or issue that is bringing stakeholders and the organization together. The second is quality. The quality of the interaction is crucial because it influences the likelihood and nature of future interactions. Last is a time dimension. This dimension allows us to look at how the interactions between stakeholders and the organization evolve. Interactions that feature a topic that is important both to the organization and to the stakeholder, are multi-directional to improve quality, and are timely for informing decision-making make it easier to build ongoing relationships with stakeholders and to improve the organization's value creation.

In the last chapter, I concluded that facilitated participation might be necessary to achieve these kinds of interactions. Stakeholder engagement goes beyond facilitated interactions. Interactions, whether they are facilitated or not, are short-term and designed for stakeholder management. Stakeholder relationships are long-term and are can lead to ongoing stakeholder engagement. Facilitated interactions have as their purpose enhancing responsiveness. Stakeholder engagement regimes have as their purpose enhancing transparency, accessibility, responsiveness and accountability (Rosener, 1982, p. 459; Strange, 1972, p. 467).

Accountability, as a long-term outcome for the organization, is enhanced when organizational processes (Stivers, 1990, p. 93) for motivating stakeholder participation and facilitating interactions with specific stakeholders occur. There are other significant long-term, often intangible outcomes to be gained as well, such as the development of ongoing relationships that can make gathering input in the future faster and at a lower cost. Also, relationships reveal shared values and build trust. The bridging and bonding effects (Putnam, 2000) can be valuable when changes are necessary. In the next section, we examine the benefits delivered from stakeholder engagement.

6.3 Benefits of Stakeholder Engagement Regimes

One benefit an organization that embraces stakeholder engagement receives is a process for knowing who the organization's stakeholders are and a strategy for monitoring their satisfaction with and preferences for the organization's activities. In

Chap. 5, I concluded that thoughtful selection of different sources of input could be based on the relative costs and benefits, as well as the purpose for which the data are to be used. Doing so would improve the data available to inform decisions. Additionally, a commitment to stakeholder engagement, such as that suggested by a commitment to corporate social responsibility, can help align an organization's decisions and activities with the preferences of their stakeholders (Arnold, 1990; Rosener, 1982). Stakeholders' understandings arising from facilitated interactions and relationship development can also provide more accurate perceptions about the competing interests that may influence the organization's decisions (Miller & Stokes, 1966).

There are other reasons why stakeholder engagement enhances value creation. Stakeholder engagement processes institutionalize information channels to decision-makers and improve communication between administrators and stakeholders (Wondolleck, Manning, & Crowfoot, 1996, p. 253). These attributes of stakeholder engagement can foster decisions "...made based on a formed consensus, rather than on majority strength" (Donovan & Bowler, 2004, p. 51). Stakeholder engagement can enhance the organization's reputation for competency, efficiency (Berman, 1997, p. 106), and effectiveness (Buck, 1984, p. 468).

In the empirical literature, there is a blending of findings and recommendations for gathering stakeholder input and building long-term relationships (Graves & Waddock, 2000). Often these activities are discussed using labels such as customer relationship management, which is often passively data-driven with an emphasis on retaining stakeholders through ongoing transactions that drive sales growth. Customer relationship management has the same emphasis but is a continuous activity.

Another label is stakeholder relationship management (Dohnalová & Zimola, 2014). This focuses more on direct interactions for resolving issues facing the organization (Olander & Landin, 2008) as well as to improve stakeholder satisfaction and corporate financial performance (Choi & Wang, 2009; Moneva, Rivera-Lirio, & Muñoz-Torres, 2007).

Stakeholder relationship management can be beneficial in three specific situations: first, when stakeholder monitoring identifies shifts in the operating environment that may influence the organization's activities; second, during strategic planning and environmental scanning to plan for the future; and third, when the strategic plan is the impetus for planned changes in the policies or activities of an organization.

Recognizing the different data needs suggested by these three situations (Bourne, 2016), general stakeholder engagement activities would be appropriate for the first situation when ongoing monitoring can discern changes that necessitate small but rapid adjustments for stability in the organization's activities. For the second and third situations, more intensive engagement with the specific stakeholders who will have the most influence, or be influenced the most in a particular emergent situation, positively or negatively would be appropriate. The differences in how stakeholder relationship management occurs are explored in the next two subsections.

6.3.1 *General Stakeholder Engagement*

General stakeholder engagement leverages the input voluntarily provided by motivated stakeholders. General stakeholder engagement can be used to establish a baseline of perceptions and preferences depicting the stakeholders who commonly interact with the organization and how they feel about the current activities of the organization. These activities are particularly important for customer relationship management. A wide-ranging selection of participation opportunities should be institutionalized for general stakeholder engagement. When this is done, the ability to conduct trend analysis and triangulation over multiple sources is higher. More importantly, stakeholders will increasingly become aware of and avail themselves of opportunities to interact and to communicate their preferences.

Administrators responsible for general stakeholder engagement must consider the appropriate format and then select between issuing a general or a selective invitation to stakeholders. A general invitation is appropriate when many participants are desired, existing communication modalities can be used, and the representativeness of the input is not a concern. Selective invitations are issued when the organization desires input from representatives of specific sub-populations (Callahan, 2002). Selective invitations require the administrator to determine whom to invite as well as how to custom tailor communications across multiple modalities to make sure these are the mechanisms preferred by the stakeholders from whom input is desired.

6.3.2 *Situational Stakeholder Engagement*

Situational stakeholder engagement refers to intermittent activities to gather data on emerging issues in the external operating environment or for considering windows of opportunity where the organization may change its activities to improve its competitiveness or net worth. It can also refer to periodic data collection to inform specific strategic management activities such as routinized planning processes for fine-tuning organizational activities and strategic decisions promoting agility in policy implementation. In these kinds of situations, the organization can benefit from having custom-tailored preference data.

To acquire this data may require extending selective invitations so that the preferences of particular stakeholders, such as those who are highly influential in or influenced by the organizational activities or those most likely to be positively or negatively impacted by a decision, are gathered. Alternatively, the organization may need a particular kind of preference data, such as sincere preferences or willingness to pay or willingness to share to assess the viability of a planned change or proposed decision. These types of data may not be routinely gathered via general stakeholder engagement. When these kinds of information are necessary, situational stakeholder engagement is preferred.

A best in class stakeholder engagement function plans for both general and situational stakeholder engagement. This function should be a routine component of the strategic management functions in an organization alongside planning, resource management, program activities, performance monitoring, and evaluation. Information from each of these components must be fed forward to the other. Doing so aligns activities. The shared focus is on contributing to accountability for results that improve value creation and the organization's net worth.

Stakeholder engagement is more than making the organization's decisions and activities transparent, offering participation mechanisms that make it accessible, and purposefully facilitating stakeholder access to provide representative input to inform decisions. It is also a collaborative and synergistic process that benefits the organization and stakeholders in more profound ways, such as accountability, efficacy, empowerment, and sustainability. Dyson (1999, p. 411) emphasizes the need for a collaborative structure that includes cooperative relationships and accountability between actors.

As Freeman (2004, p. 233) reminds us, an organization's enterprise strategy should commit to making stakeholders better off and improving any trade-offs that may exist between stakeholders. Organizations that adopte corporate social responsibility policies and practices recognize the importance of attention to the social performance of the organization (Graves & Waddock, 2000; Peloza, Loock, Cerruti, & Muyot, 2012; Sachs & Maurer, 2009), and they monitor how it is achieved through stakeholder engagement. They also adopt processes and practices for managing stakeholder relationships, which is the topic of the next section.

6.4 Managing Stakeholder Relationships

To fully obtain the benefits offered through stakeholder engagement regimes, relationship management must be purposeful. Doing this recognizes that, like interactions, relationships can have positive, neutral, or negative tendencies due to the actions of the organization or the stakeholder. The nature of relationships is not static.

Consider this: two organizations in a particular industry may be in direct competition, suggesting a negative relationship based on a winner take all approach and zero-sum interactions. However, since these organizations are in the same industry, they may also cooperate, such as in situations where one organization has insufficient capacity to meet customer demand or when planning innovations to expand the industry and make it sustainable in the long-term future. Another example of when organizations must both cooperate and compete is when the government intervenes to avoid the formation of monopolies or industry control by oligopolies that could detrimental to the collective.

In Chap. 5, when discussing the ten purposes for stakeholder interaction, I noted three types of relationships with stakeholders that one could expect. In my analysis, one-half of the purposes could result in adversarial relationships, while educating and exploring purposes can foster neutral relationships. However, seven of ten purposes hold out the prospect of cooperative, rather than adversarial relationships.

Administrators have the opportunity to make facilitated interactions more cooperative if they pay attention to satisfying stakeholders' process-based expectations and communicate from the very first interaction how the process works and what action will be taken to assure that decision-makers know the information stakeholders have provided (Buckwalter, 2014, p. 36).

Freeman (2004) concludes that it is the relationship with and between stakeholders that is the useful unit of analysis. This is consonant with the observation of Williamson (1979) that it is preferred for businesses to be involved in relationships that are stable since they reduce the transaction costs associated with repeated interactions. Repeated interactions can create an environment of collaboration or cooperation, as well as an expectation for continued transactions and interactions. They can also lower the costs associated with gathering stakeholder preferences as participants gain knowledge about the organization's activities and become more skilled in providing input.

When organizations commit to stakeholder engagement, there is an indirect benefit related to building stakeholder efficacy that comes from purposeful interactions. A stakeholder with enhanced efficacy can better contribute to a marketplace of ideas (Lindblom & Woodhouse, 1993) and dialogue to collaboratively identify a course of action that is mutually value-producing. To fully reap the benefits of stakeholder engagement, the organization needs to communicate to stakeholders that for some activities, stakeholder input is binding; for others, it is advisory. In either situation, the take-away is that the organization values the input and seriously considers it.

There are differences in the level of attention that will be paid to some stakeholders. In the early literature, the preferences of the owner, like the stockholders for organization, were the ones considered to be primary and legitimate. As stakeholder theory has evolved, a number of concepts and tools have been introduced to help gauge how much effort should be put into stakeholder relationship management as our understanding of the number and types of stakeholders has improved. For example, Nutt and Backoff (1992) suggest assessing stakeholders' position (support, oppose, or neutral) on an issue or in a specific context and then assessing the stakeholder's importance on this issue. Using a matrix, they advise mobilizing supportive stakeholders to bring those who are neutral on an issue into the supportive column. Preble (2005) advocates for considering the salience of the stakeholder which is a construct encompassing the concepts of legitimacy, power, and urgency. Writing more than a decade later, Bourne (2016) utilizes the bulls-eye approach to stakeholder identification and urges consideration of the depth of a stakeholder's power, proximity, and urgency as represented by deep coverage through the outer rings of the bulls-eye.

The reality of an organization's subjective assessment of a stakeholder's input will be more acceptable if the organization is clear about the amount of attention that will be paid to some stakeholders over others based on the nature of the relationship particular stakeholders have with the organization. For example, input from stakeholders with a mixed role that is simultaneously both internal and external to the organization may receive more attention than a single external stakeholder who is not a client. It is also important to be transparent about the venue and criteria that will be used for decision-making. For example, the organization's decision-makers may operate in a forum-style venue and strive for Pareto optimality. Alternatively, they may adopt a Kaldor-Hicks criterion suitable for using a court-like venue that weighs costs and the ability of perceived winners to compensate perceived losers.

When stakeholder input is gathered through facilitated interactions, the appearance of making a zero-sum decision should be avoided. This could lead to perceptions that the stakeholder engagement processes were actually pseudo-empowerment (Arnstein, 1969). This reduces the likelihood that input will be provided in the future through direct interactions. Instead, stakeholders will choose other and likely more hostile participation activities for making their preferences known. It would be better to make it known that an arena-style decision approach will be used and the last alternative standing will be accepted. No matter which decision rule is adopted, stakeholders may perceive that there are winners and losers. These perceptions are ok as long as the organization follows the decision rules that were established and communicated how stakeholder preference data were considered (Ebdon & Franklin, 2006).

Maintaining and not jeopardizing relationships with stakeholders through process transparency is essential for engaging stakeholders. In Chap. 2, I organized the range of relationships with the static labels of cooperative, neutral, or adversarial. These categories create a useful heuristic suggesting relationships can be described with labels that are mutually exclusive and exhaustive. However, these labels do not fully capture the shifting nature of relationships over time nor do they reflect the fact that degrees of difference exist in each category.

To analyze the potential for managing stakeholder relationships in a dynamic environment using labels that are more precise for capturing the interactive nature of the relationships, I explored classification schemes used in the natural sciences. The ecological sciences have identified six relationships that can occur between two species that exist in the same ecosystem. We can borrow these relationship labels to describe human interactions (instead of species) and communities of interest (instead of ecosystems) to analyze by analogy potential stakeholder relationships that an organization could manage.

In Table 6.1, I substitute the word stakeholder for species and adapt the physical sciences approach for ecological systems to accommodate different organizational sectors or markets for goods and services. Doing this allows us to analyze the current condition of an organization's relationship with a stakeholder. With this knowledge it is possible to design interventions to move the relationship from one that has negative impacts to one that is mutually value-producing.

Next, I expand the list of the six naturally occurring relationships to nine possible combinations of positive (+), neutral (0), and negative (−) relationships so that both the organization and the stakeholder can experience all possible combinations. The categories in Table 6.2 can be useful for determining the status quo relationship an organization has with a stakeholder. These categories can also help the organization to identify areas where negative stakeholder relationships can be improved. Also,

Table 6.1 Definitions of stakeholder relationships

Ecological relationship	Encyclopedia Britannica Definition [modified to apply to stakeholders]
Mutualism	Relationship between [stakeholders] in different [sectors or markets] that is beneficial to both
Parasitism	Relationship between [stakeholders] in different [sectors or markets] in which one benefits at the expense of the other, but both can co-exist
Predation	Relationship between [stakeholders] in different [sectors or markets] where one pursues another to capture or terminate the other Note: This relationship can exist in two relationship forms for the organization: organization positive and stakeholder negative or organization negative and stakeholder positive
Commensalism	Relationship between [stakeholders] in different [sectors or markets] in which one benefits without harming or benefiting the other
Amensalism	Association between [stakeholders] in different [sectors or markets] where one is inhibited or destroyed and the other is unaffected Note: This relationship can exist in two relationship forms for the organization. One is organization neutral and stakeholder negative. The other is organization negative and stakeholder neutral
Competition	A relationship where [stakeholders] exist in the same or different [sectors or markets], but there are insufficient resources to meet everyone's needs

Table 6.2 Combinations of stakeholder relationships

Relationship	Organization outcome	Stakeholder outcome	Potential organizational strategies
Mutualism	+	+	Monitor
Parasitism	+	0	Maintenance (input)
Predation (S1 on S2)	+	–	Provide resource support (input)
Commensalism	0	+	Seek benefits (process)
Neutral	0	0	Monitor
Amensalism (S1 on S2)	0	–	Enable partner (process)
Predation (S2 on S1)	–	+	Neutralize (process)
Amensalism (S2 on S1)	–	0	Appeal to partner (process)
Competition	–	–	Compete, find new partner

In Table 6.2 S1 is stakeholder 1 and S2 is stakeholder 2. The table has two lines for predation and amensalism since the positive and negative (or neutral) effects are reversed, plus a neutral category is added

since the organization's operating environment changes organically or can be changed purposefully by the organization, these categories help anticipate strategies that could be possible in response to dynamic changes in relationships.

For our analysis of the types of stakeholder relationships and strategies to manage these relationships, we will assume that the stakeholder and the organization are both self-interested. Further, they both have to or want to continue their relationship.

Lastly, the organization seeks to identify solutions to fix or avoid a negative condition. In Table 6.3, I present the nine relationships arranged so that the relationships with negative outcomes for Stakeholder #1, which is the organization, are in the second column. On the bottom row, I present the negative relationships for Stakeholder #2.

The arrows in Table 6.3 move from the left and away from the negative outcomes for the organization. The various moves that would be possible for the organization are considered sequentially. The criteria for each move would be to achieve mutually value-producing outcomes. For the organization, the Pareto optimal decision criteria would apply so that each move would improve the organization's outcome by moving from - to 0 and then to + in the least amount of moves. Further, the choice of action taken by the organization would not deteriorate the current condition of Stakeholder #2.

There are differences in who experiences negative relationship outcomes after a move is made. In the left-hand column, the organization is always subjected to negative relationship outcomes. Moving up a level yields no benefits. In the relationships at the bottom of the table, Stakeholder #2 experiences negative outcomes for the first two moves.

For the organization to gain benefits and not impose adverse outcomes on the stakeholder, the first preferred strategy is moving to the right to improve the organization's condition while maintaining the stakeholder in the same condition. The preferred strategy for the second move is to move upward toward the outcome. However, moving to the right again is also acceptable since it holds Stakeholder #2 in the same condition while improving the relationship for the organization (Stakeholder #1).

When analyzing relationships using this chart, the organization must proactively decide if it wants to attempt to change a relationship. This decision will depend on the direction in which the organization is heading. It is easy to imagine a relationship of competition where there is no need to change the status quo. There are also conditions where a stakeholder would allow predation to occur. One is when the organization is seeking horizontal or vertical integration to have more control over the factors of production. An example is Amazon developing its dedicated delivery services rather than relying on the US Postal Service or for-profit carriers.

Table 6.3 Improving stakeholder relationship outcomes

Negative relationship outcomes for Stakeholder #1 (the organization in our analysis) are in the left column and positive relationship outcomes are in the right hand column.	-,+ Predation	→	0,+ Commensalism	→	+,+ Mutualism
				↑	↑
	-,0 Amensalism	→	0,0 Neutral	→	+,0 Parasitism
				↑	↑
	-,- Competition	→	0,- Amensalism	→	+,- Predation
	Negative relationship outcomes for Stakeholder #2				

What if the predatory behavior were directed toward the organization? Then, the organization could analyze its legal obligations and consider options for changing the relationship. Alternatively, the organization could move into different activities that provide a niche or that are outside the market served by the competitor.

For a public organization, activities that are considered to be predatory may be a sign that the government no longer needs to provide the good or service since a market exists. In the other direction, if the reason for providing the good or service shifts from transactions with individuals to assuring the availability of publicly valued goods or services for groups or the collective, then the government may take action to stop or to regulate predatory behavior. An example of this followed the 2008 housing market crisis with the creation of the Financial Industry Regulatory Authority (FINRA).

Acknowledging that competition and predation exist is just one component of stakeholder engagement and the management of stakeholder relationships. The second component is to adopt a stakeholder mindset supported by principles the organization has articulated to the guide the implementation of stakeholder engagement practices (Freeman, 2004, p. 233). One example would be a policy for how conflicts with stakeholders will be resolved (Dohnalová & Zimola, 2014).

The corporate social responsibility literature provides evidence that for-profit firms make decisions about policy and everyday activities that benefit stakeholders other than their owners, clients, or employees. Since 2007, FedEx has published a Global Citizenship Report detailing their two-prong commitment to financial value production as well as sustainable societal benefits through organizational activities. This is a policy decision. FedEx and other large organizations, including DHL, UPS, and other carriers and airlines and even the US military, regularly make decisions to support direct and indirect stakeholders when they participate in relief missions when a weather disaster has occurred anywhere around the world. When this happens, social performance outweighs economic performance goals.

It is likely that organizations that dedicate resources to corporate social responsibility programs and place a value on monitoring levels of social performance would agree with the conclusion that the organization should not diminish and, in fact, may attempt to improve the condition of an identified stakeholder, group, organization, or collective. It is well documented in the social entrepreneurship literature that economic and social performance should be a concern for all organizations (Ghosh Moulick & Taylor, 2016). The successful adoption of hybrid institutional logics that balance economic and social goals has occurred in formal as well as informal organizations in all sectors (Franklin, Krane, & Ebdon, 2013; Krane, Ebdon, & Franklin, 2020; Scholtens & Zhou, 2009; Waddock & Graves, 1997).

Before we end the discussion on ways to strategically manage dynamic stakeholder relationships, I must put on my scholar's hat and point out that the competition and predation examples in this section address only three of the nine cells in Table 6.3. They are provided as illustrations of how knowing these nine relationships can be useful for the organization to organization to analyze and take action to manage stakeholder relationships.

For theory building, the presence or absence of all relationship types for human relationships needs to be tested before definitive guidance about what strategies can be useful can be offered. Empirical research can lead to a better understanding of what stakeholders and organizations do in different situations and if they are acting in their own best interest, acting in the interests of the stakeholder concurrently, or motivated by other factors.

Accountability for economic and social performance can be enhanced by institutionalizing a commitment to continuously engaging stakeholders rather than waiting for stakeholders to engage the organization. Purposefully building relationships with stakeholders and strategically pursuing transactions and interactions that limit or mitigate negative externalities for the organization can enhance value creation for the organization. However, building relationships with stakeholders takes an organizational commitment and administrative resources. In addition, there can be possible indirect costs associated with an organizational culture that resists collaboration with outsiders. The empirical evidence on resistance to stakeholder input is discussed next.

6.5 Resistance to Stakeholder Engagement

Organizational officials considering a commitment to stakeholder engagement can learn from extant literature that resistance is likely. There are many sources of resistance. First is a desire to insulate the organization from the environment (Kweit & Kweit, 1980, p. 604). This can lead to an over-emphasis on organizational routines (Thompson, 1967, p. 659). Greenstone and Peterson observe that "A bureaucracy whose very structure requires rationalization runs contrary to the requirements of participation ..." (Greenstone & Peterson, 1973, p. 220).

The second source is resistance by (s)elected officials to giving administrators responsibility for facilitating participation activities that may create an expectation of decision-making influence (Chapman & Cleaveland, 1973). Administrators with subject matter expertise are in a commanding position to develop and manage policy (Levine, 1979). This position may be perceived as threatening to organization officials. When this occurs, the delegation of stakeholder engagement activities may not occur.

The third source of resistance by (s)elected officials arises when they suspect that delegation of responsibilities will encourage self-serving behaviors by internal stakeholders such as administrators similar to greedy bureaucrats (Niskanen Jr, 1971), like enhancing their position and over-valuing the input from stakeholders with preferences similar to their own. This type of resistance can complicate relationships between the stakeholders, the administrator, and (s)elected officials (Cunningham & Olshfski, 1986, p. 104).

Time constraints may prevent (s)elected officials not to move forward with stakeholder's ideas, thus limiting the influence of stakeholder input (Onibokun & Curry, 1976, p. 272). Concerns about sharing decision-making on complex issues may lead to subtle resistance to offering widespread participation opportunities (Cain, Ferejohn, & Fiorina, 1987, p. 226; O'Toole, Marshall, & Grewe, 1996; Thomas, 1995). Inviting stakeholders to interact can lead to a loss of administrative efficiency for the organization (Hallman, 1972). Additionally, it takes time and resources to gather input (Aberbach & Rockman, p. 508), and it creates an opportunity cost for work that must be set aside. The challenge, according to Hallman (1972), is finding a way to balance day-to-day administrative duties with coordinating decision-making processes that encourage stakeholder participation. Gathering stakeholder input may also be perceived as making employee's jobs even harder (Bland & Rubin, 1997; Thompson & Jones, 1986) since participatory processes are inefficient and can cause delays and increase red tape (King, Feltey, & Susel, 1998, p. 319). Koontz (1999, p. 273) identifies expenditures of time, personnel resources, and money as three costs to consider. Rosener (1978, p. 458) adds administrative energy and the cost of expertise to this list.

The stakeholders themselves may be resistant to engagement with an organization based on prior interactions. The subject matter expertise of organization employees can lead stakeholders to perceive that employees are too controlling of the process. Alternatively, professional expertise may lead employees to think that participant input is less valuable since stakeholders are not part of the organization (Buckwalter, 2014). Irland (1975, p. 263) portrays the challenge of inclusiveness as the ability to minimize an emphasis on technocratic values, arguing that bureaucratic professionals are leery of the expertise of citizen participants, preferring instead to rely on their professional standards.

A disparity in subject matter expertise for the (s)elected officials and administrators relative to other stakeholders can create uneasy relationships when professional expertise conflicts with the preferences of stakeholders. The right thing to do can be dramatically different when one is guided by scientific management principles versus concerns for fostering equality. Leonard White (1948, p. 20) made this prescient comment: "The reconciliation of democratic institutions and a professionalized bureaucracy… is one of the major perplexities of the future."

6.5.1 Administrator Resistance

Administrators may be resistant to stakeholder engagement since their primary task is to use business-like principles and best practices knowledge to promote cost efficiency. Scholars (Kweit & Kweit, 1980, 2004; Van Meter, 1975) maintain that the basic premises of organizational theory (expertise, regularity and routinization, and efficiency) reduce the tolerance of administrators for stakeholder participation. Alternatively, administrators may believe that organization activities are too complex for gathering useful input from the stakeholders (Long & Franklin, 2004). Administrator's subject matter expertise generally exceeds the knowledge of most external and mixed stakeholders. Rather than accepting that stakeholders should participate in decisions that affect them and their community directly, Bachrach (1967) found that administrators devise solutions that maximize net social gains based on their expertise rather than on trust in the ability of stakeholders to understand complex decisions. Given the disparity in knowledge, administrators may perceive stakeholder input as usurping their expertise or diminishing their discretion.

Resistance may also arise from conflicting values. For example, the bureaucratic emphasis on treating people like a case (Wilson, 1991) can discourage stakeholder engagement in order to avoid charges of unequal access or unfair treatment (Allison & Zelikow, 1999). Alternatively, resistance may lead to administrators manipulating participants or participation processes or making input only advisory in order to reduce stakeholder impact (Schaller, 1964, p. 178). Benveniste (1972) calls attention to the resistance of bureaucratic experts who tend to become suspicious of client beneficiaries who request changes out of self-interest. This tension is well documented by others (Belasco & Alutto, 1969; Rourke, 1960).

Another explanation for resistance is that administrators may think it is the responsibility of other internal actors – especially (s)elected officials or executives – to initiate it (Miller & Evers, 2002). Alternatively, (s)elected officials and administrators may be reluctant to encourage facilitated participation because they may feel that stakeholders already have sufficient access through existing participation activities (Franklin & Ebdon, 2004).

Under conditions of resistance, it is not unusual to have distrust and conflict (Cunningham & Olshfski, 1986, p. 105) between the three categories of stakeholders, external, mixed, and internal. The challenge, then, is to overcome the tyranny of expertise (May, 1965), so that participation becomes a meaningful dialogue rather than a façade (Van Meter, 1975, p. 807). There may be a wish to avoid the perception that the organization is unable to resolve problems related to everyday activities. In this situation, participation by outsiders may be viewed as an intrusion that will expose the organizations shortcomings (Baum, 1982). Overcoming resistance requires a shared understanding of how stakeholder preferences can and will inform decisions and improve organizational activities.

Designing strategies to overcome resistance from external, mixed, and internal stakeholders could be the task of an administrator housed in a stakeholder relations department. Creating this type of administrative unit in an organization is not unprecedented since there are organizations that have stockholder relations or public relations units. Staff units regularly release information to promote transparency. They are also a point of entry into the organization, making accessibility less of a concern. Encouraging facilitated interactions and embracing stakeholder engagement for relationship building and management could be staff functions as well.

Relationships that cross the organization's boundaries, while necessary, create their own unique challenges (Koopenjan & Klign, 2004; Olsen, 2002). Since it is necessary to balance the needs for representation and results, administrators need to think creatively about nurturing stakeholder relationships, structuring negotiations, and building coalitions (Berry, Portney, & Thomson, 1993, p. 41). Bardach (1998) argues that administrators who are active collaborators need to embrace a problem-solving ethos and to become experts in consensus building processes. Additionally, stakeholder engagement activities will benefit when administrators have group facilitation and conflict management skills. Through stakeholder engagement practices, administrators are the human interface between the organization and its stakeholders (Hord, 1992; Svara, 1994). Resources for training and technical assistance may be necessary to develop techniques that emphasize meaningful interactions and stakeholder inclusion to gather input (Koontz, 1999, p. 276).

Being responsive to stakeholders is not only useful for engaging stakeholders, but it also is vital in building support and legitimacy between interdependent actors (Kotter, 1977) and strengthening civic discourse (Reich, 2002). For a mutually value-producing discourse, stakeholders' voices must be clear, loud, and equal (Verba, Schlozman, & Brady, 1995). When this occurs, organizational officials learn what stakeholders want and need. These officials have an incentive to pay attention to what they hear. When the organization pays attention, the democratic ideal of equality in responsiveness to the preferences and interests of all is served and external accountability is enhanced.

Stakeholder engagement processes that consider and value participant inputs utilize this preference data alongside other inputs for decisions and communicate widely the results of participation activities. Doing so offers the potential for attaining the governance ideals scholars describe. When this happens, the organization's activities are more impactful than what can be measured by economic performance. Stakeholder engagement also produces social impacts that enhance the function of society as a collective. In the next section, I describe how to structure stakeholder engagement processes so that there is a higher likelihood of fulfilling these normative expectations.

6.6 Utilizing Stakeholder Preference Data

The main argument in this chapter is that stakeholder engagement is a valuable activity for building productive relationships. Proactive management of stakeholder relationships can reduce the costs of gathering preference data that is representative of the full range of stakeholders for the organization. This can include data for general activities as well as for specific issues such as proposed policy or activity changes. Having data is necessary, but not sufficient. The real value comes from sharing the data with mixed and internal stakeholders in ways that encourage use in all the strategic management activities of the organization.

Evaluation literature has long considered how best to communicate policy and program evaluation results in ways that foster utilization. Utilization is defined as the use of evaluative information for communicating, learning, motivating, improving the delivery of goods and services, decision-making, monitoring, and evaluating.

The key to accomplishing all these tasks is to identify and engage primary users of the data when designing the evaluation and then to work with them to identify and prioritize intended uses of the results (Patton, 2008; Wholey, Hatry, & Newcomer, 2010). Utilization-focused evaluation is based on the premise that the value from evaluations should be judged by their utility and actual use (Patton, 2008). In 2011, USAID established an evaluation policy with standards for high-quality, relevant, and transparent evaluations to demonstrate results, generate evidence to inform decisions, promote learning, and ensure accountability. A stakeholder engagement regime is strengthened by adopting the same criteria.

In 1982, Cronbach concluded that evaluative data are intended to serve decision-makers, yet evidence of this occurring was scant. His concerns about utilization continued for decades and are still important although progress has been made. In a 2006 survey of American Evaluation Association members, 68% self-reported that their evaluation results were not used (Centers for Disease Control and Prevention et al., 2013). A 2013 report states that there is a need to take reports off the bookshelf and get them in the hands of the intended audience to encourage use (Centers for Disease Control and Prevention et al., 2013). By 2016, an evaluation of commissioned evaluations reported a 93% utilization rate. The results included "[reports that]...stimulated learning in USAID and, to a degree, among its partners as well. Ninety percent of these evaluations were reported to have resulted in decisions being made and actions being taken at appropriate stages in USAID's Program Cycle" (Hageboeck & collaborators, 2016, p. vii).

To encourage the use of stakeholder input data, the administrator must design reporting tools for communicating stakeholders' preferences. Some features of reports that can contribute to increased utilization include using the language of the intended report user; presenting the information in a way that is visually appealing including especially tables, charts, and figures; and making sure the information is available when needed to inform decision-making (Wholey et al., 2010).

Concerning the distribution of the report's findings, administrators need to be creative and have a mixed-method communication strategy that considers the audience's needs and the timing for which the information will be helpful. Different ways of delivering evaluation findings include (Patton, 2008; Posavac & Carey, 2002; Rossi, Lipsey, & Freeman, 2003; Wholey et al., 2010):

- Presenting findings at annual meetings of the organization and staff meetings
- Posting a short video version of findings
- Sharing findings on the knowledge management platform
- Creating infographics to share with listserves
- Producing action memos for internal and selection mixed stakeholders and potentially external stakeholders with whom the organization has partner relationships

Perhaps the most crucial step in terms of promoting the utilization of stakeholder preference data is to assign responsibility for distribution of the aggregated data to a specific person. This person is also responsible for creating a dissemination plan. In the plan, the administrator can determine how to disseminate reports that have content that is relevant to the audience and to demonstrate the urgency of using the findings and recommendations to make changes. There is also a need to follow up with primary intended users to facilitate and enhance use. The administrator can support the use of the information by creating a data use calendar and keeping a record of what is done with the recommendations, making the process transparent. Finally, on a regularized basis, it is crucial to find out how internal and mixed stakeholders use the preference data. Doing so will allow the administrator to be accountable, learn, and to improve utilization. The bottom line is this, to fully leverage data from stakeholder engagement, administrators need to identify the users and create reports and dissemination strategies that facilitate use.

6.7 Summary

In this chapter, I argue that organizations should institutionalize an expectation for the systematic and continuous engagement of their stakeholders to be accountable. One outcome from stakeholder engagement, as a strategic management function, is the development of ongoing relationships that can make gathering input faster and at a lower cost. In addition, the organization can manage relationships that are adversarial by interacting with the stakeholder and finding out preferences and areas where coproduction may be possible. Stakeholder relationship management can reveal shared values and build trust. Accountability through the development of relationships that are mutually value-producing for the organization as well as the stakeholder can lead to enhanced economic and social performance.

With institutionalized communication channels and continuous availability of usable preference information through stakeholder engagement, it is hoped that de jure utilization will become a reality. What is not known is the extent to which the benefits derived from these actions may outweigh the additional costs. By deliberately considering the enhanced value creation that can be expected from stakeholder engagement, organizations determine the appropriate answer. In the next chapter, the potential for identifying competing values and identification of performance gaps in stakeholder engagement is considered.

References

Allison, G., & Zelikow, P. (1999). *Essence of Decision: Explaining the Cuban Missile Crisis* (2 edition). New York, NY: Pearson.

Arnold, R. D. (1990). *The logic of congressional action*. New Haven, CT: Yale University Press.

Arnstein, S. R. (1969). A ladder of citizen participation. *American Institution of Planners Journal, 35*(7), 216–224.

Bachrach, P. (1967). *The theory of democratic elitism: A critique*. Boston, MA: Little, Brown and Company.

Bardach, E. (1998). *Getting agencies to work together: The practice and theory of managerial craftsmanship*. Washington, DC: Brookings Institution Press.

Baum, H. S. (1982). The advisor as invited intruder. *Public Administration Review, 42*(6), 546–552.

Belasco, J. A., & Alutto, J. A. (1969). Line staff conflicts: Some empirical insights. *The Academy of Management Journal, 12*(4), 469–477.

Benveniste, G. (1972). *The politics of expertise*. Berkeley, CA: Glendessary Press.

Berman, E. M. (1997). Dealing with cynical citizens. *Public Administration Review, 57*(2), 105–112.

Berry, J. M., Portney, K. E., & Thomson, K. (1993). *The rebirth of urban democracy*. Washington, DC: Brookings Institution Press.

Bland, R. L., & Rubin, I. S. (1997). *Budgeting: A guide for local governments*. Washington, DC: International City/County Management Association.

Bourne, L. (2016). *Stakeholder relationship management: A maturity model for organisational implementation*. Oxfordshire, United Kingdom: Routledge Routledge.

Buck, J. V. (1984). The impact of citizen participation programs and policy decisions on participants' opinions. *Western Political Quarterly, 37*(3), 468–482.

Buckwalter, N. D. (2014). *The potential for public empowerment through government-organized participation*. Public Administration Review

Cain, B., Ferejohn, J., & Fiorina, M. (1987). *The personal vote: Constituency service and electoral independence*. Cambridge, MA: Harvard University Press.

Callahan, K. (2002). The Utilization and Effectiveness of Citizen Advisory Committees in the Budget Process of Local Governments. *Journal of Public Budgeting, Accounting and Financial Management, 14*(2), 295–319.

Centers for Disease Control and Prevention, Mirambeau, A., Elmi, J., Losby, J., & Gervin, D. (2013). *Evaluation reporting: A guide to help ensure use of evaluation findings*. Washington, DC: U.S. Department of Health and Human Services.

Chapman, R. L., & Cleaveland, F. N. (1973). The changing character of the public service and the administrator of the 1980's. *Public Administration Review, 33*(4), 358–366.

Choi, J., & Wang, H. (2009). Stakeholder relations and the persistence of corporate financial performance. *Strategic Management Journal, 30*(8), 895–907.

Cronbach, L. J. (1982). Designing evaluation of educational and social programs. Thousand Oaks, CA: Sage.

Cunningham, R., & Olshfski, D. (1986). Interpreting state administrator-legislator relationships. *The Western Political Quarterly, 39*(1), 104–117.

Dohnalová, Z., & Zimola, B. (2014). Corporate stakeholder management. *Procedia – Social and Behavioral Sciences, 110*, 879–886.

Donovan, T., & Bowler, S. (2004). *Reforming the republic: Democratic institutions for the new America*. Upper Saddle River, NJ: Pearson Pearson Prentice Hall.

Dyson, L. L. (1999). Developing a university-school district partnership; researcher-district administrator collaboration for a special education initiative. *Canadian Journal of Education, 24*(4), 411–425.

Ebdon, C., & Franklin, A. L. (2006). Citizen participation in budget theory. *Public Administration Review, 66*(3), 437–447.

Franklin, A. L., & Ebdon, C. (2004). Aligning priorities in local budgeting processes. *Journal of Public Budgeting, Accounting and Financial Management, 16*(2), 210–227.

Franklin, A. L., Krane, D., & Ebdon, C. (2013). Multilevel governance processes–citizens & local budgeting: Comparing Brazil, China, & the United States. *International Review of Public Administration, 18*(1), 1–24.

Freeman, R. E. (2004). The stakeholder approach revisited. *Zeitschrift Für Wirtschafts-Und Unternehmensethik, 5*(3), 228–254.

Ghosh Moulick, A., & Taylor, L. L. (2016). Fiscal slack, budget shocks, and performance in public organizations: Evidence from public schools. *Public Management Review*, 1–16. https://doi.org/10.1080/14719037.2016.1243813

Graves, S. B., & Waddock, S. A. (2000). Beyond built to last... Stakeholder relations in "Built-to-Last" companies. *Business and Society Review, 105*(4), 393–418.

Greenstone, J. D., & Peterson, P. E. (1973). Race and authority in urban politics: Community participation and the war on poverty. New York, NY: Russell Sage Foundation.

Hageboeck, M., & collaborators. (2016). *Evaluation utilization at USAID*. Management Systems International, a Tetra Tech Company. https://pdf.usaid.gov/pdf_docs/PA00KXVT.pdf

Hallman, H. (1972). Federally-financed citizen participation. *Public Administration Review, 32*, 421–428.
Hord, S. M. (1992). *Facilitating leadership: The imperative for change*. Austin, TX: Southwest Educational Development Laboratory..
Irland, L. C. (1975). Citizen participation: A tool for conflict management on the public lands. *Public Administration Review*, 263–269.
King, C. S., Feltey, K. M., & Susel, B. O. (1998). The question of participation; toward authentic public participation in public administration. *Public Administration Review, 58*(4), 317–326.
Koontz, T. M. (1999). Administrators and citizens: Measuring agency officials' efforts to foster and use public input in forest policy. *Journal of Public Administration Research and Theory, 9*(2), 251–280.
Koopenjan, J., & Klign, E. H. (2004). *Managing uncertainties in networks: A network approach to problem solving and decision making*. New York, NY: Routledge.
Kotter, J. P. (1977). Power, dependence and effective management. *Harvard Business Review, 55*(4), 125–136.
Krane, D., Ebdon, C., & Franklin, A. L. (2020). Social entrepreneurship and the challenge of collaborative governance of civic events: Brazil, Korea, and the United States. In M. N. Iftikhar, J. B. Justice, & D. B. Audretsch (Eds.), *Urban studies and entrepreneurship (pp. 119–142).* Springer International Publishing. https://doi.org/10.1007/978-3-030-15164-5_7
Kweit, R. W., & Kweit, M. G. (1980). Bureaucratic decision-making impediments to citizen participation. *Polity*, 647–666.
Kweit, R. W., & Kweit, M. G. (2004). Citizen participation and citizen evaluation in disaster recovery. *American Review of Public Administration, 34*(4), 354–373.
Levine, A. L. (1979). The role of the technoscience administrator in managing national science policy. *Public Administration Review, 39*(2), 122–128.
Lindblom, C., & Woodhouse, E. (1993). *The policy making process* (3rd ed.). Prentice-Hall.
Long, E., & Franklin, A. L. (2004). The paradox of implementing the government performance and results act: Top-down direction for bottom-up implementation. *Public Administration Review, 64*(3), 309–319. https://doi.org/10.1111/j.1540-6210.2004.00375.x
May, J. D. (1965). Democracy, organization, Michels. *The American Political Science Review, 59*(2), 417–429.
Miller, G. J., & Evers, L. (2002). Budgeting structures and citizen participation. *Journal of Public Budgeting, Accounting & Financial Management; Boca Raton, 14*(2), 233–272. https://doi.org/10.1108/JPBAFM-14-02-2002-B005
Miller, W. E., & Stokes, D. E. (1966). Constituency influence in congress. In A. Campbell (Ed.), *Elections and the political order (pp. 351–372).* New York, NY: Wiley.
Moneva, J. M., Rivera-Lirio, J. M., & Muñoz-Torres, M. J. (2007). The corporate stakeholder commitment and social and financial performance. *Industrial Management & Data Systems, 107*, 84.
Niskanen Jr., W. A. (1971). *Greedy bureaucrat*. Chicago, IL: Aldine-Atherton.
Nutt, P. C., & Backoff, R. W. (1992). *Strategic management of public and third sector organizations: A handbook for leaders* (1st ed.). San Francisco, CA: Jossey-Bass.
Olander, S., & Landin, A. (2008). A comparative study of factors affecting the external stakeholder management process. *Construction Management and Economics, 26*(6), 553–561.
Olsen, J. P. (2002). Maybe it is time to rediscover bureaucracy. *Journal of Public Administration Research and Theory, 16*(1), 1–24.
Onibokun, A. G., & Curry, M. (1976). An ideology of citizen participation: The metropolitan Seattle transit case study. *Public Administration Review, 36*, 269–277.
O'Toole, D. E., Marshall, J., & Grewe, T. (1996). Current local government budgeting practices. *Government Finance Review, 12*(6), 25–29.
Patton, M. Q. (2008). *Utilization-focused evaluation* (4th ed.). Thousand Oaks, CA: Sage Publications.

Peloza, J., Loock, M., Cerruti, J., & Muyot, M. (2012). Sustainability: How stakeholder perceptions differ from corporate reality. *California Management Review, 55*(1), 74–97.

Posavac, E. J., & Carey, R. G. (2002). *Program evaluation: Methods and case studies* (6th ed.). Upper Saddle River, NJ: Prentice Hall.

Preble, J. F. (2005). Toward a comprehensive model of stakeholder management. *Business & Society Review, 110*(4), 407–431.

Putnam, R. D. (2000). *Bowling alone: The collapse and revival of American community*. New York, NY: Touchstone/Simon & Schuster.

Reich, R. B. (2002). Policy making in a democracy. In P. Kobrak (Ed.), *The political environment of public management* (pp. 122–149). New York, NY: AB Longman.

Rosener, J. B. (1978). Citizen participation: Can we measure its effectiveness? *Public Administration Review, 38*, 457–463.

Rosener, J. B. (1982). Making bureaucrats responsive: A study of the impact of citizen participation and staff recommendations on regulatory decision making. *Public Administration Review, 42*, 339–345.

Rossi, P. H., Lipsey, M. W., & Freeman, H. E. (2003). *Evaluation: A systematic approach*. Thousand Oaks, CA: Sage Publications.

Rourke, F. E. (1960). Bureaucracy in conflict: Administrators and professionals. *Ethics, 70*(3), 220–227.

Sachs, S., & Maurer, M. (2009). Toward dynamic corporate stakeholder responsibility. *Journal of Business Ethics, 85*(3), 535–544.

Schaller, L. E. (1964). Is the citizen advisory committee a threat to representative government? *Public Administration Review, 24*(3), 175–179.

Scholtens, B., & Zhou, Y. (2009). Stakeholder relations and financial performance. *Sustainable Development, 16*(3), 213–232.

Stivers, C. (1990). The public agency as polis: Active citizenship in the administrative state. *Administration and Society, 22*(1), 86–105.

Strange, J. H. (1972). The impact of citizen participation on public administration. *Public Administration Review, 32*(Special Issue), 457–470.

Svara, J. (1994). *Facilitative leadership in local government: Lessons for successful mayors and chairpersons*. San Francisco, CA: Jossey-Bass.

Thomas, J. C. (1995). *Public participation in public decisions*. San Francisco, CA: Jossey-Bass.

Thompson, F., & Jones, L. R. (1986). Controllership in the public sector. *Journal of Policy Analysis and Management, 53*(3), 547–571.

Thompson, J. D. (1967). *Organizations in action*. New York, NY: McGraw Hill.

Van Meter, E. C. (1975). Citizen participation in the policy management process. *Public Administration Review, 35*(Special Issue), 804–812.

Verba, S., Schlozman, K. L., & Brady, H. E. (1995). *Voice and equality: Civic volunteerism in American politics*. Cambridge, MA: Harvard Harvard University Press.

Waddock, S. A., & Graves, S. B. (1997). Quality of management and quality of stakeholder relations: Are they synonymous? *Business & Society, 36*(3), 250–279.

White, L. D. (1948). *Introduction to the study of public administration* (3rd ed.). Macmillan.

Wholey, J. S., Hatry, H. P., & Newcomer, K. E. (2010). *Handbook of practical program evaluation* (3rd ed.). San Francisco, CA: Jossey-Bass.

Williamson, O. E. (1979). Transaction-cost economics: The governance of contractual relations. *Journal of Law and Economics*, 233–261.

Wilson, J. Q. (1991). *Bureaucracy: What government agencies do and why they do it* (1st ed.). New York, NY: Basic Books.

Wondolleck, J. M., Manning, N. J., & Crowfoot, J. W. (1996). Teetering at the top of the ladder: The experience of citizen group participants in alternative dispute resolution processes. *Sociological Perspectives, 39*(2), 249–262.

Chapter 7
Stakeholder Engagement Outcomes

Abstract This book uses a process model of organizational actions and the influence of the external environment to consider what can be gained by organizations that embrace stakeholder engagement activities. The external environment contains stakeholders who have varying levels of motivation that push them to provide input and engage in participation activities. Inside the organization's boundaries, a decision can be made to take action to pull stakeholders into interactions with the organization designed to gather input to inform decisions and enhance the organization's activities. This happens through facilitated interactions and relationship building. Each of these elements inside and outside of the organization contributes to stakeholder engagement. These activities are a means for the organization to be transparent about participation activities and decisions, gather input while assuring access and representativeness, and be responsive to stakeholders. When the organization's purposeful interactions with stakeholders provide usable information to guide decision-making, then stakeholder engagement processes increase accountability for economic performance and sustainability when economic and social performance goals are met.

7.1 Introduction

In the preceding chapters, I analyzed stakeholder engagement using the components of Easton's (1965) black box model of the policy process, where inputs are transformed through the administrative processes of an organization. The inputs were stakeholders, participation activities, and motivations to participate. The organizationally hosted processes intended to pull stakeholders into participation, facilitate interactions, and engage stakeholders to create valued outputs. The outputs were representativeness, transparency, accessibility, responsiveness, and accountability. These outputs when combined create an economic performance sustainability outcome and can enhance long-term social performance sustainability. When this happens, then the organization through stakeholder engagement becomes sustainable.

A. L. Franklin, *Stakeholder Engagement*,
https://doi.org/10.1007/978-3-030-47519-2_7

In this chapter, I analyze how stakeholder engagement can enhance the long-term outcomes and impacts. I compare ideals and values related to stakeholder engagement to current organization activities via gap analysis, as a tool to continuously improve the organization's prospects for sustainability. The analysis culminates with a hybrid logic model for stakeholder engagement.

7.2 Components of Stakeholder Engagement

The topic of Chap. 2 is stakeholders, who are an input to the organization. I suggested the label external stakeholders to refer to individuals, groups, organizations, or collectives that exist outside of the organization but can be influenced by or influence the organization's activities. A second label for stakeholders is mixed, to denote persons who have a dual relationship with the organization and who can offer perspectives on the external and internal environment simultaneously. The internal stakeholder label refers to (s)elected officials, administrators, and subject matter experts who work for the organization.

These categories are not mutually exclusive; however, understanding the category from which a stakeholder is communicating input in a specific situation is essential. I organized stakeholders along six continua as a way to determine who typically interacts with the organization and who may need to interact with the organization. Ideally, a broader and more representative range of stakeholders' preferences can be encouraged through stakeholder identification. Doing so can better align the organization's and the stakeholders' preferences.

Participation activities, as described in Chap. 3, are another input to the organization. There is a wide range of participation activities available from which stakeholders can passively and actively communicate preference data. Administrators charged with stakeholder engagement should consider the frequency and direction of the interactions to make sure that data are being gathered to benefit organizational activities and decision-making. The different combinations can influence the nature of the interaction, which could range from cooperative to neutral or even adversarial. Considering the frequency and direction of interactions would make the organization more accessible to stakeholders who wish to provide input. Ideally, the transparency of the organization's activities and decision-making processes are improved, and the cost of stakeholder engagement is minimized through the purposeful selection of a combination of passive and active stakeholder participation activities.

Stakeholder motivation is both an input from the external environment and an internal process occurring inside the organization's black box of activities. Seven motivational push factors were identified in Chap. 4. These influence a stakeholder's decision about voluntarily interacting with an organization. There are also pull factors that can be used to motivate interaction. The administrator can identify stakeholders most likely to participate based on the push factors and then take actions to pull specific stakeholders into interactions. Many times, this can be accomplished by offering incentives. A recursive organizational process for leveraging push and pull factors to encourage participation creates a dynamic relationship with stakeholders. To be judged successful, stakeholder engagement encourages perceptions of an accessible organization and results in stakeholders who proactively participate.

Chapter 5 introduced the concept of facilitated interactions. These occur when an organization sponsors an administrative process that invites stakeholders to take advantage of the transparency and accessibility of the organization to provide input and register their preferences. Combining information from Chaps. 2, 3, and 4, I described ten different purposes for facilitated interactions. Then, the relative costs and benefits of each can be analyzed by the administrator. Facilitated interactions provide an opportunity for organizations to learn stakeholders' preferences. They can also be useful for communicating the organization's activities and decisions. Doing this may enhance the acceptance of or lead to better support of decisions. Ideally, facilitated interactions create a positive perception of organizational responsiveness and help the organization to identify sincere stakeholder preferences.

Stakeholder engagement was described in Chap. 6 as the organizational commitment of resources for an administrative function tasked with the goal of being more responsive to stakeholder's preferences by developing and managing relationships. These activities are intended to enhance the accountability of the organization. This can be done through a combination of general and situational stakeholder engagement that continuously monitors the external operating environment plus periodically gathers input to be used throughout the strategic management cycle to manage for results. Ideally, a stakeholder engagement process is institutionalized, and the combined net economic and social value of the organization is enhanced.

In this chapter, I continue the discussion of the utilization of stakeholder preference data. From the organization's perspective, purposefully considering stakeholders' input can lead to decisions that enhance the organization's sustainability. Informing decisions is one component of my argument that organizations can benefit by engaging stakeholders.

A second component that makes stakeholder engagement important is that it can be mutually value-producing. From the stakeholders' perspective, evidence that the preference data were considered during decision-making would make the organization transparent, responsive, and accountable. Knowing that their participation mattered could also increase stakeholders' efficacy, which contributes to the organization's social performance goals.

When successful, stakeholder engagement processes can minimize transaction costs (Williamson, 1979) by aligning the organization's activities with what is desired by the marketplace and minimizing the decisions that generate stakeholder dissatisfaction which could potentially disrupt activities. Successful stakeholder engagement can lead to long-term sustainability when the organization proactively responds to changes in the external environment in ways that incorporate stakeholders' preferences.

7.3 The Duality of Stakeholder Engagement

When organizations commit to stakeholder engagement, the goal is to foster a marketplace of ideas across all venues and to systematically gather preference data for organizational decisions. For some decisions, stakeholder input is binding; for other decisions, stakeholder input is advisory. Decision-makers may strive for Pareto optimality (as opposed to using Kaldor-Hicks criterion or making a zero-sum decision) as a decision goal. However, for most decisions, stakeholders will perceive that there are winners and losers. That is ok as long as the input and decision processes observe the decision rules of the venue and the organization communicates how stakeholder preference data were considered (Ebdon & Franklin, 2006).

There are other challenges for stakeholder engagement since it communicates a commitment to reciprocal relationships. Unfortunately, participation processes do not always achieve the ideals expected. This is problematic since, as Arnstein (1969) observes, participation can be an empty ritual with no real power to affect outcomes. The Advisory Commission on Intergovernmental Relations indicated that one of the ultimate objectives of participation "… is to change … behavior so that [organizational] units respond better to citizens' needs and desires and refrain from the arbitrary, capricious, insensitive, or oppressive exercise of power" (1979, p. 79). Forester (1999) concludes that the participatory rituals of stakeholder engagement processes offer dialogue and argument venues that have more relevance than anticipated. They can create more value than at first anticipated and foster relationships that promote deliberative political rationality, which is superior to rational decision-making processes.

One of the reasons why decisions are improved is that stakeholder engagement processes institutionalize information channels to decision-makers and improve communication between administrators and stakeholders (Wondolleck, Manning, & Crowfoot, 1996, p. 253). This can foster decisions "…made on the basis of a formed consensus, rather than on majority strength" (Donovan & Bowler, 2004, p. 51). Stakeholders' understanding arising from improved transparency and access can also provide more accurate perceptions of decisions (Miller & Stokes, 1966) and can help align an organization's policy actions with the preferences of their stakeholders (Arnold, 1990; Rosener, 1982). Further, stakeholder engagement can enhance the organization's reputation for competence, efficiency (Berman, 1997, p. 106) and effectiveness (Buck, 1984, p. 468).

From the stakeholder's perspective, continued interactions can result in a positive emotional attachment to the organization. Long-term relationships can also improve stakeholder efficacy and, over time, empower stakeholders. Increasing the capacity of stakeholders is mutually value-producing; the stakeholders benefit from enhanced efficacy, and the organization benefits from decisions better aligned with stakeholder preferences and reduced costs for stakeholder engagement activities.

Stakeholder engagement is more than making the organization's decisions and activities transparent, offering participation mechanisms that make it accessible, and purposefully facilitating stakeholder access to provide input to inform decisions. It is also a collaborative and synergistic process that benefits the organization and stakeholders in more profound ways, such as enhancing sustainability. Dyson (1999, p. 411) suggests four essential elements for structuring collaboration processes to achieve all these values. First is a developmental process of determining the mutual goals of the collaboration. Second is a professional communication protocol. The third is a collaborative structure that includes cooperative relationships and accountability between actors. Fourth is a process supporting the creation of outcomes that benefit all who interact. In the next section, I suggest how these four elements can be integrated into a governance structure that fosters strategic stakeholder engagement.

7.4 Managing Competing Values

Much of my prior work examined stakeholder interactions in public organizations. In these settings, it is clear that there are multiple, and often conflicting, values that must be considered during decision-making. Pareto optimal solutions in this situation are seldom possible, particularly when accountability is measured by both economic and social performance. In these situations, values such as those described in each chapter of this book must be reconciled and balanced. One tool organizations can use to assess their fulfillment of stakeholder engagement values is the spider chart typical for benchmarking activities (Keehley & Abercrombie, 2008). This tool can also identify areas where performance gaps exist so that the organization can design strategies and allocate resources for continuous improvement.

An example of how a spider chart could be used to assess the organization's performance on stakeholder engagement values is presented in Fig. 7.1. For those unfamiliar with this analytical tool, here is how I explain it to my students. What

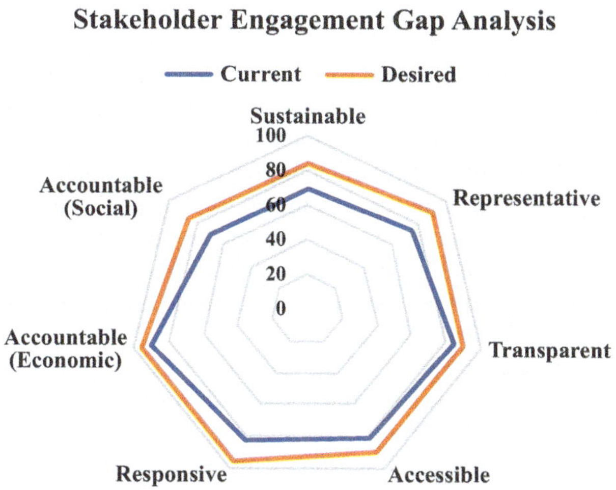

Fig. 7.1 A spider chart of stakeholder engagement

kind of web should a spider have in order to catch a sufficient amount of food to stay alive? From a nutritional perspective, enormous webs will capture more food than smaller webs. From an engineering perspective, the web needs to be anchored to something, and more anchors make it stronger. Like a spider web, the benchmarking spider chart suggests a small web at the inner core representing low performance and a more substantial web on the outer circle representing the ideal performance. The seven axes on the web are labeled with the value that is enhanced by each element of stakeholder engagement. These anchors contribute to sustainability.

To use the spider chart (which is called a radar chart in excel) for measuring value attainment, the organization assesses current performance levels on each of the anchors on a scale from 0% to 100% of possible or desired. The range from 0% to 100% allows for the use of objective and subjective performance data. To do this, a decision must be made, will the 100% value be an ideal, an expectation, or the best performance level achieved by competitors. After performance is charted on each axis, the administrator can compare the level of performance to what is possible, what is desired or even a competitor's performance. Where gaps exist, the organization can decide if additional efforts to enhance performance levels are necessary.

I acknowledge that the presentation of the seven stakeholder engagement values in Fig. 7.1 has limited utility. Organizations are not monolithic: some values will be embraced; others will not. In addition, values not included in my analysis may matter to a specific organization. That is a strength of the spider chart; organizations can change the values represented by each anchor and can add or reduce the number of anchors for assessing the outcomes from stakeholder engagement activities.

7.5 A Hybrid Logic Model of Stakeholder Engagement

The values in this spider chart are the same as what I presented in the logic model in Chap. 1, the logic model borrowed from the black box metaphor of Easton (1965). This model was designed as a simple heuristic helpful for understanding that the organization gets inputs and transforms them into stakeholder engagement outputs. These outputs promote sustainability outcomes from an economic performance perspective. They are not sufficient for guaranteeing sustainability because the second component is social performance, which is not under the control of the organization. Instead, social performance is co-produced with stakeholders and, hopefully, enhanced when the organization institutionalizes a stakeholder engagement regime designed to be impactful for society.

The black box metaphor for organizational processes is common in public policy scholarship. In the evaluation literature, a slightly different metaphor is used to understand organizational processes. The logic model, developed by Mohr (1988), emphasizes the articulation and measurement of values to be achieved via the sequential organizational process model.

Both metaphors have informed the analysis and arguments presented in each chapter. Table 7.1 combines the two metaphors to introduce a hybrid logic model reflecting the interrelationships between the concepts that constitute the stakeholder engagement construct. In the top row of the hybrid model are the inputs, processes, outputs, and outcomes which are critical for achieving the goals of the organization. The values enhanced by the organization's activities are noted in the bottom row of the model according to the time perspective moving from outputs, to outcomes, and, finally, to impacts. The chapters in the book follow the columns from left to right. The arrows from the outcome, output, and process are the feedback loops that go back to the beginning of the stakeholder engagement logic model.

Stakeholders and participation activities are two inputs needed for stakeholder engagement. A stakeholder engagement regime will analyze the current level of inputs for each and will develop strategies to enhance the value that can be produced through purposeful interactions with stakeholders. In doing this, two outcomes can be enhanced. The first outcome of stakeholder engagement is enhanced representativeness of the input that the organization receives from stakeholders and upon which it makes decisions about organizational policies and activities. Presented below is the ideal condition for the value of representativeness in stakeholder input.

Table 7.1 Hybrid stakeholder engagement logic model

	Input	Input	Input=push Process=pull	Process	Output	Outcome
	Stakeholder	Participation activities	Stakeholder motivation	Facilitated interactions	Stakeholder engagement: Internal	Stakeholder engagement: External
Output	Stakeholder identification	Passive and active data collection	Input repre-senting all who can/are impacted	Data to change activities and inform decision	Net value is enhanced	Mutually value producing relationships
Ideal	Better align actions with preferences	Minimize interaction costs	Stakeholders choose to interact	Identify sincere preferences	Economic performance	Social performance
Value Served	Representative	Transparent	Accessible	Responsive	Accountable	Sustainable

- *Representativeness:* Organizations should robustly identify a universe of stakeholders who are influenced by or can influence the organization's operations.

The second outcome desired from stakeholder engagement is enhanced transparency. To achieve this, an organization can use passive and active participation activities to inform, educate, and interact with stakeholders to learn preferences and guide action. Presented below is the ideal condition for the value of transparent organizations.

- *Transparent*: Organizations should gather stakeholders' preferences from a range of participation activities to inform decisions and communicate actions.

The third outcome from stakeholder engagement is an understanding of what factors motivate participation. Ideally, the motivating factors will lead to a representative sample of stakeholders who communicate preference data without intervention by the administrator. However, this ideal is not realistic. To enhance access, the administrator can identify missing stakeholder perspectives and offer incentives to motivate participation. Presented below is the ideal condition for accessible organizations.

- *Accessible*: Organizations should offer participation activities that encourage stakeholders' participation at low cost to the stakeholders and the organization.

When unrepresented stakeholders are identified, then facilitated interactions can be a strategy for engaging these stakeholders. The ideal for facilitation interactions is to be responsive to all stakeholders. When successful, preference data are gathered and reported in ways that encourage utilization to inform decisions. Presented below is the ideal condition for responsive organizations.

- *Responsive*: Organizations should offer facilitated participation to stakeholders to fulfill a variety of purposes in a way that balances costs and benefits and informs decisions.

A fifth outcome from stakeholder engagement is accountability. Ideally, the organization purposefully institutionalizes a strategic management function and tasks a staff unit or administrator with deliberately designing, implementing, overseeing, and evaluating stakeholder engagement processes. Presented below is the ideal condition for accountability in organizations.

- *Accountability*: Organizations interact with stakeholders to offer goods and services that enhance the organization's economic value.

The impacts from stakeholder engagement are dependent on the co-production of social desired outcomes with stakeholders. An organization's activities that are mutually value-producing enhance organizational sustainability. Presented below is the ideal condition for the value of sustainability in organizations.

- *Sustainability*: Organizations should commit to continuous stakeholder engagement activities that are mutually value-producing and assure future transactions and interactions.

To have theoretical (normative) value, the propositions embedded in the hybrid stakeholder engagement logic model have to be generalizable and predictive. I have made attempts to ground my ideas and analysis in literature drawn from many different disciplines. However, as I have noted in the chapters, there are areas where additional confirmation or knowledge development is required.

7.6 The Value of Stakeholder Engagement Regimes

Stakeholder engagement processes provide an avenue for exploring the shared values we expect an organization to uphold. Participation serves an essential information and education function. Participation is a means for registering our individual preferences about what course of action we should expect from organizations in society (Forester, 1999). It can improve the efficacy of both stakeholders and organizations. Verba, Nie, and Kim (1971, pp. 15–19) documented the fact that there will be more significant concurrence about collective problems between stakeholders and organizational officials when participation occurs.

The sheer size and reach of organizations in society today, as well as the challenge to remain sustainable in a globally competitive market, makes it unlikely that stakeholder engagement practices will have the highest prioritization. Organizations must puruse multiple goals including economic and social performance simultaneously. Further, it is not realistic to achieve the 100% performance level envisioned by the spider web. Unfortunately, decision-makers can never have the luxury of complete consultation with their stakeholders on every issue they confront. Nor, do organizations have unlimited resources to make every stakeholder happy. For some decisions, organizations may continue to compensate for these shortcomings by relying on decision-makers to fill the role of trustees with stakeholders. This is a reasonable approach given that decisions made in this fashion are typically more efficient in terms of the time and resources necessary. Even in these situations, it is reasonable to expect stakeholder engagement to enhance value more than a lack of attention to the importance of stakeholder engagement does.

Decision-makers can seldom wholly satisfy, but instead must attempt to balance, competing preferences held among the stakeholders they serve. As a consequence, they act in a variety of roles such as delegate, trustee, mediator, facilitator, subject matter expert, and so on to try and align preferences with action and to explain decisions when alignment is not possible. When successfully performed, these activities can still strengthen perceptions of organizational accountability.

The question of accountability has been an enduring one, particularly for organizations that serve public purposes and that have decision-makers who are expected to function as the stakeholders' representative. In a time where good citizenship has come to mean perfunctory and sporadic voting for political elites, the revival of stakeholder engagement is essential (Freeman & Harris, 2009; Hart, 1972; Putnam, 1993, p. 612, 2000; Skocpol & Fiorina, 2004). Hansen (1975, p. 1198) was fearful that conditions for effective participation were weakening, and this condition could lead to increased citizen frustration and a perceived lack of effective control over leaders' actions. Stivers (1990, p. 95) reinvigorates this argument suggesting that apathy is a by-product of what stakeholders have learned from life experiences and the media, suggesting that voting and other forms of civic engagement are a waste of time. However, Thompson (1970, p. 3) maintains that stakeholders must share in governing and they are willing to do this. Unfortunately, there has been a tendency to view participation "…as a cost to both citizen and bureaucrat rather than as a benefit to society" (Stivers, 1990, p. 87).

Without institutionalizing expectations for stakeholder engagement, there is no incentive for an organization to change its behavior and no motivation for stakeholders to become better informed. "…[I]ncreasing channels of communication and participation will improve levels of political trust and increase confidence in public authorities" (Cole, 1975, p. 776). Changing organizational behavior to expect higher levels and more variety in stakeholder engagement to the point that it becomes an institutional value will make organizations more responsive to stakeholders' needs and desires. It will serve as a check on "…the arbitrary, capricious, insensitive, or oppressive exercise of power" (Cole & Caputo, 1984, p. 414). Stakeholders are afraid of losing personal contact with and control of large bureaucratic organizations (Creighton, 1981). A role exists for administrators to ensure that stakeholders have adequate skills and perspectives to avoid this outcome (Clark, Croddy, Hayes, & Philips, 1997).

Finally, even though my thesis is that organizations can benefit economically from stakeholder engagement, as a governance scholar, I have a normative bias for value production that goes beyond revenue generation, transparency, permeability, and accountability. My ideal for stakeholder engagement is that it should not only be institutionalized but that it should also be meaningful – meaning it is mutually value-producing not only for the organization but also for the stakeholders. This can assure attention to social value creation as well. Accomplishing this will require higher-level abstract thinking that goes beyond the descriptive and prescriptive findings we now have.

In this treatise, I have taken a qualitative meta-analysis approach to the chapter topics to offer a lot of descriptive categorizations and analytical tools. Some readers may prefer one categorization or tools; others may like another. The purpose is not to authoritatively decide what is best. Instead I offer a variety of tools that can be practiced and models that can be tested empirically to find out which are robust and which need to be refined or discarded. The next step is to empirically test models of stakeholder motivation and engagement to explain better and then predict how it can lead to sustainability. Lastly, we need better guidance on how to transmit and adapt these findings into organizational practices. When this is successful, then the values to be enhanced through meaningful stakeholder engagement can be realized.

From a normative perspective, I argue that organizations are improved when they are responsive to the external environment and to stakeholders within that environment. To borrow from Dwight Waldo: "Participation is unquestionably 'right' in my view. But the issues involved are of all but mind-paralyzing complexity, inconsistency and confusion abound, and we need to get above the level of *ad hoc* partisan agreement" (1971, p. 264).

While researching and writing this book, I have come to appreciate the veracity of Waldo's observation. The development of the hybrid stakeholder engagement logic model at times featured mind-paralyzing complexity and confusion abounded. Nevertheless, I sought to organize what we know, identify what we do not know, and suggest how we might find out. This exercise convinced me that participation was unquestionably right.

The intent of the book is to mobilize the communities of scholars and practicing professionals to answer this urgent question: How can we design and encourage stakeholder engagement practices so that relationships between organizations and stakeholders is institutionalized? I look forward to engaging in this deliberation and dialogue.

References

Advisory Commission on Intergovernmental Relations. (1979). *An agenda for American federalism: Restoring confidence and competence*. Washington, DC: US Government Printing Office.

Arnold, R. D. (1990). *The logic of congressional action*. New Haven, CT: Yale University Press.

Arnstein, S. R. (1969). A ladder of citizen participation. *American Institution of Planners Journal, 35*(7), 216–224.

Berman, E. M. (1997). Dealing with cynical citizens. *Public Administration Review, 57*(2), 105–112.

Buck, J. V. (1984). The impact of citizen participation programs and policy decisions on participants' opinions. *Western Political Quarterly, 37*(3), 468–482.

Clark, T., Croddy, M., Hayes, W., & Philips, S. (1997). Service learning as civic participation. *Theory Into Practice, 36*(3), 164–169.

Cole, R. L. (1975). Citizen participation in municipal politics. *American Journal of Political Science, 19*(4), 761–781.

Cole, R. L., & Caputo, D. A. (1984). The public hearing as an effective citizen participation mechanism: A case study of the general revenue sharing program. *The American Political Science Review, 78*, 404–416.

Creighton, J. L. (1981). The public involvement manual. Cambridge, MA: ABT.

Donovan, T., & Bowler, S. (2004). *Reforming the RAlbanesepublic: Democratic institutions for the new America*. Upper Saddle River, NJ: Pearson Prentice Hall.

Dyson, L. L. (1999). Developing a university-school district partnership; researcher-district administrator collaboration for a special education initiative. *Canadian Journal of Education Revue Canadienne de l'Education, 24*(4), 411–425.

Easton, D. (1965). *A framework for political analysis*. Englewood Cliffs, NJ: Prentice-Hall.

Ebdon, C., & Franklin, A. L. (2006). Citizen participation in budget theory. *Public Administration Review, 66*(3), 437–447.

Forester, J. (1999). *The deliberative practitioner*. Cambridge, MA: The MIT Press. https://mitpress.mit.edu/books/deliberative-practitioner

Freeman, R. E., & Harris, J. D. (2009). Creating ties that bind. *Journal of Business Ethics, 88*, 685–692.

Hansen, S. B. (1975). Participation, political structure and concurrence. *American Political Science Review, 69*, 1181–1199.

Hart, D. K. (1972, October). Theories of government related to decentralization and citizen participation. *Public Administration Review, 32*, 603–621.

Keehley, P., & Abercrombie, N. (2008). *Benchmarking for best practices in the public sector* (2nd ed.). San Francisco, CA: Jossey-Bass.

Miller, W. E., & Stokes, D. E. (1966). Constituency influence in congress. In A. Campbell (Ed.), *Elections and the political order* (pp. 351–372). New York, NY: Wiley.

Mohr, L. (1988). *Impact analysis for program evaluation*. Chicago, IL: Dorsey Press.

Putnam, R. D. (1993). *Making democracy work: Civic traditions in modern Italy*. Princeton, NJ: Princeton University Press.

Putnam, R. D. (2000). *Bowling alone: The collapse and revival of American community*. New York, NY: Touchstone/Simon & Schuster.

Rosener, J. B. (1982, July/August). Making bureaucrats responsive: A study of the impact of citizen participation and staff recommendations on regulatory decision making. *Public Administration Review, 42*(4), 339–345.

Skocpol, T., & Fiorina, M. P. (2004). *Civic engagement in american democracy*. Washington, DC: Brookings Institution Press. http://www.brookings.edu/research/books/1999/civicameric

Stivers, C. (1990). The public agency as polis: Active citizenship in the administrative state. *Administration and Society, 22*(1), 86–105.

Thompson, R. H. (1970). The administrator's battleground. Conflict among values. *Peabody Journal of Education, 47*(5), 310–314.

Verba, S., Nie, N. H., & Kim, J. O. (1971). *The modes of democratic participation*. Beverly Hills, CA: Sage Publications.

Waldo, D. (1971). *Public administration in a time of turbulence*. Scranton, PA: Chandler.

Williamson, O. E. (1979). Transaction-cost economics: The governance of contractual relations. *Journal of Law and Economics, 22*(2), 233–261.

Wondolleck, J. M., Manning, N. J., & Crowfoot, J. W. (1996). Teetering at the top of the ladder: The experience of citizen group participants in alternative dispute resolution processes. *Sociological Perspectives, 39*(2), 249–262.

The manufacturer's authorised representative in the EU is Springer Nature Customer Service Centre GmbH, Europaplatz 3, 69115 Heidelberg, Germany. If you have any concerns regarding our products, please contact ProductSafety@springernature.com

Printed and bound by CPI Group (UK) Ltd, Croydon, CR0 4YY
30/09/2026
02225710-0007